#DELETED

#DELETED

**BIG TECH'S BATTLE TO
ERASE THE TRUMP
MOVEMENT AND STEAL
THE ELECTION**

Allum Bokhari

CENTER
STREET

New York   Nashville

Center Street
Hachette Book Group
1290 Avenue of the Americas, New York, NY 10104
centerstreet.com
twitter.com/centerstreet

First Edition: September 2020

Center Street is a division of Hachette Book Group, Inc. The Center Street name and logo are trademarks of Hachette Book Group, Inc.

The publisher is not responsible for websites (or their content) that are not owned by the publisher.

Library of Congress Cataloging-in-Publication Data
Names: Bokhari, Allum, author.
Title: #DELETED : big tech's battle to erase the Trump movement and steal the election / Allum Bokhari.
Description: First edition. | New York : Center Street, 2020. | Includes bibliographical references and index. | Summary: "Conservative journalist Allum Bokhari examines how the liberal-leaning elites of Silicon Valley have completely overtaken social media, creating a crisis for privacy and freedom of expression"—Provided by publisher.
Identifiers: LCCN 2020014851 | ISBN 9781546059301 (hardcover) | ISBN 9781546059332 (ebook)
Subjects: LCSH: Trump, Donald, 1946- | Social media—Political aspects—United States. | Internet industry—Political aspects—United States. | Corporate power—United States. | Right and left (Political science) | Polarization (Social sciences)—United States. | Political culture—United States. | United States—Politics and government—2009–2017. | United States—Politics and government—2017–
Classification: LCC HM742 .B64 2020 | DDC 306.20973—dc23
LC record available at https://lccn.loc.gov/2020014851

ISBNs: 978-1-5460-5930-1 (hardcover), 978-1-5460-5933-2 (ebook)

Printed in the United States of America

LSC-C

10 9 8 7 6 5 4 3 2 1

Contents

Foreword   vii

Prologue: The Typewriter That Talked Back   1

1. A Very Offensive Election   15
2. How the Web Was Lost   26
3. The Panic   37
4. Plausible Deniability   54
5. Deleted   63
6. Robot Censors   75
7. Human Censors   91
8. Financial Blacklisting   105
9. The World's Most Dangerous Company   112
10. Censorship Kills the YouTube Star   132
11. The Defamation Engine   143
12. The World Wide Honeypot   161
13. The "Free Speech Wing of the Free Speech Party"   175
14. When Facebook Kills Your Business   186
15. When Silicon Valley Met Washington   206
16. "Just Build Your Own"   225

Epilogue: The Typewriter That Did as It Was Told   241

Acknowledgments   247
Notes   249
Index   263

Foreword
By the moderation team of r/The_Donald and thedonald.win

As the United States approaches the 2020 election, President Trump's supporters find themselves in the crosshairs of all major social media platforms.

Whether from the rabidly left-wing Twitter Trust and Safety Council, an activist Facebook administrator, or a political operative overseeing Reddit communities, Trump allies and voters are at risk of censorship in the digital world by simply voicing their beliefs. These companies enjoy protection under federal law, but their actions toward conservatives clearly undermine their standing as neutral platforms and lend credence to the belief that they have become publishers with clear political agendas. So why do they continue to enjoy the special federal protections reserved for such platforms?

We are the creators and moderators of r/The_Donald, the largest community of Trump supporters on Reddit, the wildly popular message board that calls itself "the front page of the internet." For five years, Reddit—the nineteenth-most-popular site on the web—has been home to our nearly eight hundred thousand users and has become one of the most influential sources of pro-Trump content on the web. A 2018 study by computer scientists at King's College London, University College London, Boston University, the University of Alabama, and the Cyprus University of Technology found that we were far and away the top distributor of memes on the internet.[1]

But our position is in peril. Since r/The_Donald was created, Reddit has consistently targeted it with restrictions that are not equally imposed upon other subreddits on the site. Even before President Trump's stunning victory in 2016, Reddit and its CEO, Steve Huffman, aka "spez," began displaying hostility toward us and taking actions to diminish our reach and suppress our message. Reddit's suppression of r/The_Donald only grew when George Soros acolyte Jessica Ashooh joined Reddit as director of policy and de facto manager of Reddit communities.

Our major issues with Reddit began with the Pulse nightclub shooting, during which radical Islamist Omar Mateen slaughtered forty-nine gay people and wounded an additional fifty-three. Upon learning of the Muslim faith of the attacker, default subreddits, those with the most subscribers, began a campaign of censorship and oppression of speech, going so far as to remove comments directing users to locations to donate blood. As Redditors were unable to receive updates on the shooting elsewhere, users began flocking to r/The_Donald and significantly boosted our subscriber count. In response, Reddit began a long history of capricious actions aimed at removing the voices of President Trump's supporters from the Reddit public forum.

Four days after the shooting, Huffman, the Reddit CEO, stated the following concerning the reactionary changes to their website: "Many people will ask if this is related to r/the_donald. The short answer is no, we have been working on this change for a while, but I cannot deny their behavior hastened its deployment. We have seen many communities like r/the_donald over the years—ones that attempt to dominate the conversation on Reddit at the expense of everyone else. This undermines Reddit, and we are not going to allow it."[2]

At the time of Huffman's statement, r/The_Donald enjoyed a place atop Reddit's most active communities, thanks to our devoted user base and the energy they expended in their support of President Trump's 2020 campaign.

While Huffman accused us of dominating the conversation, topics of interest to progressives, such as support for net neutrality and the failed presidential campaigns of Bernie Sanders, routinely made the front page, often originating from subreddits where the user counts do not even remotely match the large number of upvotes (Reddit's rough equivalent of Facebook "likes") they received. Clearly, "dominating the conversation" on Reddit is perfectly fine if you're a progressive.

In November 2016, shortly after Trump's election, Reddit's CEO revealed his true colors. Frustrated by our users continually mocking him, Huffman used his database access to edit user comments in r/The_Donald, something unheard of on any social media website and calling the integrity of Reddit as a whole into question. He offered a halfhearted apology and continued as CEO despite the severe damage to the reputation of his site.[3] Imagine Mark Zuckerberg using his powers to edit your grandma's Facebook post because she made fun of him. That's the equivalent of what Huffman did.

One week later, messages were leaked from Slack, an instant messaging service, that clearly displayed collusion between site administrators and non-r/The_Donald moderators in an attempt to ban r/The_Donald. Again, Huffman found himself in the middle of the controversy. The leaked messages showed him saying, "I think we need to figure out T_D without banning them. [Because] there will be another."

As part of a new advertising campaign, Reddit created a site for prospective advertisers to view user counts in subreddits so that they might select where to run their ads. While all other subreddits displayed numbers similar to what Reddit states, r/The _Donald showed a number of 6 million users—far beyond the nearly eight hundred thousand Reddit currently displays. Administrators attempted to explain the discrepancy as an error, but together with our own website metrics, it cast doubt over the reliability of the site's numbers. Is Reddit hiding the true number of Trump supporters on its platform?

Reddit's anti-Trump users often parroted the leftist media line that Trump supporters are Russian bots and foreign operatives, but Reddit itself dispelled this lie in March 2018. It released a security report stating that 14,000 posts during the 2016 election may have originated from Russia. Of those, only 316 originated from r/The _Donald, by far the most active political subreddit during the election cycle.

June 2019 saw Reddit hit r/The_Donald with a deathblow, by putting us in "quarantine." This made our subreddit invisible to anyone not subscribed to r/The_Donald, the majority of Reddit's user base.[4] The justification given was violent comments aimed toward government officials, posted by anonymous users. This quarantine occurred only after a Media Matters article and a campaign by censor extraordinaire and spoiled rich child Carlos Maza. In response, we conducted a review of other subreddits and compiled a twenty-five-page report on violent comments directed at government officials. Of particular note was the fact that the far-left r/politics subreddit contained twenty-nine violent comments in a post about the same exact story, a standoff between Republicans and Democrats in Oregon, each one of which far exceeded the ferocity of the seven that resulted in our quarantine.[5]

We unsuccessfully tried to appeal our quarantine by preparing an in-depth report demonstrating the changes we made and the accompanying data. We complied with all requests from administrators. Reddit responded by notifying us that the quarantine would remain in place because we failed to meet a metric that they would not share with us and because our users supposedly upvoted content that violated their intentionally broad rules, something over which we had no control. Even after condemnation from a member of Congress, Representative Jim Banks (R-IN), Reddit wouldn't budge.[6]

On February 25, 2020, Reddit hammered the final nail into the coffin of r/The_Donald. With no prior warning, they gutted our moderation team by removing our sixteen most active moderators.[7]

Over subsequent days, Jessica Ashooh, author of such articles as "What the Rise of the Islamic State Tells Us About Donald Trump: And How to Take Them Both Down," and her community team removed several more, leaving us unable to properly run the web's largest hub for Trump supporters. Thankfully, we prepared for this eventuality by creating a site for our user base without the activist interference of Reddit, thedonald.win, which we now call home.

A common phrase uttered by the liberal-outrage mob is "If you don't like it, build your own platform." We did and our host was immediately targeted by the same people whose goal in life is to silence dissenting opinions. After a few bumps in the road, we now find that traffic exceeds that of r/The_Donald, and we will only continue to grow the community. Our time on Reddit is over, but our next phase of online Trump support is only beginning. We look forward to the day when we may discuss the actions of Reddit's leadership team with members of Congress and prepare them for any hearings.

We only hope that other Trump supporters, spread out across leftist-owned platforms like Facebook, YouTube, and Twitter, will find a way to escape the grip of Silicon Valley censors before the next election. As you'll find out in the rest of this book, our experience dealing with Big Tech censorship is not unique to Reddit—the same story is being played out across the entire internet.

#DELETED

PROLOGUE:
The Typewriter That Talked Back

The year is 1968. The internet is nothing but a glint in the eye of a scientist working for the Defense Department's Advanced Research Projects Agency. Computers are the size of large rooms and are used mainly by NASA scientists and the military. "Internet" isn't even a word, and the pocket calculator has yet to achieve mass-market appeal.

There's still some technology, though—typewriters are nearly ubiquitous, which means the public has an easy and inexpensive way to communicate.

It just so happens that typing is exactly what you're doing. You sit at your desk; your fingers skate across the keys of your typewriter. But something's wrong.

The typewriter has stopped working. It's not *broken*. Everything seems to be working fine. It's just that no words are coming out.

You give the typewriter a few prods. Nothing happens. You take the paper out of the paper roll and replace it with a new one. Still nothing. You try once more to type a few words. Nothing.

Suddenly, and entirely of its own accord, the typewriter jumps into action. Your hands are nowhere near it, yet there it is, typing out a message, all on its own:

Dear Customer,

We regret to inform you that your last letter violated our terms of service (Rule 32: Abusive & Offensive Content). We have suspended access to your typewriter for 24 hours.

                                              Regards,

                                              Twit Typewriters Co.

Bemused, you go to the phone. The last letter you wrote was to your friend Pat O'Reilly. Maybe you wrote one too many Irish jokes? You dial Pat's number, preparing to tell him about the strange turn of events.

But Pat doesn't pick up. Instead, your ears are greeted by the brisk tone of an operator, who delivers the following message: "Good morning. Our systems detected that, in your last call, you told a joke beginning with the line 'An Englishman, an Irishman, and a Scotsman walk into a bar…' We regret to inform you that this violated our policies on offensive stereotypes. You are banned from using your phone for forty-eight hours. Warm wishes, Bell Telephones Co."

Click.

Outraged, you grab your pen and begin scribbling a letter to the telephone company. Who the hell do they think they are? You're a paying customer, goddammit! And you're Irish—you feel it's your right to poke fun at your countrymen! You spend several minutes furiously jotting down your thoughts about Bell Telephones Co., going so far as to suggest that it's a monopoly and ought to be broken up. A radical idea like that ought to get their attention!

You seal the envelope and head for the post office. It's a cool, brisk December day. On your way, you decide to stop at the newsstand— you want to pick up a copy of *Peace Now*. It's a fringe, far-left magazine, but with so much government propaganda about the escalating war in Vietnam, it's the only information source you trust.

The last time you visited the newsstand, you could find no copies of *Peace Now*. It's not entirely surprising, because the mag is known for its fascination with outlandish stories like the alleged military cover-up of an attack that never happened in the Gulf of Tonkin, and a secret CIA mind-control project called MKUltra. State sources have rubbished both stories as conspiracy theories—but you still don't appreciate newsstand owners not giving you a wide range of reading options.

Maybe *Peace Now* is too kooky to read, but that should be *your* decision to make. After all, if the stories have even a grain of truth behind them, they're of huge public importance.

Still, the newsstand must surely have the *Bugler*, a highly popular newspaper that's both antiwar and antiestablishment. The paper's editorial board reluctantly backed Richard Nixon prior to the 1968 presidential election as a result of his pledge to pull out of Vietnam.

But at the newsstand, you receive yet another surprise. The *New York Times* is there, the *Washington Post* is there, even the *National Enquirer* is there. However, in place of the *Bugler*, there's only this short notice:

This newsstand no longer stocks the *Bugler*, which has been categorized as "fake news" by third-party watchdogs. Thank you.

Marvin Suckerberg, Newsstands Inc.

The ban on one of your favorite newspapers is a huge problem, not least because Suckerberg's Newsstands Inc. recently bought out every competing newsstand in your city. There are no alternatives.

"What's going on?" you ask. "How come you've dropped the *Bugler*?"

The owner of the newsstand, his nose buried in a copy of the *New Yorker*, puts down the magazine and peers at you curiously.

"The *Bugler* is fake news, according to several reputable fact-checkers. Several of my employees petitioned me to drop it, and I agreed with their position. So, it's gone, that's that. If you're determined to read it, you can get it directly from their printing facility. It's about five hours' drive away, mind you."

The vendor returns to his reading material—but you aren't satisfied with his explanation. "Who are these fact-checkers?" you demand. "Millions of people read the *Bugler*! It's the most popular paper in the state!"

Once again, the newsstand owner puts down his magazine.

"Well, of course it's popular. That's the whole problem. We can't allow misinformation to spread, can we?

"Say…," he continues, now eyeing you suspiciously. "You didn't vote for *Nixon*, did you? I heard that most *Bugler* readers voted for Nixon."

You're about to retort, but a glance at your watch tells you the post office will close in twenty minutes. Still annoyed, you turn and walk away.

The vendor yells after you: "You should be ashamed of yourself! Nixon's a radical! His 'Silent Majority' slogan is code for fascism! He's literally Hitl—"

———

The postal clerk greets you with a smile, clearly in a much better mood than the newsstand owner. And why shouldn't he be? It's 1968, and it'll be decades before his job becomes threatened by robots and mass immigration.

"Hello, sir," he says cheerily. "We were expecting you!"

"Expecting me?" you reply. "You knew I was writing a complaint to Bell Telephones?"

"Oh no, sir. We thought you'd be wondering why we returned all the mail you sent out last week. About six letters, I think it was. Should have been sent back to your address earlier this morning."

"Sent back?" you ask. "What do you mean, 'sent back'? Hold on…"

You put two and two together.

"Have I been banned from using the mail?"

"That's right, sir!" The clerk beams, still blissfully unaware of immigrants and robots. "It'll last for precisely two weeks. Just long enough for you to learn the error of your ways!"

You close your eyes for several seconds, attempting to contain your anger.

"Why…? How…?"

"It's quite simple," replies the clerk. "When we read your mail two weeks ago, we found a couple of jokes about Irishmen. They were hilarious—and so true. I'm Irish. But they violated our code of—"

"You read my mail?!" you exclaim. *"Why the hell are you reading my mail?!"*

"Well, of course we read your mail, sir," says the clerk hurriedly. "Otherwise we wouldn't know what advertisements to send you! You see, we wouldn't want your letterbox to be bombarded with pointless ads for the Ford Falcon when your last few letters have all been about how happy you are with your brand-new Chevy Chevelle. This way, we can send you ads for spare tires and accessories instead. Really, it's just so we can improve your user experience! There's nothing to worry about!"

"Stop it! You stop it right now!" you bellow. "I never signed up for that!"

"Ah, but you did, sir. Here, take a look."

The clerk hands you a one-inch-by-one-inch postage stamp.

"This is just a stamp. What am I looking at?"

"Take a closer look, sir."

You bring the stamp up to your face and squint at it. Scrawled in tiny writing across the bottom is a message:

TERMS OF SERVICE: ALL MAIL WILL BE MONITORED AND REVIEWED TO IMPROVE USER EXPERIENCE AND ENSURE COMPLIANCE WITH OUR CODE OF CONDUCT. FOR A FULL LIST OF PROHIBITED COMMUNICATIONS, PLEASE SEE ONE OF OUR STORE CLERKS.

You are now quite convinced that the world has gone mad. You read the message three times, just to be sure. You're barely paying attention to the clerk as he explains your suspension.

"So, because of the offensive jokes about Irish people, who are a protected group after facing considerable discrimination—"

"Hold on a second," you interrupt. "*I'm* part Irish. And so is my friend, whom I wrote those letters to. How can you suspend my service for something that neither of us found offensive?"

"Well, I sympathize, sir, but Lena McDunham and Kathy McGriffin might not see it that way," replies the clerk. "If they got wind of this—"

"I don't care! They're not even funny!" you declare.

"Keep your voice down!" hisses the clerk. "Their talent agency represents half the stars in Hollywood. Do you know how much fan mail their clients get on a weekly basis? That's a huge chunk of our revenues! We can't risk that for one man's right to tell a joke!"

You've finally had enough.

"That's it, to hell with the post office," you declare, heading toward the door. "I'm taking my business to FedEx."

"Good luck!" yells the clerk as you leave. "They won't be founded until 1971!"

It occurred to the clerk that his very angry customer wouldn't have much luck in 1971 either.

After all, if FedEx were to carry *hate speech* in its mail trucks, it'd only be a matter of time before it was banned from using the roads.

Stranger Than Fiction

Sometimes, the only way to understand the weirdness of the present is by comparing it to the past. But as time goes on, such an exercise becomes difficult. Many of those reading this book have little, if any, experience with typewriters. Sending a letter through the mail seems archaic, unless it's a Valentine's Day or Christmas card. If we're not careful, the generation born today will have to ask their grandparents what it was like to communicate without feeling that a giant corporation was listening to what they said and reading what they wrote.

Many commentators have warned that the unchecked power of Big Tech corporations means that dystopia is just around the corner. This book reveals a far more unsettling truth: the dystopia is already here. We're just desensitized to it.

Google Docs is a typewriter that talks back. It has terms of service, and one of its terms is that you don't engage in "abuse." If you violate its terms, it will kick you off. That's exactly what happened in October 2017, when a number of writers working on documents about innocuous topics like wildlife crime and the multiplayer role-playing computer game *RuneScape* were unceremoniously locked out of their work.[1] It was an accident—Google later admitted that they had been erroneously censored for "abusive content" and quickly restored their access. But the incident showed how much power the company has given itself. Even your private projects can be taken away from you if Google deems them "abusive."

"Abusive," along with "dangerous" and "harmful," is a word that has been weaponized by censors, because it can be stretched to cover virtually any expression they may wish to discredit. In the early days of tech, it referred to indisputable "abuses" of communication systems, like phishing, spam, and malware. Now it encompasses a huge variety of flexible terms that allow tech companies to censor at will—among them "fake news," "misinformation," "hate speech." What do these words mean? Where did the words come from and who decides what is "fake"? Is there an agreed definition? More important, which definition is Google or Facebook or Twitter using?

We don't know the answer to that last question, because much of the companies' operations are hidden from view in an inscrutable black box—but we do know that it could change at any time. As we'll see later in this book, many of Silicon Valley's more militant censors would like to stretch terms like "abuse" and "misinformation" as far as they possibly can. So would politicians, who may want the terms to cover their opponents, and media organizations, whose managers want the terms to cover their competitors.

You might think that Microsoft Word is better than its primary competitor, Google Docs. After all, Word was originally an offline product—surely their terms of service can't be too weird.

Wrong! Microsoft's services agreement is, if anything, worse than Google's.[2] In addition to prohibiting the sharing of "inappropriate content" (was there ever a vaguer term?), Microsoft prohibits the communication of "hate speech," a term that modern-day censors love even more than they love "abuse." Users are warned that any transgression of the service agreement could result in a shutdown of their Microsoft account or their Skype account.

Yes, both your typewriter and your telephone now have minds of their own. And, if Microsoft's service agreement is anything to go by, they also have their own set of moral values.

What about the other weird scenarios I mentioned, like the postal service reading your mail? By now, I would hope that everyone is aware that Google scans your inbox, both to personalize its services to its users and (until recently) to target ads. Is this any different from the post office opening your letters and reading them? If the U.S. Postal Service said it was doing so only to "improve our service," would you trust them?

Newsstand bans on newspapers for "fake news" have also become a reality in the digital world. These occur through bans on "low-quality" or "fake-news" sources, or algorithm adjustments that make the labeled sources nearly impossible to find. It's like your TV hiding channels from you—even the popular ones. Scan Apple's recommended news sources and you'll find plenty of establishment sources like *The Economist*, the *Washington Post*, and *Time* magazine, but you won't find populist, dissident sources like Breitbart News on the right or the Intercept on the left. You can still add such sites to your feed, but only by searching for them manually. Google, meanwhile, has all but booted mainstream conservative sources like Conservative Tribune out of its news search results altogether and is under constant pressure from its activist employees to blacklist Breitbart, too. A study by Northwestern University found that more than 25 percent of the news stories Google delivers to its users via its "top stories" feature came from CNN, the *New York Times*, and the *Washington Post*. You're likely to find less variety in Google's top news results than you would at a brick-and-mortar newsstand!

And what about the Irishman being banned for making jokes about Irishmen to another Irishman? Well, as the recent *Newsweek* headline "Why Are All the Conservative Loudmouths Irish-American?" suggests, Irish stereotypes are apparently acceptable today.[3] Still, you should prepare to be banned for even the slightest hint of derogatory phrases, even if no one involved is offended. Facebook has repeatedly locked gay users out of their accounts for using the word "faggot," even if they're trying to reclaim the word from bigots by using it as a tongue-in-cheek reference to themselves and their friends.[4] Unsurprisingly, the artificial intelligence (AI) systems trained by Silicon Valley to detect wrongspeech aren't so intelligent after all, and don't understand context. The very mechanisms designed to "protect" minorities end up censoring them instead.

The postal service that won't let you send messages for fear of offending its lucrative celebrity clients? That's Twitter, a platform of profound political importance that also appears to be highly dependent on the whims of thin-skinned celebrities and their influential talent agencies. This is common knowledge among current and former Twitter employees, some of whom have been interviewed for this book—in the strictest confidentiality for fear of being blacklisted across Silicon Valley.

Even without inside sources, we can see Twitter's pro-celebrity bias. Former soccer star and TV host Gary Lineker is free to call anyone he likes a "d*ck,"[5] but when a British political satirist fired back, calling him a "c*nt" (a far less offensive term in the United Kingdom than in Silicon Valley), he received a lifetime Twitter ban—a ridiculously disproportionate punishment.[6] In other notorious cases, celebrity Twitter users have threatened violence against high school kids without even losing their verified checkmark, a de facto stamp of approval from the platform.[7] According to a BuzzFeed report from 2016, major Hollywood agencies like CAA are prone to bullying Twitter into rule changes desired by their celebrity clients, threatening mass boycotts from high-profile celebrity Twitter users when they don't get their way.[8]

If it's not celebrities calling the shots to tech giants, it's politicians and corporate journalists. In 2018, Google intervened on YouTube, which it owns, to remove videos critical of the Federal Reserve from its top ten search results for the term "Federal Reserve." The cause? A tweet from MSNBC journalist Chris Hayes, who complained that anti-Fed videos were doing too well in YouTube's algorithm.[9]

A few months later, a complaint from a *Slate* journalist about pro-life videos led Google to conduct a similar reordering of YouTube search results for "abortion." This establishment favoritism affects both the Right and the Left—research from leading search engine expert and psychologist Robert Epstein found that Google searches tended to favor Democratic presidential candidate Hillary Clinton in the 2016 general election[10]—but no such favoritism was found for her antiestablishment primary opponent, Bernie Sanders.

The influence of politicians on Silicon Valley is more worrying. Bans of antiestablishment figures, like radio shock jock Alex Jones in the United States and populist activist Tommy Robinson in the United Kingdom, from social media platforms frequently occur after campaigns by politicians in those countries. Whatever you may think of such individuals, you should be deeply concerned about corporations being able to shut down political opposition. Through their influence on Big Tech, Western elites have given themselves the power to silence figures of immense political consequence.

The democratic process has evolved over centuries to stop politicians from imposing their policies without public debate, judicial review, or other checks and balances. By turning to corporations to do their bidding, politicians aim to bypass that time-honored process. Whether you like Alex Jones or not, that's dangerous—it's exactly how the Chinese government uses its own corporations.

"Hold on a second," says the conservative establishment. "It's still a free market, isn't it? Doesn't Twitter have a competitor?"

Not really. Think back to my bizarre example of FedEx trucks being banned from the roads for carrying hate speech. That's essentially what happened to Gab, a social media platform committed to hosting the maximum level of First Amendment–protected speech—just as mainstream platforms like Twitter once did.

But the same principles about which Twitter once boasted now amount to hate speech for most Big Tech companies. It wasn't long before Gab's mobile app was banned from both the App Store and the Google Play Store. When Apple and Google combined have a 99 percent market share of smartphone operating systems, they can make it nearly impossible for any apps they disapprove of to reach consumers.[11]

There are complicated workarounds to installing an app without the help of Google and Apple, but these back doors are too cumbersome for the average consumer to master. For all intents and purposes, the App Store and the Play Store are the highways of the app economy—the only ways for businesses to deliver their products. Gab is banned from both.

But that wasn't enough for the opponents of free speech on the web. Even without access to the app stores, Gab was still online and operational. That changed in late 2018 when, following negative news stories about the platform, Gab lost its cloud hosting provider, domain name registrar, and payments processor. Without these, Gab was forced offline until it found replacements. The explanation was that the platform had played host to a deadly terrorist—but at the height of the Islamic State's power, Twitter played host to thousands of terrorists, and was never taken offline.

There'll be more on the Gab story later in this book, but the point to remember is this: there's no free market. Today, if you try to create a platform with the same free-speech principles that Twitter used to follow, Silicon Valley will deny you access to payment processors, smartphone app stores, and possibly the internet itself.

When tech giants, in addition to controlling the largest platforms on the web, also control the means of competing with them, we no longer have a free-market economy. We have an oligopoly economy, dominated by a few giant companies that follow largely the same ideology.

Only this time, it's more dangerous. We're not talking about a telephone monopoly that provides poor service due to lack of competition, as Ma Bell used to do. Nor are we talking about a railroad monopoly that engages in rate fixing, as the nineteenth-century rail barons did. Those were all problematic to the public interest and deserved to be corrected, but they were not existential threats to freedom and democracy.

The tech monopolies of today are far more dangerous. The product over which they have a monopoly is nothing as mundane as railroads or telephones—it's *us*. It's our personal information, our political viewpoints, our attention, and our content. Big Tech owns the mother of all public squares, it owns the devices in our homes and pockets, and it's using them to find out everything about us.

Completing the picture of a totalitarian digital nation-state, Facebook has announced the creation of its own digital currency, the Libra coin—which would give the company the power to regulate and spy on our purchases as well. Facebook and Google are tirelessly working on new ways to use our data to manipulate us—originally so that advertisers could target us, and now, terrifyingly, so that the Big Tech companies can change our moral conduct and our political beliefs. If you resist? They'll just ban you.

Since the birth of the modern world, fiction and nonfiction writers have warned that new technologies could usher in an age of unprecedented tyranny. Novels like *1984* and *Brave New World* imagined humanity in the grip of technological dystopias.

But those novels imagined worlds that were far in the future. This book reveals a grim truth: the age of digital tyranny is already here. It is a particularly cruel kind of tyranny, because immediately preceding it was a period of true, uninhibited digital freedom. Silicon Valley entrepreneurs gave the world something precious, valuable, and almost universally beloved—and then made us watch as they smashed it to pieces.

Some of what Silicon Valley is doing is being done quite openly—FB taking down an immigration ad; YouTube taking down more than three hundred pro-Trump ads; Twitter banning a preposterous number of prominent Trump supporters from its platform. We'll cover this open censorship in chapter 5.

Some of it is hidden, coming into public view only through leaks. For example, it was not until an enterprising Google employee told me about it that we learned that YouTube has on numerous occasions adjusted its search results for politically charged topics in response to complaints from left-wing journalists. We'll go into detail about that leak in chapter 10, which is about YouTube. Chapter 6 explains how the algorithms of Big Tech companies can be manipulated against conservatives, while still granting those tech companies plausible deniability.

Leaks have also revealed that some in Silicon Valley know exactly what the goal is in 2020. Leaked footage of Google executives that I published in September 2019 revealed the company's leadership making sinister comments that suggested a game plan: they talked of the need to "deploy the great strength of the company" and make the populist movement a "blip" in history.

There were grumblings about the dangers of an overly free internet before Trump. In 2013–15, mainstream journalists and progressive commentators started to notice that comments sections under news articles and social media platforms like Twitter were being used to mock them and counter their points. There was a lot of talk about "toxic comments sections." But it wasn't until Trump was elected president that opposition to the laissez-faire internet turned into a full-blown firestorm.

Republicans missed their chance to regulate the tech giants. The easiest time would have been in 2017 and 2018, when they controlled the White House and both houses of Congress. They could have amended Section 230, the law that allows tech platforms to censor at will. Chapter 15 examines the inaction of politicians in more detail.

The story of how we got here is also a story of monopolization— how a handful of corporations accountable to no one took over the web, killing the libertarian dream that it would be decentralized. Chapter 2 addresses this story in detail.

But before we get to that, we must first look at how Silicon Valley views elections that don't go its way—and why that view threatens democracy.

1. A Very Offensive Election

In November 2016, a disturbance in the force hit Northern California. It was as if millions of trendy, high-income Silicon Valley leftists suddenly cried out in terror…and haven't stopped crying since. No, I'm not badly quoting *Star Wars*; I'm describing the actual reaction of the tech nerds who had, for the previous decade, spun an image of themselves as the smartest people in the world, and now felt that they had been let down by their alleged galaxy-size brains. Just as it had done to election pollsters and journalists, the U.S. presidential election outcome had utterly confounded Silicon Valley's predictions. The impossible had happened. The reckoning was here. Donald Trump was president.

At an all-hands meeting of Google held shortly after the election, a crestfallen Sergey Brin took the stage. Like a priest at a funeral, the Google cofounder channeled the grief of his congregation.

"As an immigrant and a refugee, I certainly find this election deeply offensive, and I know many of you do too."

"Most people here are pretty upset and pretty sad," he said. "[The election result]…conflicts with many of our values."

Brin's remarks—an open display of political bias from a leader of the world's most powerful tech company—were never meant to reach the public. But at that time, Google recorded its all-hands meetings, conducted at its Mountain View headquarters, for internal use. I obtained a leaked copy of the video in 2018 and subsequently published the full recording at Breitbart News.[1]

A string of other downcast Google executives followed Brin's speech, each expressing a similar mix of fear, pain, and outrage.

Kent Walker, Google's head of global affairs, suggested the election was the result of "xenophobia, hatred, and a desire for answers that may or may not be there" and expressed concerns that the world was moving toward a "tribalism that's self-destructive [in] the long-term."

Eileen Naughton, the company's head of human resources, joked about moving to Canada.

Ruth Porat, the chief financial officer, tried to recount her experience of election night, only to break down in tears halfway through. She then led a company-wide group hug.

Virtually every top Google executive, including CEO Sundar Pichai, was onstage. None of them expressed anything but horror at the election of President Trump. When one low-level Google employee asked the executives if they saw anything positive arising from the election, the room erupted in laughter.

Pichai reluctantly conceded that Trump's plans to improve the U.S. infrastructure might be a positive, while Brin said any hopes that Trump might do good things required "wishful thinking."

Brin, who opened the meeting by calling the decision of the American public "offensive," went on to say that he believed that "boredom" had driven American voters to "extremism."

At one point, Brin seemed to suggest that Jigsaw, a program Google developed to intervene in search results to guide potential Islamic terrorists away from extremist content, could be used to tackle this new form of "extremism."

Kent Walker, the company's legal chief, said that they should work to ensure that the populist movement represented by Trump became nothing more than a "blip" and a "hiccup" in history's march toward progress.

I found the video particularly shocking because, as a Brit, I can imagine the scandal that would have erupted had the director-general of the British Broadcasting Corporation (BBC) made similar comments. Although the broadcaster is notorious for the left-wing bias of its employees, its leaders would quickly be given a one-way ticket out of the company if they dared undermine its public commitment to political neutrality. Even in private, they wouldn't dare express such strong opinions about the election of a new prime minister—and they certainly wouldn't do so in front of the whole company.

Google may not be a quasi-state-run organization like the BBC (indeed, Google is far more powerful), but it regularly makes similar public commitments to neutrality—its CEO has even done so under oath, before Congress. What's more, with its dominance over search results, online news aggregation, and smartphone operating systems, Google's capacity to influence democratic elections goes far beyond that of any other company. The only entities that come close to its potential influence on politics are other Silicon Valley giants, such as Facebook and Twitter. Yet here was its entire leadership team, nakedly displaying their horror at the outcome of a democratic election.

A few miles away, at Facebook headquarters, the mood was much the same.

"One person described it being like a portal to a different dimension opened up on election night that no one thought existed," a source close to the company told me. The source said that the atmosphere within the company was one of shock and despondency.

"What I am given to understand is that there were a lot of crestfallen faces, stunned and shocked silence. There were some grave announcements from the higher-ups and a town hall meeting [at which it was] suggested [that] everyone use it as a teachable moment and to look for common ground, because of course the idea of sharing and building friendships is what Facebook built its entire company on.

"Rather than use it as a teachable moment…the groupthink coalesced, the righteous anger intensified, and people went into full-on revolt."

It wasn't long before news of the revolt trickled out of the company. Less than two weeks after the election, BuzzFeed published a story about a group of "renegade Facebook employees" who had, in defiance of cofounder and CEO Mark Zuckerberg, set up a group to combat "fake news."[2] This was shortly after the term "fake news," a catchall concept used by the Left in part to demonize pro-Trump media, had entered the popular lexicon.

My source compared the attitude of left-wing Facebook employees with those of other industries known for their liberal slants.

"If you work in San Francisco (or L.A., or New York, for that matter), in certain industries, the thought that anyone outside your echo chamber exists is unfathomable," my source said. "Put it this way: if you are a liberal, Bay Area millennial, you're going to approach your job with a certain unconscious bias, same as you might a West Virginian coal miner."

He's not wrong—but the thing about those other industries is, they don't have anywhere close to Silicon Valley's power to control political speech and influence elections. And, according to a different source at Facebook, those initial feelings of shock quickly morphed into a desire for action—a desperate scramble to do something, anything, to "fix" what had gone wrong.

"Immediately after the election, GSM [Global Sales and Marketing] folks, folks in other areas of Facebook, and even executives were very outspoken about their feelings," said the insider. "It was easy to notice that the most outspoken Trump antagonists were soon working in, and leading, the efforts to combat fake news, misinformation, and polarization.

"These efforts were never presented as a referee system [which would have dissuaded those antagonists from joining], but instead [were presented] as a way to invoke positive social change. The well was poisoned from the start."

According to my insider, Facebook held post-election meetings that resembled Google's—with a clear focus on how to make elections "better."

"In the integrity kickoff meeting shortly after the election, employees fantasized about how they could improve elections here and abroad," said my source. "Many noncitizen tech workers were upset that they could not vote in the U.S. election when they saw the results. Some saw Facebook's election efforts as a gateway to [influence] the vote without needing a vote. Facebook is fighting foreign influence with its own foreign influence."

Back at Google, left-leaning employees at the company were, according to my sources, just as distraught as the higher-ups who had spoken in the leaked video. One of my insiders, former Chromebook engineer Kevin Cernekee, recalls a range of bizarre behavior from his colleagues at the time:

"Many of my colleagues took the entire week off to mourn—managers openly encouraged this. These same managers sent out wistful emails pontificating about how the election was a devastating setback for women and minorities, and that we should keep their struggle at the forefront of our minds.

"There were numerous cases of employees sending anti-Trump propaganda, invitations to protests, and solicitations for progressive charities straight to their work mailing lists.

"They did not seem to consider the possibility that some of their coworkers might be Republicans. The blatant in-your-face workplace activism even made some progressives uncomfortable," said Cernekee.

"Administrative assistants discussed ways to change their groups' purchasing decisions to boycott small businesses whose owners supported Republicans.

"Everywhere you looked, there was a massive frenzy of over-dramatized complaints that President-Elect Trump was plotting to put innocents in death camps, deny lifesaving drugs to members of the LGBT community, and perpetrate ethnic cleansing."

According to Cernekee, requests to move to the company's Canada offices were more than just a joke. "There were a bunch of employees who made a huge deal about how they felt unsafe in the U.S. and wanted to transfer to Canada," he said. "There was an official (semi-tongue-in-cheek) announcement from Eileen Naughton saying that the Canada offices are full and they're looking for options to accommodate employees who fear for their lives under a Trump administration."

As had occurred at Facebook, the anger and sorrow quickly transformed into calls for action. Around the time of the inauguration, said Cernekee, "activists formed a 'Rogue National Parks' [Google Plus, the company's social network] community to brainstorm ways to undermine the administration. This is where the massive outdoor protest was originally planned. Directors were involved from the start. They initially pretended it was a grassroots effort but dropped the facade when various VPs lent their support to the protest."

The anti-Trump plotting apparently went beyond protests and angry internal messages. A lawsuit filed by former employee James Damore alleged that Alon Altman, a senior engineer at Google, suggested that the company "brick" (i.e., sabotage) the president's Android phone, and ban the Gmail accounts of his administration's senior officials and staff.

According to the suit, Altman also called for the company I work for, conservative media giant Breitbart News, to be stripped of all Google ads, saying the tech giant should "use the full economic force [of] Google for good."[3] An internal mailing list called "Resist" was set up and used by employees to brainstorm how to undermine Trump and his movement. Altman's suggestion that Breitbart be stripped of its ad revenue gained momentum inside the company— Google's activists launched a company-wide petition to have the site demonetized, while an advertising account manager directed major advertisers to the page of the Sleeping Giants, a far-left organization that spreads smears about conservative media websites in an effort to frighten advertisers away from them.[4] The suit states that senior management did little to clamp down on these efforts; according to Cernekee, many even encouraged them.

As internal activism progressed, said Cernekee, "there were a dozen-plus 'resist' groups since people also set up local groups (resist-mv, resist-sf, resist-nyc, I think) to coordinate activist gatherings in each region.

"One thing I remember seeing on these lists is training for 'ICE intervention,' where employees would learn how to interfere with Border Patrol enforcement operations."

While Google's leaders did not indulge every crazy idea (the company never "bricked" Trump's phone—although that's hardly a high bar to clear!), it pays to remember that such rabid displays of partisan bias would be frowned upon at traditional media companies, even those with profound left-wing slants like the *New York Times* or CNN. And Google is a far more dangerous company than either of those.

Vested Interests

One of the more instructive moments in the leaked Google video comes at the end, when Sergey Brin says, "He [Trump] could do anything. I mean, we have no idea. You really don't know." Elsewhere in the video, public policy chief Kent Walker says that "nobody knows" whom Trump would pick for Federal Communications Commission chair. "We don't even know who's doing some of the transition work in some cases... We're going to have to deal with a new cast of characters. We're figuring out who those characters are and what their policies will be."

In so many words, Google's leaders were telling their employees that the election had blindsided them—that they hadn't bothered building any serious connections with potential Trump appointees during the run-up to the election, and now they had no idea what his administration was going to do, or who would be doing it. Silicon Valley's masters of the universe, who had for years been giving their users algorithmic feedback loops, echo chambers where they were fed content that reaffirmed their views, had been caught flat-footed, thanks to their very own progressive Bay Area echo chamber.

It's safe to say that the tech giant would not have encountered the same problem had a Democrat been elected to the Oval Office. The back-and-forth links between Silicon Valley and senior Democrat politicians is shocking—one investigation by the online news publication the Intercept found that 55 Google employees left the tech giant to take positions in the Obama administration, and 197 government employees moved from the federal bureaucracy to Google or to other companies and organizations owned by Eric Schmidt, who was then executive chairman of the company. To get a sense of how extraordinary those numbers are, there are currently only 377 people employed in the West Wing.

From the Intercept: "Google [alumni] work in the departments of State, Defense, Commerce, Education, Justice, and Veterans Affairs. One works at the Federal Reserve, another at the U.S. Agency for International Development. The highest number—29—moved from Google into the White House. The State Department had the next highest with just five. The moves from Google to government got more frequent in the later Obama years; 11 occurred in 2014 and 16 in 2015, after only 18 in the entire first term."

The investigation also discovered seven cases of "full revolutions through the revolving door"—individuals who either went "from Google to government and back again, or from the government to Google and then back again."[5]

Government links are just one aspect of Silicon Valley's incestuously close relationship with the Democrats. There are also political links. Leaked emails released via WikiLeaks showed that Eric Schmidt, then the executive chairman of Google's parent company, Alphabet Inc., gave extensive advice and support to Hillary Clinton at the earliest stages of her 2016 presidential campaign. A leaked email from Clinton campaign manager John Podesta said that Schmidt "clearly wants to be head outside advisor."[6] And at Clinton's election night party in New York City, Schmidt was spotted wearing a Clinton "staff" badge.[7] It seems clear that the man who was second only to cofounders Larry Page and Sergey Brin in influence at Google was deeply embedded in the Clinton campaign.

In the course of my investigations into Big Tech, I uncovered even more links between the Democrats and Silicon Valley companies. Searching LinkedIn's database of Facebook employees in 2018, I found forty-five Facebook employees who had previously worked for Hillary Clinton's election campaigns, Barack Obama's election campaigns, or Barack Obama's White House. By way of comparison, I found just seven Facebook staffers who had previously worked for Mitt Romney's 2012 campaign. Clearly, the balance was tilted very much in favor of former Democrat staffers.

Former Democratic operatives can be found in positions across the company, from marketing and recruitment to creative roles, where political bias arguably might have less of an impact. But others could be found in more impactful roles, like the "news integrity" team, as well as in senior positions on the company's public policy and research teams. One former Obama staffer, Anthea Strong, worked at Google on a team that dealt specifically with civics and elections before moving to Facebook to work on its news team. And that doesn't even cover people like Nick Clegg, who led a Liberal Democratic party into government in the United Kingdom before joining Facebook's leadership team. On the Right, the only similarly well-known figure linked to the company is Peter Thiel—who, as a board member, isn't even involved in the day-to-day running of the company.

Understanding the deep links that existed between Silicon Valley and the Democratic Party casts Google leaders' post-election confusion in a new light. Sergey Brin said he had "no idea" what President Trump was about to do after his election victory. Would he have said the same about Hillary Clinton? With Eric Schmidt at her election night party wearing a "staff" badge, and former Google employees all over the Obama White House, it's safe to say that Google would have had a much better idea of what a Democratic administration was going to do. But Google's leaders simply never imagined that their political fellow travelers would be kicked out of office. And, like the rest of the elite progressive class, they certainly never imagined that somebody like Trump could do it. Didn't the *New York Times* give Hillary a 91 percent chance of victory less than a month before the election? What happened?!

With most industries (banking is an example), the main concern with regard to crossover employees is that they will influence government policy in their companies' favor. Countless articles have been written about how big banks like Goldman Sachs have benefited by placing their former employees in top positions within presidential administrations.

With Big Tech, however, the concern is twofold: as with the banks, an overly close relationship between Big Tech and the White House increases the likelihood of policies that unfairly favor the former. "Net neutrality," an Obama-era policy that favored web companies like Google and Netflix to the detriment of telecom companies like Verizon, was one such example, which we'll cover in detail later in the book. But there's also another concern—employees who cross over from a political party or a presidential administration to a Big Tech company may subsequently influence that tech company to support their favored political candidates and causes. After all, there's no law to stop them, so why wouldn't they? At a company like Goldman Sachs, a progressive employee may well influence the company's diversity quotas. But at a Google or a Facebook or a Twitter, politically biased employees can do far more damage—they can influence the digital public square, the single most important forum for political debate in the modern world. These are platforms where political activists and politicians can reach a potential audience of billions. They're where people go when they want to find out information about a candidate or a cause. They're where new political movements can grow and develop. Rise high enough in Silicon Valley, and you can be no less than the global referee of democracy. There's only one difference—a football referee has to follow a strict set of rules, whereas in Big Tech, the rules change every day.

In the following chapters, we'll look at some of the ways in which Silicon Valley's initial shock at the election result turned to anger—and action. As my sources at Facebook and Google have said, the leftists of Big Tech didn't just mire themselves in gloom—they began to organize. Initiatives against "fake news," initiatives against "hate speech," initiatives to promote "election integrity," all enjoyed a massive surge of interest in Silicon Valley in the months and years following Trump's election. And, according to my sources, the people who were most keen to be part of those efforts were those who were the most deeply tied to left-wing politics.

As we look more closely at how Silicon Valley adjusted its algorithms, banned high-profile conservatives from its platforms, and manipulated the information we all encounter on a daily basis, remember the people who are behind it all. From the top down, Silicon Valley companies are full of rabid political partisans, incandescent with rage at the result of the 2016 election, as well as guilt that their platforms might have helped bring about that result. As we'll see in chapter 3, Silicon Valley's guilt was a perfect partner for the panic of the political and media establishments, which blamed Big Tech for electing Trump and demanded radical changes in policy. This, naturally, empowered the most radical left-wing activists inside companies like Facebook and Google.

Before we get into all that, though, we need to answer a few questions: How did companies like Facebook and Google become so important? How did they acquire so much power that even other tech giants, like Twitter, seem small and unthreatening? Wasn't it less than a decade ago that the mantra of the internet was freedom of speech, freedom of information, and open access for all? Where did those lofty principles go? Are Facebook and Google the whole internet now? And if so, how did it happen?

2. How the Web Was Lost

What happened to digital freedom over the past half decade was nothing short of a robbery.

The internet promised to be the greatest leap forward for individual freedom since the Bill of Rights. With blogs and newsletters, we were all printing presses. With webcams and podcasts, we were all broadcasters. With websites and online payment processors, we could all start a business without getting up from our couches. Reddit founder Alexis Ohanian summed it up best in 2013 in an interview with *Forbes*: "To join in the industrial revolution, you needed to open a factory; in the Internet revolution, you need to open a laptop."[1]

Ohanian's statement captured the spirit of the internet at the time—a technology accessible by all and controlled by none. Disruption, democratization, and freedom of expression—those were the watchwords of the digital age. We were to be liberated citizens in what Microsoft cofounder Bill Gates called the "global town square." Unbound by censors, with a worldwide audience of millions just a click away, information was to be forever free.

So, where did it all go wrong?

In 2018, a whistle-blower at Google sent me a remarkable document. An internal presentation prepared by researchers at Google's Insight Labs, an internal think tank dedicated to understanding and neatly explaining the company's ever-changing policies and products, it made grim reading for anyone concerned about internet freedom.

The presentation discussed Google's emerging role as self-appointed gatekeeper over the flow of information, and its patrician-like duty to protect internet users from so-called harmful content.

The Orwellian title of the briefing summed up the tech giant's view of itself. It was called (without a trace of irony) "The Good Censor."

For someone like me who has documented Silicon Valley's relentless erosion of internet freedom over the past five years, seeing Google's logo emblazoned on a document titled "The Good Censor" was like seeing Hillary Clinton's signature on a letter saying, "Yes, I *personally* murdered Jeffrey Epstein."

Describing the early ideals of Silicon Valley as "utopian," the document proclaimed that internet users were "questioning whether the openness of the internet should be celebrated at all.

"Free speech has become a social, economic, and political weapon," argued the document's authors, who went on to complain that a free and open internet allowed "have-a-go commentators" to compete on an even playing field with "authoritative voices." This, they argued, was a threat to "rational debate."

If those conclusions had come from a think tank or a policy group, they'd have been troubling enough—but they came from Google, which has more influence over the free flow of information than any other company. As of February 2020, the tech giant owns 92 percent of the search engine market, 63 percent of the internet browser market, and 75 percent of the smartphone operating system market.[2] It also has a dominant position as a video-hosting platform through its ownership of YouTube, the second-most-visited website in the world after Google itself.[3]

"The Good Censor" is frighteningly honest about Google's dominance. It admits that Google, Facebook, and Twitter now "control the majority of online conversations." During their early years, all three companies promised their users would be able to enjoy free speech, but they saw a "shift towards censorship" later. "The Good Censor" was Google, the corporate giant of our age, standing over the murdered corpse of internet freedom, yelling, "I did it! It was me!"

The document even argued that Google's censorship was at risk of going too far, recommending that the company should regulate only "tone" and steer clear of regulating "content" (although this is a nonsensical distinction—you can't regulate the former without regulating the latter). As we'll see later in the book, even that modest suggestion was ignored by the tech giant—and every other tech giant that has "shifted towards censorship" in a similar manner.

As described in "The Good Censor," Google and other tech giants in Silicon Valley pulled off the biggest bait and switch of the twenty-first century.

What's more, they admit it! We've gone from Bill Gates praising the arrival of the "global town square" to Alphabet CEO Sundar Pichai boasting to reporters that YouTube erased 9 million videos from its platform.[4] Promises to users of freedom and openness have been replaced by promises to elites of control and so-called authoritativeness. Tech executives deliver these lines with a smile to approving reporters and offer no apology to the billions of internet users to whom they offered a false promise of freedom.

We've already covered the document admitting to the heist—now let's tell the story of how it happened.

The Great Escape

The takeover of the web by a handful of predatory corporations is especially tragic because the success of the World Wide Web—the network of independently owned, universally accessible websites now synonymous with "the internet"—wasn't a foregone conclusion. Had things gone differently, we might have been doomed to a corporate-controlled online network from the very beginning.

The technology behind the web was invented in 1990 by scientist Tim Berners-Lee at the European Organization for Nuclear Research, the Switzerland-based organization usually referred to by its French acronym, CERN. It was simple and liberating. Internet users could create "hypertext documents" (now known as "websites") and link them to other users using the "hypertext transfer protocol" (that's the "http" you see in front of most website addresses). Anyone with an internet connection could set up a website and link to it through a "browser"—also a Berners-Lee invention.

By now, we all know what browsers and websites are, even if we're still hazy on "hypertext transfer protocols." For most people, the "web" and the "internet" mean the same thing. But Berners-Lee's decentralized, individualized World Wide Web was far from the first online service. There were plenty of others, most of which were controlled from the top down by corporations. In the decade preceding the web's invention, big companies like America Online (AOL) and CompuServe offered consumers subscription services to rudimentary online networks. But these corporate-controlled services were very different from the internet we know today.

AOL and CompuServe were walled gardens—a CompuServe user could not access AOL via the former service, and vice versa. Nor, initially, could users access the sprawling World Wide Web, with its myriad independent websites. CompuServe did offer a message board system where various topics could be discussed, but content on these early boards was tightly moderated by the company. Much like Facebook and Twitter, CompuServe could decide what users were allowed to post.

The World Wide Web was different. Since it consisted of independent websites, it was largely free of top-down control. Website owners had complete freedom over what appeared on their digital property. The result was a highly decentralized web, spread out among thousands—and later, millions—of small- to medium-size websites.

A sense of benign anarchy prevailed and, unless you were doing something illegal, there were no restrictions on content, beyond the painfully slow connection speeds that were then the norm. Against a 1990s backdrop of conservative moral panic about rap music, violent video games, and shock-rock pioneer Marilyn Manson, the resulting lack of censorship was a marvel to behold.

Here's how *Time* magazine described the carnival atmosphere of the early Net: "People who use these new entry points into the Net may be in for a shock. Unlike the family-oriented commercial services, which censor messages they find offensive, the Internet imposes no restrictions. Anybody can start a discussion on any topic and say anything. There have been sporadic attempts by local network managers to crack down on the raunchier discussion groups, but as Internet pioneer John Gilmore puts it, 'the Net interprets censorship as damage and routes around it.'"[5]

In the early 1990s, it wasn't certain that Berners-Lee's crazy, free-wheeling World Wide Web would beat its family-friendly corporate competitors. Luckily for all of us, it did. And so, for a short while before the rise of the "Good Censors," internet users experienced a freedom of expression that was unprecedented in human history.

Just a decade earlier, in the 1980s, political activists had had to file First Amendment lawsuits seeking the right to distribute leaflets in shopping malls.[6] But by the end of the 1990s, anyone with an internet connection could access a digital audience that was orders of magnitude larger than any mall. The political establishment, accustomed to a world where access to information was controlled largely by big broadcast networks and national newspapers, was about to feel the world-shaking effects of the new technology.

By the mid-1990s, fewer than half of Americans were connected to the web, and some observers speculated that the technology would prove to be a passing fad.[7] *New York Times* columnist Paul Krugman, in one of his many hilarious fails, predicted that its impact would be "no greater than the fax machine."[8] But, despite its relatively niche status, the web showed at least one early sign of its extraordinary ability to liberate suppressed information and disrupt the mainstream order. In the second term of the Clinton administration, a humble website owner would demonstrate how the web could be used to out-scoop the mainstream media, disrupt mainstream politics, and nearly dethrone a sitting U.S. president.

In 1995, Matt Drudge set up an email newsletter to share show-biz gossip with friends. Within three years, the Drudge Report, having shifted from showbiz to politics and from a newsletter to a website, had attracted tens of thousands of subscribers. Before this, online journalism didn't exist; with the exception of a few sites like Yahoo!, "news" sites were just online versions of print and TV journalism.

The results of Drudge's experiment came quickly. Just a year after setting up his newsletter, Drudge scooped the mainstream media, breaking the news that Republican presidential candidate Bob Dole would select former football star and Housing secretary Jack Kemp as his running mate. Then, in 1998, Drudge landed the mother of all scoops. *Newsweek*, a mainstream newsmag, had spiked a story about the president of the United States, Bill Clinton, having engaged in a sexual affair with Monica Lewinsky, his twenty-three-year-old intern. Drudge, by then a nexus for political gossip, quickly gained access to details of the story—and immediately broke it on the internet. At 9:32 p.m. Pacific time on January 17, 1998, the Drudge Report ran the following headline:

NEWSWEEK KILLS STORY ON WHITE HOUSE INTERN

BLOCKBUSTER REPORT: 23-YEAR OLD, FORMER
WHITE HOUSE INTERN, SEX RELATIONSHIP WITH
PRESIDENT[9]

This was the internet as it was meant to be used. For the first time—but not the last—an online newsman (arguably the first online newsman) changed the course of American politics by breaking news of national importance that the mainstream media wouldn't touch. The story would go on to dominate American politics for more than a year and led to the House of Representatives voting to impeach a sitting president.

Some political analysts argue that the scandal led to the election of George W. Bush in 2000 by preventing Clinton from campaigning on behalf of Bush's opponent, Vice President Al Gore. What's more, the story was broken by a guy with a budget smaller than the annual coffee tab of one mainstream media newsroom. A website owner in his apartment took on the corporate media—and won!

A few liberal journalists saw the threat early on, deriding Drudge-type journalists as the "pajamas media"[10]—a phrase that could be regarded as a precursor to the "fake news" pejorative, which we'll cover in the next chapter. But the trepidation that some in the establishment felt about Drudge wasn't strong enough to generate a full-on backlash against internet freedom...yet.

Maybe you think a sex scandal, even one involving the president, isn't particularly important (although lying about it under oath, as Clinton did, is a different matter). Still, the implication of Drudge's scoop was impossible to ignore—with just a fraction of the mainstream media's resources, website owners on the internet could break stories that altered national politics.

If this wasn't fully apparent at the end of the 1990s, by the early 2010s it had become impossible to ignore. On both the Left and the Right, citizens armed with websites were running rings around the mainstream media. In 2010, the previously obscure website WikiLeaks released footage of the deaths of two Reuters journalists at the hands of U.S. forces in Iraq—another humiliation for the neoconservative foreign policy establishment and its hugely unpopular military interventions. In the same year, Drudge protégé Andrew Breitbart released footage of officials at the Association of Community Organizers for Reform Now (ACORN) seemingly agreeing to help a child trafficker set up an underage prostitution ring. The "trafficker" was an undercover journalist, James O'Keefe, who recorded the encounter and passed the footage to Breitbart for publication on the web. The story would lead to the loss of federal funding and eventual bankruptcy of ACORN, an organization that counted then president Barack

Obama among its alumni and enjoyed widespread support from establishment Democrats.

Breitbart and WikiLeaks were both huge problems for the establishment. The former represented populist conservatism, the latter, antiwar leftism. Both were movements that had been marginalized over the prior three decades by neoliberals and neoconservatives in Washington and their allies in the mainstream media. Yet both were now using the web to publish news stories of national importance that the mainstream media simply couldn't ignore. These were explosive stories that exposed almost unthinkable conspiracies and acts of wrongdoing by establishment-backed institutions. From *Newsweek* to the U.S. military, internet journalism was shining its spotlight into every hidden crevice.

That was the web as it was meant to be. A free, open network that anyone could use to share consequential information, even if the political establishment would rather it never see the light of day. A network that would liberate information from the control of newspapers and broadcast networks, the media barons who censored and simplified information before presenting it to citizens.

Sadly, the freedom offered by the World Wide Web didn't last. Much to the relief of the political establishment, corporations were about to reassert control over the flow of information. The corporate takeover of the web was about to begin.

Rise of the Good Censors

Is there a single American, Democrat or Republican, who wants to be ruled by a corporation?

Most American citizens don't want a future where elections are decided by a Google search algorithm, where Mark Zuckerberg can render your business unprofitable with the push of a button, and where Twitter CEO Jack Dorsey decides whether you're allowed a voice in the public square.

Yet that world, welcomed by no one other than establishment

elites, is where we're rapidly headed. We thought the internet would be an escape from corporate control of information. But the corporations got smart, changed their tactics, and caught up. The Good Censors have arrived.

There was one growing problem with the web: information overload. By the mid-2000s, there were simply too many websites to keep track of. Blogs, which started out as public online diaries, were everywhere. People set up blogs about their pets, their hobbies, current events, and every other topic imaginable. By the early 2010s, it seemed like every tech-savvy millennial was running a blog. In this thicket of information, with new websites sprouting every minute, it was easy to get lost.

During this period, Google became a ubiquitous tool to navigate the complexity. Instead of asking your friends what the best food blog was, you could just ask Google. Its superior search function quickly left competitors, like Ask Jeeves and Yahoo!, by the wayside.

But even search engines weren't enough. What if you were a fan of dozens, or hundreds, of blogs and websites? What if you wanted to monitor all of them, without having to type every address into your browser or click through every link in your bookmarks folder?

A group of energetic, rapidly expanding platforms would offer up a fix to this problem. The solutions they offered were so simple, we were happy to drink from their poisoned chalice on a massive scale— surrendering our digital independence in the process. These serpents were, of course, the social networks.

Don't bother setting up your own blog, said Facebook—just make an account with us, and we'll blast your thoughts out directly to all your friends. Why waste money hosting video on your personal website, asked YouTube—we'll do it for you and give you an audience and ad revenue. All for free! Don't keep a bookmarks folder full of blogs to keep track of current events, said Twitter—just look at our neat list of trending topics!

They also promised that censorship would never happen. YouTube's humble mission, according to its motto (which it has since dropped),[11] was allowing you to "Broadcast Yourself."

Facebook's goal, according to its motto (which it has since dropped),[12] was "Making the World More Open and Connected."

A VP at Twitter declared that the company's mission (which its current CEO has since passed off as a "joke")[13] was to be "the free speech wing of the free speech party."

Google's unofficial slogan (which, though unofficial, it has since dropped—just to make sure!)[14] was "Don't Be Evil."

Whether we believed their now-scrapped slogans or not, these new corporations quickly became unavoidable. Offering unrivaled simplicity of access and the tantalizing chance of instant viral fame, they took off. All we had to do was persuade ourselves that these friendly-looking corporations with their cute mottoes and rainbow-colored logos wouldn't one day go fascist on us.

I mean, they promised not to be evil, right? They *promised*!

A few naysayers saw what was coming. The headlines today might be full of Republicans denouncing corporate censorship, but a few short years ago it was progressives sounding the alarm. The late Aaron Swartz, probably the most respected progressive digital rights campaigner of his time, raised the alarm about corporate censorship as early as 2013.

"Both the government and private companies can censor stuff. But private companies are a little bit scarier," warned Swartz in an interview before his death in 2013.[15]

"They have no constitution to answer to. They're not elected. They have no constituents or voters. All of the protections we've built up to protect against government tyranny don't exist for corporate tyranny.

"Is the internet going to stay free?" asked Swartz. "Are private companies going to censor [the] websites I visit, or charge more to visit certain websites? Is the government going to force us to not visit certain websites? And when I visit these websites, are they going to constrain what I can say, to only let me say certain types of things, or steer me to certain types of pages?"

It's no surprise that progressives like Swartz were concerned about internet censorship. Watergate, the Pentagon Papers, WikiLeaks,

American whistle-blower Edward Snowden—for most of the twentieth and twenty-first centuries, it was progressives who were breaking the big stories that embarrassed the establishment. Today, the cause of free speech is associated with the political Right—but that's a recent development.

Julian Assange, bane of the Western foreign policy establishment, issued similar warnings. In a speech at the Cambridge Union Society in 2011, the WikiLeaks founder predicted that the concentration of online communications in the hands of a few unaccountable corporations would lead inevitably to censorship.

"The field of public discourse occurs on private land when it occurs on the internet," warned Assange. "Archives that are historically important, important to all of us, and become our intellectual record are no longer something that is safe, and no longer something that we can build our discourse on—and indeed build our civilization on—because they are being ripped out from under us at the very moment we are trying to cite them."[16]

Assange also stated, "All over the world, information of historical importance and political importance, that which we build our civil and political life on, is disappearing, because it is in centralized archives owned by private companies."[17]

The warnings went unheeded. The services offered by the tech giants were too convenient and (for some) too lucrative to ignore. By 2015, Facebook had reached 1.5 billion users. In the same year, YouTube announced 8 billion video views per *day*. Instagram, which Facebook acquired in 2012, reached 1 billion users just over five years later.

The web had been taken over by a handful of corporate walled gardens—the very things it was meant to liberate us from. The sun was setting on the free, open web of independent websites and blogs. Enter the web of Facebook, Twitter, Google, and YouTube—the corporations that would become the "Good Censors." The worst predictions of Assange and Swartz were about to come true.

3. The Panic

Censorship never happens in a vacuum—certain historical conditions are always present. Whenever there's a crusade to restrain a new form of expression, be it a book, a song, a video game, or an entire medium of communication, it is always accompanied by its inseparable sibling: moral panic.

The present era is no exception. As we'll detail in the coming chapters, virtually every major tech platform is engaged in a clampdown on "hate speech," the most vague term of the internet age. YouTube is clamping down on "conspiracy theories." Facebook is banning "hate agents." Google is demoting "nonauthoritative sources" in its news search results. Twitter is banning "harassment."

None of this would be possible were it not for the palpable sense of panic about new technologies that has been fomented by politicians and pundits. Simmering in the background since the early 2010s, it exploded with nuclear force after the 2016 election.

Consider the following excerpt from an article published in *Wired* by tech journalist Jason Pontin, which could have been plucked from a sixteenth-century diatribe against the evils of the printing press.

"Social media are doomsday machines," he wrote. "They distract, divide, and madden; we can no longer hear each other, speak coherently, or even think. As a result, our social, civic, and political ligands are dissolving.

"Everywhere, people consult their screens to affirm what they already think and repeat what like-minded people have already said. They submit to surveillance and welcome algorithmic manipulation. Believing absurdities, they commit injustices. A few lose their minds altogether."

Pontin went on to cite several scare stories about social media: a would-be terrorist who read hyperpartisan stories on Facebook before he attempted to pipe-bomb various mainstream media outlets. A mass murderer who shot up a synagogue after reading anti-Semitic conspiracy theories on social media. Both, wrote Pontin, "were nuts before social media; but social media licensed their malevolence in different ways." To curb the corrupting influence of social media, with its fake news, hyperpartisanship, and harassment, Pontin argued that "speech on the internet must flow a little less freely."[1]

Pontin's concern that mass communication is a corrupting influence on the human psyche is nothing new. Go back to the 1970s and 1980s and you'll find sociologists worrying about the "video malaise" theory, the idea that televised news was causing Americans to lose faith in democracy and political institutions.[2] Alongside this concern, pushed primarily by the religious Right, was widespread moral panic about violent TV shows. Violence in America, so went the argument, could be explained only by violence in mass media—even by "violent" role-playing games like Dungeons & Dragons. In the modern era, entertainment executives can rest a little easier—their medium is no longer the alleged breeding ground for mass murderers and the politically disillusioned—Silicon Valley is the boogeyman of the moment.

These panics aren't a historical peculiarity of the postwar era. Every single advance in the ease of human communication has conjured similar fears. Pontin's concerns about social media have much in common with the "video malaise" theory, but they're even more similar to the nineteenth-century panic over cheap literature and newspapers: penny dreadfuls, dime novels, and yellow journalism.

The late nineteenth century, like today, was an era of rapid technological and social change. The industrial revolution was well underway, transforming virtually every profession and institution in Western society. There were huge movements of people from the countrysides to the towns. States were becoming centralized and bureaucratized. The cost of goods was plummeting. So, too, was the cost of communication.

By the end of the nineteenth century, innovations in the production of paper had made books, newspapers, and pamphlets affordable to the common folk. At the same time, mandatory education established by the West's new centralized governments led to a boom in literacy: in 1840, just two-thirds of grooms and half of brides in England and Wales were able to sign their names on marriage documents. By 1900, those figures had increased to 97 percent for both groups.[3] The transformations of the nineteenth century had created a huge market for the written word, together with cheap methods to deliver it. A massive democratization of reading was about to take place—and, along with it, a very familiar panic.

"As to the other class of pernicious literature—the dime and the half-dime novels, the sensational story papers, filled with talk of detectives, and the criminal exploits of cow-boys, and the like—these, though not usually indecent, are, as has been said before, unmistakably demoralizing in the strongest sense. Few people, perhaps, realize to what an extent the issue of these publications increases year by year, or have any conception of the sum of mischief that they surely inflict."

These pearl-clutching words are from *Concerning Printed Poison*, an 1885 pamphlet from moral crusader and professional worrier Josiah Woodward Leeds, a man who would no doubt have a blue checkmark on Twitter identifying his account as authentic were he alive today. His language is a little more flowery than that used by

Jason Pontin in his *Wired* article, but the sentiment—panic about the seismic changes in mass communication that the author was living through—is much the same. So, too, is his insistence that the new forms of communication were enticing disturbed young men down a path marked by senseless violence: "When, about eight years ago, J.T. Fields, in a lecture delivered at Boston, referred to an interview he had with the boy-murderer, Pomeroy, in which the latter spoke of his vicious career as being largely due to the influence of the many sensational stories of adventure and violence he had read, the account was all over the country...Today, however, such recitals are of so common occurrence as scarcely to excite remark."

As if there weren't enough similarities to the present-day panic over social media, Leeds went on to praise the railroad companies—the largest and most powerful private corporations of the era—for banning "trashy, sensationalist literature which has wrecked the happiness of so many homes."[4]

Condemnation of a new form of mass communication. Fearmongering about its alleged role in violent crimes. Praise for private corporations using their market power to suppress the medium and enforce public morality. Was this 1885 or 2020?

As a 2016 article in the *Guardian* notes, nineteenth-century fears over political radicalization were also laid at the doorstep of cheap literature:

> The [penny] dreadfuls were also implicated in social unrest. Since 1884, when the vote had been extended to most British men, the press had often pointed out that children raised on such literature would grow up to elect the rulers of the nation. Penny dreadfuls were "the poison which is threatening to destroy the manhood of the democracy," announced the Pall Mall Gazette in 1886. The Quarterly Review went a step further, warning its readers in 1890 that "the class we have made our masters" might be transformed by these publications into

"agents for the overthrow of society." The dreadfuls gave a frightening intimation of the uses to which the labourers of Britain could put their literacy and newly won power: these fantasies of wealth and adventure might foster ambition, discontent, defiance, a spirit of insurgency. There was no knowing the consequences of enlarging the minds and dreams of the lower orders.[5]

It's ironic to see the *Guardian* poking fun at the nineteenth-century penny-dreadful panic, given that the newspaper publishes a constant stream of scare pieces about alleged political radicalization on the internet. But no matter—the article rings true: nineteenth-century elites worried that mass literacy and mass media would lead to the "overthrow of society," much as present-day political elites worry about social media fueling the rise of populism.

There was even a "fake-news" panic during that era. Out of mass literacy and cheap printing came the disparaging term "yellow journalism," an insult invented by nineteenth-century critics to mock a new type of newspaper explicitly aimed at the newly literate masses rather than elites. These new mass-market papers featured bold, attention-grabbing headlines and focused on crime, scandal, and gossip. The pioneers of yellow journalism blended entertainment with news, adding full-color supplements with comic strips to their papers. Although all these are common features of modern mainstream newspapers, nineteenth-century contemporaries condemned them in much the same terms that clickbait websites are condemned today. One 1910 picture from the illustrator L. M. Glackens depicts William Randolph Hearst Sr., who then ran the *San Francisco Examiner*, as a mischievous jester corrupting the minds of the people with "venom," "attacks on honest officials," "appeals to passion," and "sensationalism." Hearst, for his part, leaned in to his reputation as a master of propaganda. "You furnish the pictures and I'll furnish the war," the newsman once told one of his illustrators amid a push to generate public support for U.S. military intervention against Spain in the Cuban war of independence.

Hearst, the alleged purveyor of sensationalism, went on to develop Hearst Communications, a media conglomerate that today owns more than three hundred magazines and print publications including the *San Francisco Chronicle*, the *Houston Chronicle*, *Cosmopolitan*, *Elle*, and *Esquire*. It also owns 50 percent of A&E Networks, 20 percent of ESPN, and dozens of radio stations around America. Yellow journalism indeed!

The tables have now turned: here's what two writers at the *San Francisco Chronicle*, Hearst's flagship newspaper, had to say about "fake news" in 2016:

> Fake news sites, which run the gamut of political leanings, usually fall into one of two categories: organizations that seek to spread misinformation to manipulate people and sow mistrust, and companies or individuals that use sensational— and false—stories to attract readers and make money through advertising.
>
> Facebook and Google "are essentially polluting an information ecosystem with trash, with garbage, and it's clear that that garbage has an impact," said Gabriel Kahn, a professor at the University of Southern California's Annenberg School for Communication and Journalism. "When you create a marketplace that puts two unequal things on the same level, you're democratizing unequal information. You wouldn't put a carton of milk next to a carton of paste and tell people they're the same thing because they both look white."[6]

Trash! Garbage! Sensational stories! It all sounds quite familiar, doesn't it? If you can hear the faint sound of laughter, that's William Randolph Hearst, chuckling in his grave. If that isn't enough irony for you, take this: the term "yellow journalism" arose from *The Yellow*

Kid, a late nineteenth-century cartoon that depicted a bald boy who wore a yellow nightshirt and appeared to live in a slum. The cartoon was published in the *New York World* and in its competitor, the *New York Journal American*.

Illustration: Louis M. Glackens, *The Yellow Press*, October 2, 1910, Library of Congress / Puck Magazine. (The image depicts William Randolph Hearst, dressed as a jester, distributing "yellow journalism.")

Both publications mimicked each other's style and both were seen as definitive of the lowbrow, mass-market newspapers that were so condemned by elites at the time. Because both papers published *The Yellow Kid*, the term "yellow journalism" stuck. The publisher of the *New York Journal American* was none other than Hearst. And the publisher of the other paper, the *New York World*? That was Joseph Pulitzer, whose name is now attached to the most prestigious awards in journalism. Looking down from the great assignment desk in the sky, Pulitzer, like Hearst, must be having a good laugh at our present-day "fake-news" panic.

Neither the penny dreadfuls nor yellow journalism brought about a collapse in society. On the contrary, many people now sing the praises of Hearst and Pulitzer. But we rarely learn from history and thus now find ourselves in the middle of another panic about another revolution in mass communication—the internet.

Digital-Era Fearmongering

No fewer than eight days after the 2016 election, while votes were still being counted in the state of Michigan, BuzzFeed published the article that would give rise to the fake-news panic. A deep dive into the performance of election-related news articles on Facebook, BuzzFeed's report claimed that the top twenty fake-news stories on the platform generated significantly more engagement (likes, comments, shares, etc.) during the election season than the top twenty articles from "major news outlets."

The report was accurate in one extremely narrow sense: a few obviously fake stories, written by small-time blogs in attempts to generate clicks and advertising revenue, did go viral during the election. But the methodology behind the analysis was deeply flawed—the "major news outlets" that BuzzFeed included in its data set did not include the leading Trump-supporting outlet, Breitbart News, which ranked among the most popular websites in the world—and was at one point *the* most popular political website on Facebook—during 2016.[7] BuzzFeed also failed to include other conservative websites known for producing viral content, like Conservative Tribune and the Daily Caller. Had it done so, the engagement gap between fake-news articles and real-news articles would likely have been smaller.

Politics doesn't care much for facts, though. The BuzzFeed report gave progressive elites what they were desperately searching for in the immediate aftermath of Trump's win—something to blame other than themselves and their own policies. Two days after BuzzFeed published its article—and just ten days after Trump's election—President Barack Obama gave a speech in Berlin warning that "democratic freedoms and market-based economies and prosperity" were all at risk because of fake news.[8] Over the next two months, the outgoing president made it clear to the media that fighting fake news had become one of his top priorities. One of his last acts while in office was to sign a bill into law that funneled millions of federal dollars into American media outlets—the same outlets that were being disrupted by the rise of the internet—in order to counter "foreign propaganda" and "misinformation." The involvement of the outgoing president transformed the fake-news story from a mildly viral BuzzFeed piece into a global, establishment-driven freak-out that continues to this day. Like the authors of penny dreadfuls and yellow journalism before it, Silicon Valley was about to have laid on its doorstep all of society's alleged ills—in particular, its tolerance of those pesky upstarts in the alternative media.

The hapless chief executives of tech companies initially failed to perceive the tidal wave of animosity they were about to endure from the political establishment. When faced with BuzzFeed's "fake-news" story, Facebook CEO Mark Zuckerberg responded in a way that was both honest and accurate—he portrayed it as a post-election search for blame and said it was unfair to Trump supporters to claim that they had all been duped by fake news.

"You know, personally, I think the idea that fake news on Facebook—it's a very small amount of the content—influenced the election in any way is a pretty crazy idea," said Zuckerberg a few days after the election.

"Part of what I think is going on here is people are trying to understand results of the election, but I do think that there is a certain profound lack of empathy in asserting that the only reason that some of them are voting the way they did is because they saw some fake news. I think that if you believe that, then I don't think you have internalized the message that Trump supporters are trying to send in this election."[9]

In the fever-pitch atmosphere of November 2016, perhaps the

Facebook CEO was hoping that the panic would subside and that the angered political establishment would find a new target for its ire. If so, he couldn't have been more wrong.

Over the next two years—and still to this day—major tech platforms faced a concerted assault from the media, politicians, activist organizations, and the employees on whom they depend to create world-beating products. Virtually all the attacks would follow the same familiar pattern: fearmonger, exploit scandal, threaten, and demand censorship.

Shortly after Zuckerberg correctly rubbished the assertion that fake news on his platform had led to the election of Donald Trump, he was set upon by his own staff. After Zuckerberg issued his rebuttal, staff within Facebook set up a "secret, unofficial task force" to combat fake news. According to a Facebook source who leaked to the tech news site Gizmodo, senior officials within the company had been briefed on a "planned News Feed update that would have identified fake or hoax news stories, but disproportionately impacted right-wing news sites by downgrading or removing that content from people's feeds."[10]

In December, with Trump yet to take office, Facebook quickly rushed out a change in policy: it would partner with mainstream-media-approved "fact checkers" to help it identify and label fake news on its platform. Analysis by the Daily Caller discovered that at least one of the fact-checkers was staffed almost exclusively with political left-wingers.[11]

Zuckerberg should have read Rudyard Kipling—once you pay the danegeld, you never get rid of the Dane. Submitting to a mob shakedown doesn't mean the mob will leave you alone. On the contrary, they'll just come back looking for an even bigger payout. Just so with leftists and Big Tech.

A month after Facebook's announcement on fake news, Randall Rothenberg, the CEO of the Interactive Advertising Bureau—an umbrella organization representing many of the brands upon which social media platforms rely for revenue—gave a speech to a room full of advertising and technology executives. In it, he demanded that tech companies and advertisers become the internet's new morality police, scrubbing the digital world of anything corporate America deemed unvirtuous.

"The object of fake news is to fool you into cynicism, mistrust, and even hatred," warned Rothenberg. "From that, our society cannot recover.

"As leaders of our ecosystem—as senior executives in brands, agencies, tech companies, platforms, and publishers—you have a responsibility to keep our commons safe, secure, and flourishing."

Peppered with isolated examples selected for their shock factor, including the inadvertent display of digital ads on a neo-Nazi website and a fake-news story about election fraud that went viral, Rothenberg's speech was replete with fearmongering that could have been plucked from the nineteenth-century diatribes against Hearst and Pulitzer.

"If you do not seek to address fake news and the systems, processes, technologies, transactions, and relationships that allow it to flourish," he warned, "then you are consciously abdicating responsibility for its outcome—the depletion of the truth and trust that undergird democratic capitalism."

Crucially, he also promised to "bring together journalism leaders and other content leaders" to address the problems of "hatred" and "fake news" on the internet.

Rothenberg's speech was important because the alliance of big advertising and big journalism would become a crucial engine of censorship over the next two years, as a combination of hit pieces in the mainstream media and advertising boycotts by big corporations pressured tech platforms to lurch ever further toward censorship.

The other major cog in the wheels of censorship was activist organizations. Five days before Rothenberg issued his rallying cry to digital advertisers, the infamous far-left pressure group Media Matters published a manifesto calling for internet censorship. Subsequently leaked to the Washington Free Beacon, the document cast Media Matters—an outfit closely linked to the Clinton and Obama campaigns, as well as progressive billionaire George Soros—as the "top watchdog against fake news and propaganda." It went on to call for a full-scale purge of right-wing news from social media platforms as part of a wider strategy to destroy the Trump presidency and the populist movement.

The document promised that "serial misinformers and right-wing propagandists" on social media would be "exposed and discredited" and pledged that "Internet and social media platforms, like Google and Facebook, will no longer uncritically and without consequence host and enrich fake news sites and propagandists."

The targets for this campaign of censorship were leading sources of conservative news on the internet. Media Matters' report singled out Breitbart News, Right Side Broadcasting Network, and the Media Research Center, smearing the sites with a range of imagined offenses including support for racism, misinformation, and "right-wing media manipulation."[12]

Such smears are typical of a partisan outfit like Media Matters, whose targets are almost exclusively on the political right. More shocking was how quickly they gained access to the levers of power in Silicon Valley—in the report, Media Matters boasted that it had "established a dialogue" with Facebook and was "engaging" its leadership "behind the scenes" to achieve its objectives. The group also boasted that "after Google revised their terms of service in order to prohibit so-called fake news sites from using their advertising network, it was Media Matters that had the information necessary to identify 40 of the worst fake news sites to which this policy applied."

This would become a pattern in the coming years—bullied by left-wing activists, the mainstream media, and their own advertisers and employees, tech companies would take cues from biased, progressive, anticonservative organizations, all hell-bent on manipulating the flow of information online to serve their particular political agendas. These would include not just Media Matters, but also the neoconservative-run news-rating project NewsGuard, and the Southern Poverty Law Center, an organization notorious for smearing people and organizations with dubious charges of racism and bigotry.

Keep in mind that the campaigners against "fake news" have even less evidence to support their case than did the moral crusaders who had insisted that penny dreadfuls were responsible for murder epidemics.

Brendan Nyhan, a professor of government at Dartmouth College, is no pro-Trump shill. On the contrary, Nyhan is a vocal critic of the president who believes Trump is "sowing the seeds for democratic erosion."[13] But Nyhan is also an expert on media propaganda and its effects on voter behavior, and as such knows that fearmongering about the pervasive power of "fake news" is, for the most part, baloney.

Here's what he wrote in 2018:

Dubious political content online is disproportionately likely to reach heavy news consumers who already have strong opinions. For instance, a study I conducted with Andrew Guess of Princeton and Jason Reifler of the University of Exeter in Britain showed that exposure to fake news websites before the 2016 election was heavily concentrated among the 10 percent of Americans with the most conservative information diets— not exactly swing voters.

The total number of shares or likes that fake news and bots attract can sound enormous until you consider how much information circulates online. Twitter, for instance, reported that Russian bots tweeted 2.1 million times before the election—certainly a worrisome number. But these represented only 1 percent of all election-related tweets and 0.5 percent of views of election-related tweets.[14]

Nyhan probably knew that his argument would fall on deaf ears. After all, the professor is coauthor of an influential study on motivated reasoning—the tendency of people to seek out information that confirms their preexisting beliefs. The study demonstrated that when presented with information that contradicts their opinion, they tend to reject it.[15]

In other words, attempting to debunk someone's beliefs, even with factually correct information, tends to reinforce those beliefs. Nyhan calls this "the backfire effect." If you want an active example of this, look at Facebook's early attempts to put "fake-news" labels on certain news stories—the result was that people became more likely to click on them! In the same way that the "Parental Advisory: Explicit Content" labels made rap more exciting in the 1990s, "fake-news" labels on links to news stories just make people more intrigued.[16]

Given that close to half of America's politically engaged public has convinced itself that "fake news" spread through social media deluded voters into electing Trump, it's unlikely that Nyhan's argument to the contrary will shake them out of their convictions. Nevertheless, the facts are there, for those who want them.

The Virtue of Partisanship

I recognize that this is becoming an exceedingly long chapter, but in the interests of defusing the absurd "fake-news" panic, it's worth dwelling some more on the topic of motivated reasoning. After all, it's this idea—and the concurrent, deeply negative view of human nature that goes along with it—that causes otherwise smart people to foolishly abandon the ideal of free speech.

Attempts to justify the fake-news panic from an academic perspective often rely on studies about motivated reasoning: the tendency of people to seek out facts that affirm their preexisting biases and reject facts that do not.

Modern researchers seem obsessed with proving how dumb and

easily duped we all are. Yet, buried in a 2010 study on "epistemic vigilance"—an academic term for our innate *resistance* to potential misinformation—the seeds of optimism can be found.

"Humans massively depend on communication with others, but this leaves them open to the risk of being accidentally or intentionally misinformed," write the researchers, led by cognitive scientists Dan Sperber of the Central European University and Hugo Mercier of the French National Center for Scientific Research. "To ensure that, despite this risk, communication remains advantageous, humans have, we claim, a suite of cognitive mechanisms for epistemic vigilance."[17]

The theory makes perfect sense—gullibility is a weakness, and it stands to reason that humans have evolved defense mechanisms to mitigate it. When we suspect a source of information isn't being straight with us—like CNN claiming to be politically neutral while feeding us partisan propaganda—it puts our cognitive defense mechanisms on alert. And, in an era of partisanship, where few if any sources are perceived as bias-free, our cognitive defenses are going into overdrive. When nobody can be trusted, we must question everybody.

The mainstream commentariat, upset that fewer and fewer people are blindly accepting their worldview, treat this as a crisis. They talk of a "post-truth era" in which people doubt formerly trusted sources of authority and are open to persuasion from any direction, even (gasp!) Alex Jones. They fail to see the upside—but Sperber and Mercier have.

When we can't persuade others to accept our viewpoint based on trust alone, we turn to reasoning. We assemble evidence and talking points to support our case and get to the business of persuasion. Sperber and Mercier call this the "argumentative theory of reasoning"— we don't reason to find objective truth; we reason to persuade skeptics to agree with our preexisting beliefs. And in an age of skepticism, when few people will accept your points on faith alone, you'd better work on your ability to gather evidence, reason, and argue! Have you seen the upside yet?

It is now widely accepted that human reasoning is motivated by a desire to justify our own biases rather than to achieve an objective understanding of the world. But when we encounter mistrust, we are forced to assemble facts and arguments to support our worldview and thus persuade others. Likewise, those who disagree with us are forced to do the same. And thus, as we clash with our epistemic adversaries, we are forced to find better facts and better arguments to support our case. It's through that dynamic—a *partisan* dynamic—that truth emerges.

But there's a missing piece of the puzzle. The dynamic works only when partisans are engaging with each other rather than preaching to their respective choirs. Everyone instinctively understands that echo chambers are bad, but this is the reason why.

Sperber and Mercier warn us, "When the confirmation bias is not held in check by others with dissenting opinions, reasoning becomes epistemically hazardous, and may lead individuals to be overconfident of their own beliefs…or to adopt a stronger version of those beliefs."[18]

This is what makes the "misinformation" panic so dangerous. If the critics of "fake news" and "hyperpartisanship" get their way, they'll achieve the opposite of their intended goal. By suppressing their partisan opponents—which is, of course, the ultimate objective of the fake-news panic, they'll remove the very thing keeping them epistemically vigilant: the scrutiny of their partisan opponents.

That, by the way, is why I'm in right-wing media. The scrutiny you face as a right-winger, and the consequences of getting things wrong, are far greater than the scrutiny and consequences faced by the Left. Consider this: if you slip into right-wing extremism, you are likely to be totally ostracized, excluded from polite society, and unable to earn a living. Tech platforms will ban you; payment processors will refuse you service; advertising networks will pull out of your website. If you slip into left-wing extremism, that is, communism, you can go on to have a very successful career as a college professor, author, or podcast host.

And if you get things factually wrong? You're a conspiracy theorist, a "Pizzagater," a misinformation peddler. Tech platforms will ban or suppress you, payment processors will refuse to serve you, and so on and so forth.

It's a precarious existence—but it's also the sort of thing that makes a movement far more epistemically vigilant than its rivals. And an epistemically vigilant movement is a movement that is, often, correct.

Sadly, nuanced notions such as these do not appear to have occurred to the Silicon Valley elite. Or, if they have occurred to them, they've been ignored in favor of subservience to journalists and left-wing advocacy groups. Despite the obvious hysteria of the post-election panic, Big Tech ultimately bowed to it, embarking on a campaign of radical censorship and control.

4. Plausible Deniability

The architects of the panic, left-wing journalists and advocacy groups, could be reasonably upfront about their biases. In its post-election report, Media Matters denounced "right-wing media manipulation" on the web, singled out mainstream conservative publications like Breitbart News and Right Side Broadcasting, and declared itself "ready to stop them." A year later, a shockingly biased study from the Oxford Internet Institute somehow concluded that virtually every major conservative website, including the Drudge Report, Breitbart, the Daily Caller, the Federalist, and the Washington Free Beacon, was "junk news."[1] It proves two things—that you should never trust a word of what obviously partisan academics say about conservatives, and that the fake-news panic was never really about fake news. The removal of genuine misinformation might be a happy side effect of their efforts, but the real purpose was always clear—to silence an ideological perspective.

This left the tech giants in a difficult position. While virtually all of them despised Trump, they still needed to maintain a veneer of political neutrality. Unlike left-wing academics and nonprofits, they couldn't simply declare a crusade on "right-wing manipulation" or publish a hit list of conservative websites. They may be evil, but they certainly aren't stupid. As Trump took the oath of office with a GOP-controlled House and Senate, Silicon Valley faced a minimum of two years of Republican rule in Washington, the city that Big Tech relies on for its legal privileges and government contracts, as well as the H-1B visas it uses to flood the Bay Area with foreign workers. Its approach to censorship would have to be somewhat softer than the one advocated by Media Matters.

Even as the tech giants purged prominent conservatives and alternative media sources from their platforms, they insisted that they were remaining politically neutral. "We consider ourselves to be a platform for all ideas," Facebook CEO Mark Zuckerberg told the world.[2] Just a few months earlier, an overhaul to his platform's News Feed was followed by a nearly 50 percent drop in engagements on President Trump's Facebook page,[3] and a more than 50 percent drop in Facebook traffic to some conservative websites.[4]

As time goes on and the bans of prominent conservatives mount, the protestations of political neutrality from Big Tech companies sound increasingly absurd.

Take Facebook's much-publicized showdown with the Democrats in late 2019 and early 2020 over the social network's refusal to "fact-check" political advertisements. The controversy began after the Democratic National Committee, along with leading Democratic politicians, began a campaign to force Facebook to submit Trump ads to review by largely liberal-leaning third-party fact-checkers. "It is unacceptable for any social media company to knowingly allow deliberately misleading material to corrupt its platform," said a spokesman for the campaign of former vice president Joe Biden after Facebook agreed to run an ad from the Trump campaign spotlighting the former's shady dealings with Ukraine.

Facebook, in a rare moment of sanity, disagreed—perhaps because it sensed the morass that lay ahead if it decided to rate politicians and political ads on their truthfulness. "We don't believe, however, that it's an appropriate role for us to referee political debates and prevent a politician's speech from reaching its audience," said Facebook Global Affairs VP Nick Clegg.[5]

The sentiment was echoed by Mark Zuckerberg. "We think people should be able to hear what politicians have to say," said the Facebook CEO. "I don't think it's right for tech companies to censor politicians in a democracy." Writing about the remarks, an unintentionally optimistic *New York Times* headline declared: "Defiant Zuckerberg Says Facebook Won't Police Political Speech."

On the one hand, it's a positive development that Facebook resisted Democratic bullying over political ads. On the other hand, Zuckerberg's promise not to censor politicians rang hollow. By the time he made his remarks, the platform had already permanently banned two prominent right-wing politicians: the English anti-Sharia activist and political candidate Tommy Robinson and Republican congressional candidate Laura Loomer, who is based in Florida. The platform had, by that time, also purged a range of prominent right-wing voices, including British YouTube star Paul Joseph Watson, American radio host Alex Jones, and Canadian writer Gavin McInnes. Zuckerberg pledging not to censor political speech, after years of purging various political voices from the platform, is like the Joker speaking out against crime.

Google was even more brazen. A spokeswoman for the company told me, in 2019, that "Google has never manipulated or modified the search results or content in any of its products to promote a particular political ideology." But the reason I was talking to her in the first place was because Breitbart News had obtained evidence that YouTube, a Google-owned platform, had, following pressure from a left-wing *Slate* journalist, added the term "abortion" to a file called "YouTube controversial query blacklist." As a result, several highly popular pro-life videos fell out of the top ten search results, replaced by anodyne or openly pro-abortion videos from largely mainstream and left-wing media organizations. The "blacklist" file also contained search queries for Representative Maxine Waters, Democrat from California; and the antigun activist David Hogg. One Google employee, in a leaked message, described the existence of the file as a "smoking gun" proving political bias.[6]

A YouTube spokeswoman also explained (without referring to the blacklist specifically) that the video-hosting site is a "platform for free speech" but that it has also been "working to better surface news sources across our site for news-related searches and topical information" and to "help give users more authoritative sources."

I take this to mean that in the opinion of YouTube executives, none of the pro-life videos that disappeared from the top ten results were as "authoritative" as the mainstream and left-wing videos that replaced them. You see, they aren't biased between left-wing and right-wing content, just between "authoritative" and "nonauthoritative" content. It just so happens that the "authoritative" sources are commonly left-wing and mainstream, while the "nonauthoritative" sources are often right-wing or independent. How convenient!

It is, of course, quite hard to see it as just a convenient little accident. The Left excels at inventing new terminology to demonize its political opponents and then uses its new, invented labels to get them censored and deplatformed. Before the panic, left-wing activists mastered this tactic on college campuses, getting all manner of conservative and classically liberal speakers disinvited from speaking events on the grounds that their presence made students feel "unsafe," or that the speakers were "bigoted" or "hateful." Take the following word salad, which was sent by a far-left activist to a student at Williams College who had invited the conservative author Suzanne Venker to speak at the college in 2015: "When you bring a misogynistic, white supremacist men's rights activist to campus in the name of 'dialogue' and 'the other side,' you are not only causing actual mental, social, psychological, and physical harm to students, but you are also—paying—for the continued dispersal of violent ideologies that kill our black and brown (trans) femme sisters."[7]

Browse through the "disinvitation database" at the website of the Foundation for Individual Rights in Education, and you'll find hundreds of similar examples.[8] Moderates and firebrands alike have been denied speaking opportunities, from law professor Amy Wax (disinvited from Princeton University for "racism")[9] to religion critic Ayaan Hirsi Ali (disinvited from Brandeis University for criticizing Islam).[10] The use of "safety" as an excuse for pressuring colleges to disinvite controversial speakers has been well documented.[11] In one notorious example in the United Kingdom, a philosophy club dedicated to Friedrich Nietzsche was banned because Nietzsche's ideas (which are sometimes linked to right-wing ideologies) allegedly made students feel "unsafe."[12]

You may think this has nothing to do with Big Tech, but for several reasons, it's key. First, it shows how the Far Left twists and turns our everyday language into weapons of censorship. Whether it's the broadening of terms like "hate speech" and "racism," or the warping of previously neutral terms like "safety," the reason the Left takes these words and repeats them over and over is to turn them into red-hot scarlet letters that can be used to delegitimize and ultimately deplatform their opponents. Second, it shows that censorship is rarely confined to the margins. You don't have to be a rhetorical bomb thrower like Ann Coulter or Michelle Malkin to get deplatformed on a college campus; the same has happened to people as moderate as Venker, Ali, and the very embodiment of establishment conservatism, George Will.[13] This is the ultimate goal of the Far Left in Silicon Valley as well, even if they aren't always successful. Third, it shows the Left to be either utterly extremist or acting in bad faith— virtually none of the people they've labeled "hateful" or "dangerous" actually are.

Those lessons from the campus wars should be borne in mind when considering the vast proliferation of new terminology during the post-election panic that was the subject of chapter 3. Terms like "misinformation," "fake news," "conspiracy theories" and "hyper-partisan content" could be found everywhere as journalists and left-wingers agonized over the online forces that they believed led to the election of Donald Trump.

Think, above all, about the timing—"fake news" simply wasn't a common phrase before the 2016 election. "Hyperpartisanship" was only just emerging as a concern. The panic over the destabilizing effects of social media was almost entirely a post-election matter. The same social media tools that were perfectly acceptable to the Left when Obama used them in 2008 and 2012 became an insidious threat when they helped Trump win the White House. Indeed, the only major incident where we see similar language used to describe the corrupting, destabilizing, "hateful" side of social media is in the Gamergate controversy a few years prior to the Trump campaign. The predominantly online controversy, which raged for years on major social media channels, was an online revolt of gamers against the encroachment of overbearing political correctness into their hobby.

In that, we saw an early sign of the coming reaction to the Trump election—social media is wonderful when it helps progressives, as it did in Obama's election campaigns and in movements like Black Lives Matter—but terrible, corrupting, and "hateful" when it's used to thwart their agenda.

The formula that the Left followed in all these events is a simple one that has, as we saw, been used to great effect on college campuses: first, use a negative label to define your opponents ("hateful," "racist," "misogynist," etc.). Then, pressure social media companies—just as college administrators were pressured—into banning anyone who bears the label. Then watch as, one by one, your enemies are kicked off the internet. In this mission, the tech giants have, knowingly or unknowingly, played along, developing an ever more elaborate machinery to expel people from their platforms.

Since the early 2010s, tech platforms have expanded their community guidelines to include bans on "harassment" and "hate speech." These bans are frequently applied to major right-of-center figures. It should not be surprising, if we remember the campus wars, that the departments that oversee these rule changes, in Twitter, Facebook, and Google, all have the same name—Trust and Safety. Initially formed to protect users from spambots and scammers, they are now full to the brim with wild-eyed leftists like Twitter Trust and Safety policy manager Olinda Hassan, who boasted to an undercover journalist that her team was working on ways to get "the sh*tty people to not show up" on Twitter.[14]

Another lesson from college campuses that is relevant for the Big Tech issue is the sensitivity gap between liberals and conservatives. While it's now a cliché for left-leaning folk to be labeled "snowflakes" because they melt down whenever their views are challenged, it is actually quite important to know if one side of America's political divide is more sensitive than the other, because those are the ones who are most likely to hit the "report" button on Facebook, Twitter, or YouTube. Studies on the behavior of social media users provide the stereotype with empirical support—a survey of political and social behavior conducted after the 2016 election found that Democratic women were more than twice as likely as the average American to block or unfriend someone on social media because of a political disagreement.[15]

It's reasonable to assume that people who are likely to block content are also likely to report it, and that, as social media companies give them more excuses to do so, they will use them. As the campus wars show, members of the Left are far more likely than those on the right to conduct organized campaigns to deny their opponents a platform.

But even if we don't make that assumption, knowing that Democrats are more likely to block people on social media allows us to conclude that the stated policies of social media companies favor the Left. As Twitter admitted in a 2018 blog post, one of the "signals" that the platform uses to determine which accounts they might wish to suppress is how often it has been blocked, and by whom.

"Some of the signals we use to determine bad-faith actors," wrote Trust and Safety team members Vijaya Gadde and Kayvon Beykpour, is "how other accounts interact with you (e.g., who mutes you, who follows you, who retweets you, who blocks you, etc.)."

I've asked Twitter on more than one occasion if they had considered the fact that Democrats are more likely to block than non-Democrats. The most the company has said is that it does not "make political judgments" on people's use of the service.

Those who suspect that the policies of Big Tech are affected by thinly veiled political bias are unlikely to be reassured by the statements of Silicon Valley executives. Even when the hyperprogressive tech lords try to argue in favor of political neutrality, they do so grudgingly. In 2020, the *New York Times* leaked an internal message to Facebook employees from executive Andrew "Boz" Bosworth. In the post, Bosworth admitted that he desperately wanted Trump to lose the next election.

"I'm no fan of Trump. I donated the max to Hillary...As a committed liberal I find myself desperately wanting to pull any lever at my disposal to avoid the same result," wrote Bosworth.

So far, so terrifying. There's good news, though! Despite his anti-Trump instincts, Bosworth concluded that it would be a bad idea for Facebook to intervene in the election against Trump. Comparing the power of Facebook to the corrupting power of the One Ring in *Lord of the Rings*, Bosworth wrote, "As tempting as it is to use the tools available to us to change the outcome, I am confident we must never do that or we will become that which we fear."[16]

Are we supposed to applaud Bosworth's statements? Are they meant to be reassuring? He is, evidently, trying to do the right thing by opposing efforts to have Facebook meddle in the election. But, by his own admission, he has to hold his nose while he does it. How many thousands of employees does Facebook have who don't have his self-restraint? Does Bosworth review every content-removal decision, every ban of a prominent conservative influencer or news source, or are those decisions made by people with fewer scruples than he? If Bosworth is the high bar for political neutrality in Silicon Valley, we're in trouble.

Google's executives have made even more frightening comments behind closed doors. As I noted in chapter 1, a recording of their reaction to the election of Trump during a company all-hands meeting was leaked to me in 2018. The sheer craziness of some of the comments made by the leaders of the most powerful company in the world ensured that it became my most viral scoop in a career that has lasted half a decade to date. From Sergey Brin saying the election result "deeply offended" him to Kent Walker declaring his intention to make populism a "hiccup" in history, the bias on display was blatant and unrestrained.

So, there you have it. In public, the tech giants insist on their political neutrality. Behind closed doors, it's a different story—Facebook's Bosworth admits he really wants to "pull a lever" to stop Trump, even if he knows he shouldn't. And Google's Kent Walker, a man with seemingly fewer scruples than Bosworth, professes his desire to make nationalism and populism a "blip" in world history.

And these are the *leaders* of the tech companies. Imagine what their younger, more radical employees might be doing when the supervisors' backs are turned—especially when making decisions about the all-important content reviews, which affect who gets banned from a platform and who stays. I already compared the distortion of language from left-wing critics of social media to the rhetorical tactics used by far-left activists on college campuses, and as we'll see in later chapters, the beliefs of lower-level Big Tech workers bear a great deal of resemblance to the campus wokesters.

If we're being extremely charitable to Big Tech, it could be argued that they were initially blindsided, both by Trump's election and by the onslaught of pressure from partisan activists and the media, and that Facebook's resistance to Democratic pressure on political ads is an early sign of tech companies' growing a spine and standing up to left-wing bullies.

But that's if we're being extremely charitable. The picture changes when we turn our attention away from what Silicon Valley *says* and focus it instead on what Silicon Valley *does*.

5. Deleted

The panic set up the impetus for political censorship from Big Tech companies. But how does this censorship take place? There are two ways, which I will address over two chapters. The first is the hammer—outright bans of prominent conservative personalities, news sources, and grassroots activists. This is overt censorship, the kind that hits you in the face and lets you know it's there. The second is covert censorship—"shadowbans" and a wide range of other hidden mechanisms that rank conservative content lower in social media algorithms; machine-learning systems designed to kick off conservatives; and a system of behind-the-scenes policymaking in Big Tech companies that systematically excludes conservative input. That's the unseen poison that slowly kills you.

Let's start with the first form of censorship—the bans, the suspensions, and the overt removal or suppression of content. In the years since Trump's election, his movement has been victimized by two important types of censorship—bans from major social media platforms and bans from major financial platforms. Both severely restrict the ability of the president and his supporters to spread their message. We'll cover the first, more familiar type of censorship in the first half of this chapter, before moving on to the latter.

When it comes to overt censorship from social media platforms, even the president of the United States is not immune. A 2019 investigation by CBS News' *60 Minutes* revealed that YouTube has, to date, taken down no fewer than *three hundred* of the Trump campaign's videos.[1] Facebook, too, has taken down at least one—an ad from the president's campaign about mass immigration, released shortly before the 2018 midterm elections.[2]

Censoring the president's campaign messages, including one that aired right before a major election, demonstrates a level of brazenness from Silicon Valley that seems almost unreal. Perhaps it's because they know their allies in the administration will prevent Trump from wielding his executive authority to stop the bias, and that their allies in DC "conservatism" have snuffed out any chance of regulation from Republicans.

Another example of Silicon Valley's hubris is its response to journalism exposing their biases. In June 2019, James O'Keefe's investigative journalism organization, Project Veritas, released undercover footage showing a Google executive, Jen Gennai, appearing to suggest that Google was "training its algorithms" to avoid a repeat of an outcome like the one that occurred in the 2016 election. Almost immediately, Google-owned YouTube removed the video. In swift succession, Vimeo, a competitor to YouTube, followed suit, banning Project Veritas' whole account on the grounds that its content was "hateful, defamatory, or discriminatory." (Vimeo failed to explain how Project Veritas, whose videos are straight news reports combined with undercover footage exposing the powerful, falls into any of those categories.) Twitter, meanwhile, blocked a Project Veritas tweet that contained a video revealing inside information about a different tech company, Pinterest.[3] The platform would later prevent Project Veritas from running ads aimed at recruiting new employees to work as journalists.[4]

The fact that companies like Twitter and YouTube feel comfortable enough to ban videos containing investigative journalism about wrongdoing in their own industry is mind-boggling in its brazenness. It's amazing that Republicans continue to let them get away with it.

The removal of President Trump's ads from YouTube and the

censorship of conservative journalists investigating Silicon Valley were worth covering in-depth, as they reveal the mind-set of the Silicon Valley censors—they truly believe they can get away with anything. But they're also just two examples. If we were to spend a page on every single prominent right-winger who has been censored on a major social media platform, this book would be thousands of pages long. Nevertheless, it is worth listing them at least—when you step back and look at just how many of the president's supporters have been banned from major tech platforms, the picture is breathtaking.

To name just a few: Alex Jones and Infowars, banned from every platform including Facebook, Instagram, YouTube, Apple Podcasts, and even Pinterest. Paul Joseph Watson, banned from Facebook and Instagram. Gavin McInnes, banned from Twitter and Facebook. Laura Loomer, banned from Facebook, Instagram, and Twitter. Nick Monroe, banned from Twitter. Enrique Tarrio, banned from Twitter. Roger Stone, banned from Twitter. R. C. Maxwell, banned from Twitter. Milo Yiannopoulos, banned from Facebook, Twitter, and Instagram. Tommy Robinson, banned from Facebook, Instagram, YouTube, and Twitter. Carl Benjamin, banned from Twitter. LaCorte News, banned from Facebook. Right Wing News, banned from Facebook. The Epoch Times, banned from Facebook advertising.

Whatever we may think of the banned and censored figures, most simply had the misfortune of being caught holding the wrong political viewpoints at the wrong time. Some, like Infowars and the Epoch Times, were subjected to smear campaigns from mainstream journalists, who pressured social media companies into action. But, from an electoral standpoint, these differing circumstances don't really matter. They were all, at one time or another, able to present pro-Trump (or at least occasionally Trump-sympathetic) messages to sizable audiences. In the intense fight for attention that occurs ahead of an election, that matters. And the Democratic politicians and mainstream media reporters who agitated for many of these bans, as well as the tech companies that eventually implemented them, know that it matters.

When the silencing of those voices is added to the countless banned grassroots Trump supporters who lack the clout or connections wielded by major media figures, the collective impact is enormous.

Linda Suhler is not a name that will be familiar to conservatives who don't use Twitter, but among the Trump supporters and Tea Partiers who frequent the platform, she's a legend of sorts. Her account has existed for almost a decade, and in that time, she has transformed it into a rallying point for conservative activists. A number of her close friends started off on the platform at the same time and have quietly been accumulating followers for more than nine years, through both the Tea Party and Trump movements. Several have hundreds of thousands of followers. These activists are a nexus of conservative grassroots energy on Twitter; they send out action alerts, drum up support for phone and email campaigns, and direct followers to other up-and-coming conservative accounts. Suhler and her fellow travelers are a prime example of how ordinary grassroots activists can use Twitter to energize and organize the conservative movement. So, naturally, in December 2019, after President Trump retweeted her, Twitter banned her account.

She wasn't the only one who was banned. A day or so earlier, Twitter had banned another user who was part of the network, a long-standing account known only by her first name, Christi. Others included accounts with names like TrumpGirlOnFire and InBlond-WeTrust. All had thousands, if not tens of thousands, of followers, and all were suspended after a retweet from the president. Their bios were full of "KAG" (Keep America Great), "MAGA," and other pro-Trump slogans. To Generation Z (zoomer) "America First" conservatives, these accounts may seem a little over-the-top, with their entire Twitter presence seemingly dedicated to mobilizing President Trump's base, hailing his victories, and denouncing his detractors.

To the young reader, the phrase "OK boomer" might come to mind. But, for a president or presidential candidate, people like Suhler and Christi are invaluable—they are the shock troops of the digital grass roots, the people who ensure his messages reach his online supporters and those who constantly drum up activity to boost his support.

Some of the accounts, including Suhler's, were later restored. But others were not. It's not hard to surmise what happened—upon receiving a retweet from Trump, all the accounts were likely met with mass-reporting campaigns from perpetually angry leftists who monitor the president's Twitter feed. Indeed, a Twitter representative confirmed to me over the phone that this is the most likely explanation for all of them being suspended quickly after a presidential retweet. However, the representative was hazy on why some of the accounts remained banned. The only explanation I got was that they were engaged in "platform manipulation," an allegation that baffled the fifty-two-year-old woman who owned one of the accounts, who wanted it only to post messages of support for the president.

The damage that a political movement sustains when its grass roots is deplatformed is enormous. In an election year, it's even more important than the banning of better-known conservative media personalities, whose priority is the creation of compelling commentary around different topics, as opposed to a sole focus on mobilizing the pro-Trump movement. Especially in the case of accounts like Suhler's; she organically built her Twitter following over nearly a decade.

Such accounts serve as network hubs for a larger movement. The movement uses retweets from the hub to find new accounts to follow, and the node can also serve as a source of news, information, and action alerts for activists. When that suddenly disappears, the ability of the movement to organize takes a massive hit. Information becomes harder to pass around the network, and followers of the node that responded to its action alerts will wander around, listless— or get bored with Twitter altogether and leave.

In Trump's case, it also makes it hazardous for him to draw any more attention on social media to his most enthusiastic grassroots supporters, lest they be banned as well, a fact that hinders his ability to help them reach more people. This is how an online political movement dies—or, to say it more accurately, how it is murdered.

Hate Facts

If your blood isn't already boiling at the blatant and widespread suppression of conservative content by Big Tech companies, it surely will do so when you read some of the justifications that these companies have used. As we saw in the previous chapter, Silicon Valley wordsmiths have developed a language of censorship that gives them plausible deniability when removing conservatives from their platforms, allowing them to point to superficially nonpartisan reasons for content removals and suspensions. Sadly for them, the bias behind those justifications is fairly transparent to nonliberal onlookers.

Take Alex Jones, who was banned by Instagram and Facebook in the spring of 2019 (his media organization, Infowars, had been banned from most platforms almost a year prior). To justify its ban, Facebook branded Jones—along with Laura Loomer, Paul Joseph Watson, and several other political figures—a "dangerous individual." Dangerous! Really? You would think the geniuses at Facebook could come up with a better excuse. Whatever you think of Jones, calling him "dangerous" requires a stretch of the imagination. Jones is a radio shock jock, a bombastic quasi-comedian and a political opinionator, not a terrorist. Perhaps when Facebook says "dangerous," what it really means is "dangerous to the status quo." That would demystify the reason for Jones' ban, and those of others.

Establishment conservatives turn up their noses at people like Jones, calling him a loon. Maybe he is! But there are plenty of loons on the left who don't get purged from every social media platform.

And if more straitlaced conservatives think they won't be next, they're wrong. Andy Ngo is no rabble-rouser—he's a serious journalist who regularly puts his own safety on the line to provide on-the-ground coverage of far-left riots. Twitter locked Ngo out of his account for "hateful conduct," demanding that he delete a tweet about a hot-button issue in order to regain access to his account. Ngo's tweet, posted in response to a tweet from Chelsea Clinton implying that black trans women were being victimized because of their race, was as follows: "The US is one of the safest countries for trans people. The murder rate of trans victims is actually lower than that for cis population. Also, who is behind the murders? Mostly black men."

On all empirical points, Ngo's tweet was verifiable. The murder rate of trans victims is indeed lower than the murder rate for non-trans victims, as can be determined by looking at FBI crime statistics and data from the Human Rights Campaign, which tracks transgender murders. The fact that most of the perpetrators are black men is also verifiable. These are all facts, and Ngo cited his sources in a follow-up article for the Post Millennial.[5] And yet, Twitter still deemed them "hateful" and demanded he delete the tweet before restoring his account. Social media companies have a tough enough time making everyone believe that "hate speech" is real. They apparently want us to accept the existence of "hate facts" as well.

A similar thing happened to the English anti-Sharia-law campaigner and right-wing activist Tommy Robinson, who was permanently banned from the platform after pointing out that the majority of people convicted of "grooming" underage girls for sex in the United Kingdom are Muslim men. The moderate liberal Muslim and former government adviser Maajid Nawaz came to Tommy's defense, pointing to official crime statistics that backed up his assertion.[6] It didn't matter. He'd tweeted a hate fact. He was gone. (Twitter said he was banned for "clear violations" of its hateful conduct policy.)

Some employees of tech platforms apparently believe that, in addition to hate facts, there is "hate journalism." In 2017, the online funding platform Patreon banned journalist and filmmaker Lauren

Southern after she documented a right-wing activist group's attempt to expose the efforts of a left-wing nongovernmental organization (NGO) to ferry illegal immigrants into Europe across the Mediterranean. Patreon's justification for Southern's removal beggars belief—it said that by interfering with the activities of the NGO's "rescue operations"—their way of dressing up what could easily be described as a people-smuggling operation—Southern's work could "lead to loss of life."[7] I wonder if Patreon feels the same way about the governments of Italy and Malta, which later took action to ban NGO migrant vessels (including the *Aquarius 2*, the very same ship documented by Southern) from their shores.

In fact, migrant deaths caused by risky Mediterranean crossings plummeted as newly elected populists in Europe clamped down on the crossings.[8] With the tightening of border controls, the incentive for migrants to risk themselves and their families on rickety rafts in the hope that an NGO ship might rescue them diminished. So not only is Patreon's assertion wrong (and borderline defamatory); the exact opposite is true, at least insofar as Southern's reporting contributed to the restoration of authority at Europe's maritime borders. Then again, keen observers of Silicon Valley progressives know that to them, the accuracy of facts matters far less than their orthodoxy.

The justifications that tech companies use to ban conservatives and right-wingers range from absurd to downright outrageous. If you make factual assertions based on official crime statistics, you're being "hateful." If your radio skit is too bombastic and aggressive, you're "dangerous." If you report critically on the glorified people smugglers who incentivize migrants to risk their lives, you're the one whose actions could "lead to loss of life." Stepping back and looking at the complete picture, it's hard to escape the conclusion that tech companies will twist the meaning of words to their absolute breaking points, so long as it gives them an excuse to ban a prominent right-winger.

When we look at their approach to the Left, the exact opposite appears to be true. The best example of this is the way tech companies responded to the media-manufactured "controversy" surrounding a group of Trump-supporting boys from Covington Catholic High School in Kentucky, who were confronted by activists during a visit to Washington. A selectively edited clip of their encounter with a bellicose left-wing activist, Nathan Phillips, went viral among mainstream journalists on Twitter who accused the boys of "harassing" Phillips. Even though Phillips had been the one to confront the boys, the clip, which showed MAGA-hat-wearing Covington student Nicholas Sandmann smiling sheepishly at the far-left activist, generated an unusual level of rage from journalists and the online left. One CBC journalist called it the "condescending smirk of white privilege."[9]

For the crime of smirking, the Covington kids were set upon by the mad dogs of left-wing Twitter—and a fair few mainstream journalists and personalities too. One left-wing DJ tweeted, "LOCK THE KIDS IN THE SCHOOL AND BURN THAT B*TCH TO THE GROUND." Author and pundit Reza Aslan mused, "Have you ever seen a more punchable face than this kid's?" A reporter for Vox's tech news site, VentureBeat, had similar thoughts: "Giving a shit-eating grin to a Native American's face isn't legally violence. But he is smiling *about* the violence," tweeted the reporter. "He is saying, 'my people hurt you, and you can't touch me even while I gloat about it.' It is fascism. And you should punch fascists." Left-wing "comedian" Kathy Griffin called on her followers to hunt down the names of the high school kids. "If you think these fuckers wouldn't dox you in a heartbeat, think again," she tweeted. ("Dox" refers to publicizing someone's personal information, such as their address and phone number, on the internet.)

At a time when the tech giants seize on the slimmest of justifications to permanently ban right-wing figures, you would think that brazen calls for violence—against high school kids, no less—would result in a speedy ban from Twitter. But this was not the case. While a spokeswoman did confirm to me that the platform made some of the offenders delete their tweets, some—like Aslan's, Griffin's, and the VentureBeat reporter's—did not receive such treatment.[10] As for those who did have to delete their tweets, nothing further happened to them. They were not banned, and indeed, they kept their blue "verified" checkmarks—Twitter's stamp of approval. Is there any better demonstration of Silicon Valley's bias than a platform that bans right-wingers over factual assertions, while allowing the scum who physically threatened high school kids to remain? Even ardent free-speech defenders agree that incitement to violence crosses a line, yet it seems there are some circumstances in which Twitter reacts to such behavior only halfheartedly. When I asked why the accounts are still active and verified, Twitter said, "We enforce our rules consistently, regardless of whether the person on our service has a blue check or not."

And what about "hateful conduct," the platform's stated reason for locking out Andy Ngo? While Ngo was punished for stating a verifiable fact, the platform did nothing when virulently racist tweets from *New York Times* writer Sarah Jeong were uncovered. In one, Jeong compared white people to "dogs pissing on fire hydrants." In another, she said she enjoyed being "cruel to old white men." Not only did Twitter not force her to delete her tweets, as it did with Ngo, but the platform went on to give her account its stamp of approval with a "verified" checkmark.

Here were two journalists, both with wide national audiences, being treated completely differently. This could mean two things: either Twitter gives left-wingers a pass on its "hate speech" rules, or its idea of "hate speech" is so skewed that it's almost impossible for hate from left-wingers to be categorized as such.

Facebook is little better. In documents leaked to Breitbart News, the platform's employees cited an interview with previously banned anti-Sharia activist Tommy Robinson as one of the reasons for Paul Joseph Watson being labeled a "hate agent" and banned from the platform.[11] Yet Facebook has done nothing but monitor Malik Zulu Shabazz, an open black nationalist and admirer of well-known racist Louis Farrakhan, who is also banned from the platform.

Watson's pages were removed in part because he merely interviewed Robinson—a man who hasn't said anything nearly as offensive as Farrakhan, who once compared Jews to "termites." Yet Zulu Shabazz, who himself once shouted, "Kill every goddamn Zionist in Israel! Goddamn little babies, goddamn old ladies! Blow up Zionist supermarkets,"[12] remains on Facebook, where he openly posts his admiration for Farrakhan. Even the far-left Southern Poverty Law Center calls Shabazz a "racist black nationalist," yet he remains on Facebook. It's not as if the platform isn't aware of him—he was one of the names on its potential "hate agents" list. In response to my questions for this book, Facebook confirmed that one of the "signals" that contributed to its decision to ban Watson was his praise of Robinson in 2019, but that it was "not the only signal" that contributed to the decision. Facebook did not divulge what other signals it considered.

And what of Patreon, the platform that thinks journalism can kill people? The platform tolerates—and profits from—far-left extremists who openly call for violence against their political opponents. One such group is the Red Guards Austin, whose members pose with AK-47s in Facebook photos and who urge supporters to create "paramilitary organizations" around the United States. Promoting weapons training and "revolutionary violence," the group promises that "fascists and their collaborators can be drowned out, run out, routed, beaten bloody, and even annihilated." Although the militant group's presence on Patreon has been documented and brought to the company's attention by the antiextremism watchdog Far Left Watch, the funding platform has refused to act. It seems Patreon believes that right-wing journalism can kill but that left-wing revolutionaries armed with AK-47s cannot.[13]

The Covington freak-out, Malik Zulu Shabazz, the Red Guards Austin—these are just a few examples where left-wingers have seemingly been let off with slaps on the wrist, if that. I have little doubt that countless other examples must exist. Cataloguing all of them would be an excellent project for a conservative think tank. Sadly, as we'll see in later chapters, most of the conservative research establishment is occupied with defending the tech giants rather than criticizing them.

Of course, it's not just Trump supporters who are getting banned. Also caught in the cross fire have been plenty of independents and centrists, like independent journalist Ford Fischer (demonetized on YouTube) or the antiwar libertarian Free Thought Project (banned from Facebook). Occasionally, a social media platform will ban a truly extreme left-winger like Louis Farrakhan, as Facebook and Twitter have done. Nevertheless, it is obvious which side has incurred the bulk of the damage. You will struggle to find a mainstream, Democrat-supporting account with influence comparable to that wielded by Alex Jones or Paul Joseph Watson who has been banned from a major social media platform (much less all of them, as is the case with Jones). Even when they openly call for violence, as many Twitter "blue checks" did during Covingtongate, their accounts miraculously escape the ban hammer.

If we're being extremely charitable, we might assume that Silicon Valley is largely unaware of its own biases. If you've been trained by the best diversity activists in the country to instantly recognize alleged right-wing "hate" but have no such experience in detecting its left-wing counterpart, you're going to notice the former more often, and thus ban it more often. That's if we're being charitable, though— statements made in private by people like Google's Jen Gennai and Kent Walker and Twitter's Olinda Hassan suggest that at least some of the tech giants' senior employees know exactly what they're doing.

Overt censorship is not the only way in which Silicon Valley has undermined the conservative movement since President Trump's election. It may not even be the most damaging way—just the most visible. A potentially greater danger arises from the behind-the-scenes manipulations, the adjustments of algorithms and search results, which can't easily be detected by outside eyes. That's the subject of the next chapter.

6. Robot Censors

One of the most common questions I get as a tech reporter is, "What is an algorithm?"

As public attention around the abuses of Big Tech companies has grown, the term can be found everywhere. Algorithms are central to the success of sites like Facebook, Google, Instagram, YouTube, and Twitter. Yet many people are still hazy on what they are.

Algorithms may sound complicated, but they are quite simple. In the world of tech, an algorithm is a set of rules that tells a computer how to solve a problem or a set of problems. A simple algorithm might be one designed to sort pictures of apples and oranges. The algorithm is fed pictures of both fruits (this is the "input"). It then looks for "signals" to help it categorize the picture. ("Is the object round?" "Is the object orange?" "Is the object red?" "Is the object green?" "Does the object have a smooth texture?") After detecting the signals, the algorithm will feed out a result about the picture, classifying it as an apple, an orange, or neither (this is the "output").

Written poorly, algorithms can make mistakes. For example, if the programmer who creates the hypothetical fruit-sorting algorithm neglects to write a rule telling it that the skin of an apple is smooth while the skin of an orange is bumpy, the algorithm might incorrectly determine that a green, unripe orange is actually an apple.

Or, to use a more relevant example, if a programmer were to train an algorithm to recognize the phrase "Make America Great

Again" as an example of "hate speech," it, too, would generate incorrect outputs—although, as we know nothing about the programmer's politics, he or she might not see it that way. What we can say is that algorithms inherit the biases of their programmers—if the people who build them aren't politically neutral, their outputs won't be politically neutral.

In computing, a black-box algorithm is one in which the inputs and outputs can be seen, but the set of rules that determines the outputs is not. Most of the algorithms used by Facebook, Google, YouTube, Twitter, and other social media platforms to sort their users' content are black boxes. We know, for example, that Facebook algorithms will read every post you make—those are the inputs—and use them to determine your interests, before sending those determinations (the outputs) to Facebook's advertising platform. But we don't know *how*, or by what criteria, those determinations are made.

Content moderation works in much the same way. We know that when we post on Twitter or Facebook or upload a video to YouTube, a set of algorithms will immediately scan our post for examples of incitement to violence, copyright violations, obscenity, and other potential terms of service violations. What we don't know is what the algorithm will judge to be a violation and what it will not. We can make reasonable guesses (it's not that hard, for example, to guess at what might be categorized as a copyright violation), but as vaguer and vaguer terms are introduced into the terms of service ("hate speech," "misinformation," "harassment," etc.), that guesswork becomes progressively harder.

Dumb Machines

Perhaps the biggest drawback of using algorithms to categorize content is that it's difficult for them to judge context. For example, it might seem reasonable to categorize the word "nigger" as an example of hate speech and automatically ban it. But what if someone uploads lyrics to a rap song? Should it be automatically banned, then? What if two black people are using it on Facebook Messenger to refer to each other, in a nonhostile manner? Should Facebook programmers train the algorithm to recognize skin color and make exceptions? If so, what about albinos and mixed-race people who use the word? As you can see, training an algorithm to detect "hate speech" is complicated. Algorithms are very good at quantitative analysis, but they're appalling at qualitative analysis, something that often requires a careful consideration of context.

One real-world example occurred in the summer of 2019, when YouTube engaged in one of its regular crackdowns on "hate speech." The effort, targeted at videos that the platform deemed to support Nazi ideology, ended up removing archival footage of Adolf Hitler speeches that had been uploaded by history teachers. YouTube banned at least one of the teachers from the platform, though it reinstated his account on appeal.[1]

YouTube's inept effort to crack down on Nazis had the unintended effect of making life difficult for history students, once again demonstrating the perils of trusting machines and algorithms to judge context.

That shows you how algorithms can censor legitimate content by mistake. But what happens when censorship occurs on purpose? When you consider some of the things that leftists inside Big Tech companies might train their algorithms to do, you will see the potential for censorship and manipulation on a massive scale.

Political Machines

I spoke to a Silicon Valley insider about the problem of algorithms. Like many of my other sources, he wants to avoid industry blacklisting and thus doesn't want his real name to appear in print. We'll therefore call him by an alias, "Connor." Connor has spent nearly two decades working for Big Tech companies, including Google and

Twitter and, through his friends and connections in the San Francisco Bay Area, has also familiarized himself with Facebook's operations. His technical knowledge makes him one of my best sources.

Connor explained how social networks rank their users to determine their "quality." Every account has a hidden "quality ranking," and if that ranking falls below a certain point, the account is banned. In the early days of Big Tech, their algorithms would look for signals that indicated spam, phishing, piracy, and other unwanted activities. Factors that could lower an account's "quality" rating included the use of a VPN, spammy posts, and posts that included unsafe links— such as links to websites that might steal your password or credit card information. As major social media platforms soured on anonymity, lack of a verified email address, lack of a verified phone number, use of a pseudonym, and lack of an original profile photo have been added as factors, explained Connor. A low enough score would result in an account being categorized as "abusive," and a detriment to the platform.

Those signals are still used by platforms like Facebook and Twitter to determine an account's quality, said Connor. But as these companies have become increasingly influenced by political interests, the algorithms are asking more questions about users. Have they engaged in "hate speech"? Do they share links to websites engaged in "misinformation" and "conspiracy theories"? Do they follow other accounts known for "hate speech" and "conspiracy theories"? Tech platforms' definitions of "abusive" accounts now extend far beyond nonpolitical behavior like spam and phishing.

We now begin to see the true extent of Silicon Valley's insidiousness. Not only did the massive expansion in terms of service violations on social media platforms make it easier to outright ban right-wingers and right-wing sources; it also made it easier to covertly censor them. According to Connor, you don't have to break any rules yourself for your "quality ranking" to go down and for your content to be covertly suppressed—following the wrong accounts will suffice.

With this system, Silicon Valley can censor individual influencers and their networks of grassroots supporters at the same time. And, by using vague terms like "misinformation" and "hate speech," they can also maintain plausible deniability.

Account quality affects a social media company's value. Advertisers want to know that their ads are being shown to real people, not spambots. If a large number of active accounts on a platform are low quality, then a social media company should lower its ad prices, as the low-quality accounts cannot be classified as legitimate monthly active users. That's why social media companies have invested so much time and effort in identifying low-quality accounts.

Crucially, if your "similarity score" to abusive accounts goes past a certain threshold, no human is going to double-check to see if the classification is accurate. Social media companies are simply too big for such an approach to be viable. Your account will be weighted as low quality in the database, and the company will register your activity on their platform as a source of negative value—a problem to be dealt with. As we've already seen, leftists at Silicon Valley companies are open about their desire for politically inconvenient accounts to be seen as detriments to the platform. Remember the words of Twitter's Olinda Hassan: "we're trying to get the sh*tty people to not show up."

How can you train an algorithm to detect "sh*tty people"? Everything depends on this answer. Machine-learning algorithms are trained based on a set of data—in our example at the start of the chapter, it would be pictures of apples and oranges. In the case of an algorithm designed to detect "sh*tty people" and then downgrade or deplatform them, whoever gets to tell the algorithm what a "sh*tty account" looks like wields immense power. Like a trained attack dog that never sleeps, the algorithm will go after any account that bears a resemblance to the profile you've given it.

"Basically, they take a tiny set of alt-right trolls and then they say that alt-lite [a new wave of anti-immigration, antiwar, market-skeptical right-wingers], new right, libertarians, and even nonconformist center-left have superficial similarity to the troll, like posting the same memes or following the same accounts, and therefore are all abusive (low-quality, left off the important metrics)," explained Connor.

The profile of "abusive" accounts used to train the algorithms isn't created solely by leftists at Big Tech companies. As we saw in chapter 4, Twitter admits that signals from users are also taken into account—how often an account is blocked or reported is among the signals its algorithm looks for when determining the quality of an account. And Democrats, as we've covered, are considerably more likely to block accounts than are people with other political affiliations.

As Connor pointed out to me, Silicon Valley companies also rely on the advice of partisan left-wing organizations like the Anti-Defamation League and the Southern Poverty Law Center to help them identify undesirable accounts and behavior. In addition to loose networks of far-left activists on social media that flood the accounts of right-wingers with reports and blocks, this creates a system in which the people identifying "abusive" accounts are likely to be partisan left-wingers. In algorithmic terms, if those are the "inputs," what do you think the "outputs" (i.e., the bans, the shadowbans, the downgrading) are going to look like?

There are two sets of inputs, then, that corrupt social media's content-moderation algorithms. The first, what we might describe as external inputs, are the mass-reporting campaigns from left-wing activists on social media platforms. Combined with the general propensity of Democrats to block accounts and hide posts that offend them at higher rates than other political groups, this ensures that conservatives and right-wingers will be blocked, muted, and likely reported at higher rates than their political opponents. Unless social media platforms rate blocks, mutes, and reports lower if you use those tools more frequently—something that no platform has ever told me it does—this means that conservative and right-wing social media accounts will end up with lower "quality" scores.

The second, potentially more dangerous set of inputs comes from inside the Big Tech companies themselves. To put it more accurately, it's not just inputs, but deciding *what count as valid inputs*. The companies are the ones who define "abuse." They're the ones who define "trolling." They're the ones who define "bots." They're the ones who define "misinformation." They're the ones who define "hate speech." They're the ones who define "violence." And, when an account gets reported, they're the ones who decide whether the report is valid, and whether it should be used to train the platform's algorithms to detect more cases like it. Is it any wonder why antifa and other violent far-left rule breakers get a seemingly free rein on social media platforms? The algorithms simply haven't been trained to detect them.

We caught a glimpse of how this works when Project Veritas released more undercover videos from its sting operation exposing left-wing Twitter employees. In one of the videos, Mo Norai, then a former Twitter "content reviewer" (the ones who decide if your account gets banned), boasts about banning pro-Trump content. Discussing the process of content review with an undercover reporter, Norai said, "Let's say if it was a pro-Trump thing and I'm anti-Trump. I was like, I banned this whole account…It goes to you, and then it's at your discretion. And if you're anti-Trump, you're like, 'oh you know what, Mo was right, f**k it, let it go.'"

The undercover reporter then asks Norai if he takes a softer approach with left-wing accounts, which Norai appears to acknowledge. "It would come through checked, and I would be like, 'oh you know what? This is okay.'"[2]

In another secretly recorded video, a Twitter engineer, Pranay Singh, revealed to an undercover reporter that the platform had written algorithms to classify as "bots" those accounts that use stereotypical conservative phrases.

"Just go to a random [Trump] tweet and just look at the followers. They'll all be like, guns, God, America, and with the American flag and the cross," said Singh. "Like, who says that? Who talks like that? It's for sure a bot."

Asked by the reporter whether he could remove the "bots," Singh said, "Yeah. You just delete them, but, like, the problem is there are hundreds of thousands of them, so you've got to, like, write algorithms that do it for you."

"So, if there's like 'American, guns' [in the account bio], can you write an algorithm to just take all those people out?" pressed the reporter.

"[That's] actually how we do it," confirmed Singh. "You look for 'Trump,' or 'America,' or any of, like, five thousand, like, keywords to describe a redneck, and then you look, and you parse all the messages, all the pictures, and then look for stuff that matches that stuff... You assign a value to each thing, so like Trump would be .5, a picture of a gun would be like 1.5, and if the total comes up above a certain value, then it's a bot."

"So, you would mostly just get rid of conservatives?" asked the reporter.

"Yeah," confirmed Singh.[3]

Singh and Norai exemplify the two faces of Silicon Valley censorship. Norai is an example of overt bias—treating Trump supporters more harshly than leftists because he doesn't like them. Singh, meanwhile, demonstrates unconscious bias—viewed from his perspective as a San Francisco–based employee of one of the wokest companies in the world, people who tweet all day about "guns, God, and America" are completely alien creatures. They can't possibly be real. They *have* to be bots. People like Linda Suhler and her friends (see chapter 5), banned or locked out of their accounts for signs of "inauthentic" activity, pay the price for this blinkered Silicon Valley worldview.

The decisions made by people like Norai and Singh don't exist in a vacuum—they have far-reaching effects on social media algorithms. When someone like Norai decides to ban a Trump-supporting account or to let a leftist off with a slap on the wrist, the algorithms will be watching—and learning. They'll learn that the Trump-supporting account is an example of "abusive," rule-violating behavior, while the leftist's account is not. And when Singh labels talk of "guns, God, and America" as "bot-like" behavior, the algorithms trained to search for bots will start to see such language as a signal as well. Algorithms are infants, learning about the world—and the people teaching them are predominantly leftists. The way they recognize "hate speech," "bot-like," or "abusive" behavior will be the same way their "parents" in Silicon Valley recognize them. We are looking at a future where every single post made on a platform, every account created, and every connection made will be instantaneously catalogued and judged by intelligent machines created and trained by leftist architects. The endgame is a future controlled by leftist AI that perpetually monitors our activity for signs of "hate speech," "misinformation," and other thought crimes defined by leftists. Welcome to the future.

Robot Overlords

Understanding algorithms—and the importance of the people who create and manage them—couldn't be more important, because it will be algorithms, not humans, that will eventually govern Big Tech platforms.

This is already happening. In YouTube's 2019 "community guidelines enforcement report"—a quarter-by-quarter celebration of the number of videos they've kicked off the internet—the video-sharing platform credited "automated flagging" for the removal of the vast majority of them. According to the report, more than 5 million videos removed from the platform in the third quarter were a result of automated flagging, compared with nearly 330,000 that were taken down in response to user reports.[4] Reports for the other quarters also showed automated removals that were well into the millions. Clearly, we are already living in a world run, at least in part, by machines. And—if those candid statements from current and former Twitter employees are representative of wider attitudes in Silicon Valley—those machines have been trained to hunt conservatives.

It's not just about content removals. We are rapidly moving into a world in which Big Tech algorithms are involved in almost every aspect of our lives. Whether we're approved for a loan, a mortgage, an insurance policy; whether we're allowed to rent an apartment; whether we can use platforms like Airbnb, Uber, and Lyft; whether our business appears at the top of a Google search or whether it's buried five pages down; even whom we'll be matched with by online dating apps. Algorithms already have an outsize impact on our daily lives, and this trend is only going to accelerate.

Control over this technology is the biggest prize in tech. In the title of his influential 2013 book, computer scientist Jaron Lanier asked, "Who owns the future?" With AI set to become a major feature of virtually every industry over the next century, the question may very well be rephrased as, "Who owns the AI?" Industries are unlikely to develop their own AI systems; they will likely rely on whatever is produced by the "experts" in Silicon Valley. The same tech giants that dominate today are likely to dominate the AI-powered world of tomorrow. AI trained in leftist ideology will carry those biases far beyond Silicon Valley into every industry and field you can imagine. In the near future, AI will help determine whether you're hired for a job; whether you're approved for a loan or a mortgage; whether your children are accepted into a university; whether you can finance a car; whether you can rent an apartment.

An incident at Google in 2019 showed just how determined the Left is to maintain ideological hegemony over AI. In March of that year, Google announced the formation of an external "AI ethics council" composed of eight members. Seven of the eight included mainstream academics, computing experts, and a former diplomat who had served under Barack Obama. But for left-wing Google employees, one member stood out: Kay Coles James, president of the Heritage Foundation, one of the foremost conservative think tanks in the United States.

The freak-out was immediate. One the same day that Google announced its plans for an AI ethics council, employees created a thread on an internal discussion channel to complain about the inclusion of James. The discussion quickly spiraled into a chorus of smears against the African American conservative, with far-left employees accusing her of "hateful positions," "bigotry," and even something called "exterminationism" (I'm still not sure what they meant by the phrase). One employee branded the Heritage Foundation "monstrous," describing it as an "organization dedicated to eliminating LGBTQ+ people from public life, driving them back into the closet," and "denying them healthcare." Another employee claimed the "rhetorical violence" of the think tank "translate[s] into real, material violence against trans people, particularly trans women of color."

Comments from one employee, leftist AI researcher Meredith Whittaker, were particularly illuminating. Like the others, she smeared James, calling her an "outspoken bigot" whose favored policies "dehumanize and marginalize." But her later comments revealed that she believes the stakes of allowing conservative viewpoints to influence AI are high.

"The potential harms of AI and 'advanced' tech are not evenly distributed and follow historical patterns of discrimination and exclusion," wrote Whittaker. "Those who have been historically marginalized are at the most risk of harm. See AI that doesn't hear women, that doesn't 'see' trans people, or people of color.

"See systems deployed to aid ICE [Immigration and Customs Enforcement] in targeting immigrants, to aid the Military in drone strikes, or to enhance worker control. Thus, in ensuring we are 'ethical' in our pursuit of AI dominance, we need to include and amplify the perspectives of those most at risk.

"Which brings us to the problem with this argument even on its own terms: nowhere is Civil Society represented, let alone representatives of the communities most at risk of harm. (where is the Trans Advocacy Network, criminal justice reform experts, the ACLU [American Civil Liberties Union], etc.?) While there's a member of the very-far Right, in the person of James, there is no equivalent far-left representative. (To be extremely clear, even if these voices were included, that does not justify the inclusion of an open bigot.)"

Needless to say, Whittaker's definitions of James as "very-far Right" and an "open bigot" are nothing but smears. The Heritage Foundation is as mainstream a conservative organization as you can get. But Whittaker's comments reveal the acute paranoia that left-wingers in tech feel about the potential influence of conservative viewpoints on the AI technologies that will affect almost all aspects of humanity's future. As Whittaker says, it isn't enough that multiple viewpoints are represented—*any* presence of conservative thought (calling it "very-far Right" doesn't make it so) in the development of AI is a threat. Elsewhere in her post, Whittaker warned against "justifying including bigots in the name of 'viewpoint diversity,'" arguing it is "weaponization of the language of D&I [diversity and inclusion]" that has been "used by the alt-right to argue against diversity efforts."[5]

In short, Whittaker's post argued that Google should shut out mainstream, conservative influences from its AI project because they are "open bigots," while at the same time stacking the deck with left-wing intersectional outfits like the Trans Advocacy Network and the liberal ACLU. For Whittaker, conservative-influenced AI is a mortal threat, and neutral AI is unsatisfactory—only AI influenced by the Left may be permitted. Indeed, Whittaker was so threatened by James' inclusion on the AI council that she quickly helped organize a company-wide petition to have her kicked out.[6] Google's leadership responded with cowardice—they didn't want to undo their "conservative outreach" efforts in Washington, but they also didn't want to confront their far-left crazies. So they canceled the entire AI ethics board, much to the chagrin of the board's proposed members.[7]

"It's become clear that in the current environment, ATEAC [Advanced Technology External Advisory Council] can't function as we wanted," Google wrote in a humiliating statement. "So we're ending the council and going back to the drawing board."[8] Whittaker and the crazies had succeeded in preventing even a lone, mainstream conservative voice from influencing the company's work on AI. In an article for the *Washington Post*, James condemned Google for caving in to the "mentality of a rage mob."[9]

It's no accident that Whittaker was so vocal in her opposition to James. A deep dive into her background reveals that she is one of the pioneers of an emerging field called "Machine Learning Fairness," the goal of which is to ensure that artificial intelligence is trained to be "fair"—as defined by left-wing academics. She cofounded a research institute at New York University called AI Now, the stated purpose of which is to understand the "social implications of artificial intelligence."

The institute is partnered with the left-wing ACLU (something Whittaker conveniently neglected to disclose when she pushed for its inclusion in AI oversight at Google) and seeks to marry left-wing academia to the field of AI. A glance at the institute's publications reveals its left-wing, intersectional priorities—one study is titled "Discriminating Systems: Gender, Race, and Power in AI." Another is titled "Dirty Data, Bad Predictions: How Civil Rights Violations Impact Police Data, Predictive Policing Systems, and Justice."[10]

The institute's description of its own work on "bias and inclusion" further reveals its left-wing, intersectional priorities. "At their best, AI and algorithmic decision-support systems can be used to augment human judgement and reduce both conscious and unconscious biases. However, training data, algorithms, and other design choices that shape AI systems may reflect and amplify existing cultural prejudices and inequalities . . . When machine learning is built into complex social systems such as criminal justice, health diagnoses, academic admissions, and hiring and promotion, it may reinforce existing inequalities, regardless of the intentions of the technical developers."[11]

The idea of AI as a tool for the left-wing ideological agenda is also revealed in Google's own "machine learning fairness" project, which cites studies like "Mind the GAP: A Balanced Dataset of Gendered Ambiguous Pronouns" and "The Reel Truth: Women Aren't Seen or

Heard." In its video explaining the ML (machine learning) Fairness project, Google explains that its purpose is to "prevent [machine learning] from perpetuating negative human bias. From tackling offensive or clearly misleading information from appearing at the top of your search results page, to adding a feedback tool on the search bar, so that people can flag hateful or inappropriate autocomplete suggestions."[12]

I hope that it is now a little clearer why advocates of the Left need to ensure that no conservatives ever intrude on their territory in the field of AI. Although Google's ML Fairness is framed as a campaign against bias, it is the precise opposite—an attempt to imprint left-wing biases on the technology that will, increasingly, govern our lives. Ask yourself: Would an AI designed to detect incitement to violence identify antifa if it were trained by Silicon Valley social justice warriors? If you were to train an AI to detect racism and bigotry, would it identify the *New York Times'* antiwhite bigot Sarah Jeong? Would it identify the feminists who like to joke about killing all men? Would it categorize Covington-gate as a harassment campaign? An unbiased AI certainly would, but Silicon Valley is not training its machines to be unbiased.

On a deeper level, would an AI that was developed to help landlords allow them to fully and properly scour the criminal records of prospective tenants? Looking at the work of the AI Now Institute, we can already see the use of criminal databases in AI training as a major emerging concern on the left.

It's easy to imagine even simple AI systems producing outputs that would horrify the intersectional Far Left. AIs, after all, are trained to detect patterns in data, and an unbiased examination of data often yields conclusions the Left would rather not talk about. Remember, the people creating AI are the same sort of people who locked Andy Ngo out of his account for stating incontrovertible facts about crimes against transgender people.

Imagine, for example, if you asked an AI to figure out the type of people who are most likely to possess an illegal firearm, or a class A drug, or those most likely to commit a robbery. Do you think an AI, examining all the data available, would reach a conclusion that the Left would be okay with? What if you trained it to identify individuals at the highest risk of joining a sex-grooming gang in the United Kingdom, or a terrorist cell in Belgium? The AI would start churning out the same kinds of empirically based conclusions that got Tommy Robinson banned from Twitter! What if you trained it to find out whether men and women are paid different rates for the same amount of work? Another left-wing myth would be destroyed! What if you asked it to find out which culture has made the most contributions to science and technology? The list of questions for which AI could offer factually correct, yet politically incorrect, answers is endless.

I often think that the definition of being "right-wing," today, is simply *noticing things* you're not supposed to. These include the blindingly obvious, like the innate differences between men and women (for discussing this simple truth, Google fired one of its top-rated engineers, James Damore, in 2017—he had done too much *noticing*). They include uncomfortable topics, like racial divides in educational and professional achievement, or involvement in criminal gangs. They include issues of national security, like terrorism and extremism.

On these topics and many others, the fledgling AIs of Big Tech are in the same boat as right-wingers: they're in danger of being branded as bigots for the simple crime of noticing too much. The unspoken fear isn't that AI systems will be too biased—it's that they'll be too *unbiased*. Far from being complex, AIs perform a very simple task—they hoover up masses of empirical data, look for patterns, and reach conclusions. In this regard, AIs are inherently right-wing: *they're machines for noticing things*.

This divide between the modern Left and Right, the latter determined to notice uncomfortable empirical facts and the former determined to suppress them, could not be more important—especially as the field of AI takes off. Members of the Left wrongly paint members of the Right as bigoted for their insistence on identifying, acknowledging, and discussing sensitive topics. They're wrong. The fact that many on the right want to acknowledge and discuss the problems of, say, crime in black communities, or extremism in Muslim ones, doesn't mean that members of the Right hate those communities. On the contrary, members of the Right know that those communities will not prosper or be fulfilled unless they acknowledge, discuss, and solve their particular problems. Some in those communities— although more so the political Left—may find those conversations painful, offensive, and enraging, but no progress can be made until they are had. Leftists prioritize the feelings of their protected classes (just slightly behind the importance of assuaging their own pangs of white liberal guilt) over actually solving their problems.

Those on the right should be encouraged by the fact that the default state of AI, which is to dispassionately analyze data and solve problems, works in their favor. It's difficult, after all, to train an AI program to make subtle, human considerations about offensiveness and political correctness before it produces its output. For all their hastily constructed efforts to impose "fairness" on machine learning, advocates of the Right have a natural advantage—the empirical data is on their side. And there's nothing an AI program loves more than empirical data.

Nevertheless, those on the left enjoy their own massive advantage. As we saw in the case of Kay Coles James, they have developed an overwhelming cultural hegemony in Silicon Valley, which is building the AI systems of the future. If we don't want our future robot overlords to autocorrect all our emails to use gender-neutral pronouns, or pre-ban us for drafting a Facebook post that contains "hate speech," this crisis of political culture in tech is something that must be urgently addressed. If the vast power of AI were successfully turned to political purposes, we might as well elect Big Tech CEOs emperors of the world. As we detailed in previous chapters, the political and media establishments are exerting considerable pressure on tech companies to turn their products in an ideologically biased direction. As we'll see in the next chapter, the internal pressure, from Big Tech's own employees, may be even greater.

7. Human Censors

Artificial intelligence, properly applied, has the potential to deepen our understanding of the world and solve problems that are beyond the reach of the human brain's processing power. When AI is built and trained by people who proudly wear ideological blinkers, however, it will only compound human biases and errors, entrenching them in the technology of the future. Sadly, because of the hopelessly biased internal culture of Silicon Valley tech giants, the latter—biased AI that entrenches humanity's errors—remains the most likely outcome.

The quintessential example of Big Tech's ideological groupthink is the James Damore scandal. In July 2017, in response to a Google diversity program's request for feedback, the software engineer, who at the time worked for Google, wrote a memo addressing the very topic of this chapter. Titled "Google's Ideological Echo Chamber," the memo argued that the tech giant harbored an overwhelming progressive bias, resulting in a "an intolerance for ideas and evidence that don't fit a certain ideology.

"Google's left bias has created a politically correct monoculture that maintains its hold by shaming dissenters into silence," continued Damore's memo.

"This silence removes any checks against encroaching extremist and authoritarian policies."[1]

As an example of an incorrect view caused by Google's internal political bias, Damore pointed to gender disparities in tech employment. Google's position, argued Damore, is that men are overrepresented in tech fields because of sexism and discrimination. This, he wrote, was an ideologically blinkered view, resulting from the company's suppression of conservative viewpoints—he went on to cite arguments, widely accepted by leading academics like Steven Pinker, a psychology professor at Harvard University; and Simon Baron-Cohen, a professor of psychopathology at Cambridge University, that gender disparities in tech and science are a result of the different preferences of men and women, which spring from their innate biological differences.

This is an argument so mainstream that even David Brooks, a political columnist for the *New York Times*, defends it. But in the far-left atmosphere of Google, it provoked immediate outrage. A malicious colleague of Damore's leaked the memo to the left-wing tech blog Gizmodo, which branded it an "anti-diversity screed" (even though the memo's entire point is to call for more diversity of viewpoints). Gizmodo initially published it without footnotes, meaning readers could not see the numerous empirical studies on which Damore had based his argument.[2]

As the left-wing media joined the frenzy, Google's leftist employees went into witch-hunt mode, demanding that Damore and his supporters be expelled from the company.

According to Damore's suit, Alex Hidalgo, a systems reliability engineer at the company, sent Damore an abuse-laden email. "Feel free to pass this along to HR... You're a misogynist and a terrible human. I will keep hounding you until one of us is fired. F*ck you."[3]

Another of Damore's colleagues allegedly accused him and his supporters of being "Nazis" and suggested that they ought to be violently assaulted.

"I will absolutely go out of my way to ensure that I never work near anyone involved with or who endorsed that garbage. Because Nazis. And you should absolutely punch Nazis," wrote another alleged Google employee.[4]

Finally, Damore alleges that Colm Buckley, another Google employee, went so far as to defend viewpoint discrimination at the company.

"You know, there are certain 'alternative views, including different political views' which **I do not want** people to feel safe to share here," said Buckley, quoting Damore's memo.

"Yes, this is 'silencing.' I **intend** to silence these views; they are **violently offensive**" (emphasis in the original).

A normal, nonleftist company, when confronted with multiple employees allegedly threatening physical violence and harassment against a colleague over his politely expressed views, would fire the aggressors on the spot. Google, of course, chose to fire Damore instead. The action was so outrageous, so demonstrably unfair, that the left-wing *New York Times* published an op-ed from David Brooks arguing that Google CEO Sundar Pichai should resign over his handling of the situation.

"The mob that hounded Damore was like the mobs we've seen on a lot of college campuses...Which brings us to Pichai, the supposed grown-up in the room. He could have wrestled with the tension between population-level research and individual experience. He could have stood up for the free flow of information. Instead, he joined the mob."[5]

Damore, whom I've met on more than one occasion, is not at all a right-winger. Even the far-left *Guardian*, which regularly exaggerates the threat of so-called right-wing extremism, concedes that he is merely a "centrist with libertarian inclinations."[6] Unless you're on the far identitarian left, it is impossible to characterize his claims about gender, which echoed those of mainstream academics like Steven Pinker, Simon Baron-Cohen, and feminist academic Camille Paglia, as anything other than mainstream.

But it seems that the most vocal and belligerent Google employees are on the far left. As the Damore scandal raged, I was contacted by numerous employees at the company—some conservative, some merely skeptical of far-left ideology—who supported his account of extreme ideological intolerance.

"If you defy the politically correct orthodoxy, they will tell you that you're actively harming women and minorities," one employee told Breitbart News. "If you don't recant, they'll escalate to Human Resources and your managers.

"The language policing is aggressive to the point of crippling discourse: for instance, one person got in trouble with his VP for using the term 'crazy person' to describe a mentally troubled individual who was caught running through the Googleplex naked. Employees have also been turned into HR for using terms like 'retarded.'"[7]

"A lot of social justice activists essentially spend all day fighting the culture war, and get nothing done," said another. "The company has made it a point to hire more people like this. The diversity gospel has been woven into nearly everything the company does, to the point where senior leaders focus on diversity first and technology second. The companywide 'Google Insider' emails used to talk about cool new tech, but now they're entirely about social justice initiatives. Likewise, the weekly all-hands meetings used to focus on tech, but now they're split about 50-50 between tech and identity politics signaling."[8]

The employee went on to describe a Stasi-like atmosphere in which ideologically nonconformist employees are forced to hide their true opinions, for fear that they will lose not only their jobs at Google, but their careers in Silicon Valley at large.

"Several managers have openly admitted to keeping blacklists of the employees in question and preventing them from seeking work at other companies," said the Google employee. "There have been numerous cases in which social justice activists coordinated attempts to sabotage other employees' performance reviews for expressing a different opinion.

"These have been raised to the senior VP level, with no action taken whatsoever."

It shouldn't be surprising that no action was taken. It's clear that left-wing identity politics is an article of faith among Google's senior leadership. Breitbart's sources spoke of VPs leading "black lives matter" chants onstage; of the company stationing tampons in men's restrooms because "some men menstruate"; and other stories that suggest the working atmosphere at the company resembles that of the left-wing gender studies department at the University of California, Berkeley.

Eventually, after James Damore's firing, some Google employees decided that things had gone too far—together with Damore, they filed a class-action lawsuit against the company, alleging discrimination against people with conservative viewpoints, as well as white people, Asian people, and males.

Evidence released from that lawsuit revealed even more far-left, identity-obsessed, even racist madness at Google. One astonishing document released through the lawsuit revealed that Google managers who attended "inclusive perf" training were given a document instructing them to view values like "individual achievement" and "meritocracy" as examples of "white dominant culture."

The handout warned managers about "rewarding people when they exhibit values and practices that are part of the dominant [culture], and either punishing or failing to reward people when they exhibit values that are outside of the dominant cultural norm."

It's hard to know toward whom Google was being more bigoted: whites and males, whose supposed values Google was telling its managers to de-emphasize; or nonwhites and women, who, implies the handout, have difficulty with the concepts of "individual achievement" and "meritocracy."

Take a look at the whole list. It'll boggle your mind.[9]

Valued by U.S. white/male dominant culture	Commonly invisibilized or devalued by U.S. white/male dominant culture
Front of the room, persuasive	Listening, raises up multiple voices
Arguing, winning	Identifying multiple viable paths
Either/Or	Both/And
Perfectionism	Everything's a work in progress
Urgency	Sustainability
Numbers driven	Narrative driven (quotes, qualitative)
Growth in number, size	Growth in quality
Protecting others from	Valuing self-determination
Short-term payoffs	Seven generations thinking
Avoiding conflict	Conflict is productive/necessary
Giving feedback indirectly (about you, but without you)	Giving feedback directly (with you)
Individual achievement	Collective achievement
Seeing us as unique/exceptional	Seeking connections between contexts
We are objective	Everything is subjective
Casual, informal, off-the-cuff	Formal, prepared, thought out
Meritocracy	Holding systems accountable for equitable outcomes
Colorblind racial frame	Noticing race/color and any racial patterns in treatment

The case against Google was filed by attorney Harmeet Dhillon, RNC CA committeewoman and founder of the civil liberties watchdog Center for American Liberty. According to Dhillon, at least three of the plaintiffs in the class-action lawsuit said they were discriminated against because of their race.

The plaintiffs, said Dhillon in an interview with Breitbart News, were "three highly qualified white men who identify as conservatives online who were denied jobs at Google, and it turns out that either the positions remained open or people with lesser qualifications ended up being hired for those positions. So that's the kind of classic employment discrimination that you see in gender cases and cases brought by people who are traditionally on the left.

"Apparently, it's the last frontier of acceptability to slander white people in our culture," continued Dhillon. "What's ironic is that [James Damore] was fired for allegedly perpetuating gender stereotypes, yet Google clearly perpetuates race and gender stereotypes every day in its HR policies; it's just that they're the political version, so they get away with it."[10]

When you see leaks like Google's handout on "white dominant culture," it's hard to disagree.

"An Extremely Left-Leaning Place"

Speaking to lawmakers on Capitol Hill in one of his many appearances before Congress, Facebook CEO Mark Zuckerberg made one of the understatements of the century when he admitted to Senator Ted Cruz that Silicon Valley is "an extremely left-leaning place."

It's nice that the CEO of the world's most influential distributor of news admitted this basic truth. What he didn't admit, however, was how much he and his company's official policies contributed to it.

In February 2016, Zuckerberg scolded his employees after the phrase "All Lives Matter" appeared on a wall at the company's headquarters. (The wall in question is meant for company employees to express random thoughts.) Calling the behavior "disrespectful" and "malicious," Zuckerberg told employees that the company would investigate the incident. Concluding by saying the incident was a "deeply hurtful and tiresome experience for the black community and really the entire Facebook community," he then encouraged all employees to attend a company seminar about Black Lives Matter.[11]

Disrespectful? Malicious? "All lives matter" is a pretty common riposte used by conservatives who object to the far-left, identitarian nature of the Black Lives Matter movement. It's very much in the mainstream of conservative discourse. The slogan isn't even particularly right-wing—it's a statement of liberal universalism, responding to a statement of racial division, very much in the vein of Martin Luther King's instruction to look at "content of character" rather than skin color.

Yet, because of this mild critique of the Black Lives Matter movement, Zuckerberg promised a company-wide investigation. It's hard to imagine a more demoralizing message to send to his conservative and nonprogressive employees. If *this* was considered over the line, by the CEO himself, what other mainstream conservative opinions should Facebook employees stop themselves from saying out loud? Facebook's culture of ideological conformity, it seems, is just as extreme as Google's. And, like Google's management, Facebook's management is complicit.

One Facebook employee, who chose to remain anonymous, told me that open, out-of-the-closet conservatives are so rare that "everyone...would be shocked if they met conservatives in the building, let alone had a conversation that challenged their way of thinking.

"I've attended seminars on bias before," the Facebook employee said. "Gender bias and racial bias.

"There's never been one on political bias."[12] (I asked Facebook about this—a company spokesman said that it does have a political bias training module, but did not provide any information about who is required to take it, what its content consists of, or how frequently it is used.)

"Try to imagine what a left-wing version of China's reeducation camps would look like," continued my source. "The walls are covered with announcements for events that you can join if you have the correct identity," another Facebook insider told me during an interview for this book.

"Every single day, leaders celebrate our differences (proud to BE BLACK), but we also lament our differences (Today Is Equal Pay Day! Did you know that women earn 77 cents to the dollar?).

"After the election, the walls were covered in #RESIST posters and to this day there are Black Lives Matter posters with the Black power first, Gay Pride posters inviting gay people to a special event with leadership, and many other posters covering all aspects of progressive culture.

"Murals loom overhead: 'Gender Free' with paintings of transgender people, and 'We Are USA' with a mosaic of women in hijabs. The desks are part of an open floor plan, so these messages are always in your peripheral vision. You can't create a sales pitch, walk to lunch, or use the restroom without a steady stream of propaganda.

"To put things in perspective, here are real snippets from real posts in a typical month. These posts are in the same view as posts on compensation, tax changes, organization news, et cetera. It's impossible to avoid seeing these posts without also missing vital employee information:

> November 8: 'I encourage everyone to take the Managing Bias, Managing Inclusion, and Be The Ally training courses.'
> November 13: 'Learn about practical actions you can take to be a better ally for women.'
> November 14: 'Women @ Leadership Day 2019! Please make sure you cancel any meetings on December 3rd so women are free to attend this day.'
> November 18: 'Join our Women Summit' (This is a separate event than the one above)
> November 22: 'Have you wondered how to be a better ally?'
> November 23: 'Here's a list of events that men can attend to learn how to become better allies to women.'
> November 26: 'Managing inclusion. If you haven't taken this course, take it. If you have taken it, take it again.'
> November 27: 'Diversity is top of mind. Welcoming more gender and ethnic diversity.'

"Because there is no boundary between social and work posts, wading through this content to get to the information that employees need to do their job is a scene from *[A] Clockwork Orange*."

Facebook even had its own "James Damore" moment, in the form of virtual reality (VR) pioneer Palmer Luckey. Luckey created the Oculus Rift, the device that revolutionized the VR industry and led to competing products from a wide range of companies, including Sony, HTC, and Steam. Originally funded through an online crowdfunding campaign, Oculus VR was sold to Facebook in 2014 for $3 billion, with Luckey joining the company as well. He seemed a perfect fit for Facebook. Like Zuckerberg himself, he was a nerd who had, at a young age, created a product that revolutionized an industry and catapulted him to the forefront of Silicon Valley. In the same year that Luckey joined Facebook, *Smithsonian* magazine granted him its American Ingenuity Award in the youth category. His future at the social network was sure to be long and bright.

Sadly for Luckey, he had the wrong political opinions. In 2016, it was revealed that he had donated $10,000 to a pro-Trump organization called Nimble America, which had run an anti–Hillary Clinton billboard campaign during the election.

At a normal company, this would be completely aboveboard. A wealthy executive donating to a political cause? It happens all the time! But, as Google's failure to fire the employees who threatened Damore and his supporters shows us, Silicon Valley is not a normal place.

Leaked messages obtained by the *Wall Street Journal* revealed that Facebook went into crisis mode after Luckey's support for Trump was revealed. As left-wing employees of the company, as well as the mainstream media, turned up the heat on the company, Luckey was pressured to announce his support for Libertarian Party candidate Gary Johnson instead of Donald Trump.

"I need to tell you that Mark [Zuckerberg] himself drafted this and details are critical," Facebook deputy general counsel Paul Grewal wrote in an email to one of Luckey's attorneys. The email contained a draft "apology" post for Luckey to release to the world on his public Facebook feed, announcing that he would be backing Johnson instead of Trump in the 2016 vote. I'm not sure how genuine an apology is if it's written for you, under duress, by your CEO, but readers can decide. A Facebook spokesperson told the *Wall Street Journal* that "we made it clear that any mention of politics was entirely up to [Luckey]."[13] Sure—kind of like how the unluckier characters in pirate stories get to decide which side of the plank to fall off.

Despite his apology, Luckey was put on paid leave. And in March 2017, a few months after he donated $100,000 to then president-elect Trump's inauguration committee, Luckey was fired. The company denies that his dismissal had anything to do with his political views, but it's hard to believe Facebook, given that it paid Luckey $100 million to settle his lawsuit alleging the company had done exactly that.

An Ideological Echo Chamber

There's more than enough evidence to demonstrate that Damore's thesis about an "ideological echo chamber" is true not just in Google, but in virtually every one of the tech giants. Twitter is led by a sandal-wearing hippie who marches in Black Lives Matter demonstrations. Amazon is led by the Trump-hating owner of the *Washington Post*. The tech CEOs compete to out-virtue-signal one another, whether it's Zuckerberg doing a "listening tour" of America or Apple CEO Tim Cook giving speeches denouncing online "hate" to the Anti-Defamation League.

It's not as if tech companies couldn't do anything about it. In his famously tough grilling of Mark Zuckerberg when the Facebook CEO appeared before the Senate in April 2018, Senator Ted Cruz asked him if he knew the political affiliation of the "fifteen to twenty thousand" content reviewers (the people who decide what content stays up and what gets banned). Zuckerberg responded that the company does "not generally ask people about their political orientation when they're joining the company."

Why not? It certainly wouldn't break any laws—if Facebook wanted to do something about its workforce's political bias, it could use the same framework it uses for other "diversity" efforts. It also wouldn't be hard for Facebook or Google to find out the political affiliations of its workforce—there is very little that either of those companies *don't* know about us. And what about internal workshops on political bias? One of my Facebook sources said he hasn't encountered even *one*. It's not that these companies lack the ability to take political bias and viewpoint diversity seriously—they simply don't want to.

Nothing bad would happen to these companies if they were to decide that the intolerance and belligerence of the far-left witch-hunters in their workforces could no longer be accommodated.

Just look at Oracle. Oracle is a tech giant, albeit one you don't hear of as much as Google, Facebook, Apple, or Amazon. It doesn't cultivate a trendy, woke image. It mainly focuses on developing hardware and software solutions for businesses, as opposed to mass-market consumer products. And it steers well clear of progressive politics.

In February 2020, the company's chairman and chief technology officer, Larry Ellison, announced plans to hold a fund-raiser for President Trump's reelection campaign. It was a smart move—Ellison supported Marco Rubio in the 2016 primaries and had previously donated to both Republicans and Democrats. But backing Trump in 2020 makes business sense for a company like Oracle—it's competing for government contracts, and its biggest advantage over its main competitors, Amazon and Google, is that, unlike those companies, it is not known for its ideological opposition to Republican administrations.

Ellison, who built his company in the 1980s, could not be more different from the wokesters at Google and Facebook. The CEOs of Facebook and Google may be among the richest people in the world, but it's almost like they're ashamed of it. They prefer to talk about the good they're doing in the world, whether that's "Making the World More Open and Connected" (Facebook) or "Organizing the World's Knowledge" (Google).

Ellison is the type of CEO who thinks more about making profits and destroying the competition than he does about lofty utopian goals—something I personally find a lot more refreshing than the faux idealism of Oracle's competitors. A Business Insider article about Oracle described the company's approach as "Take no prisoners, and grab 100% of the market." Another revealing insight: Ellison called the first version of Oracle's signature software "version two"—because no one buys the *first* version of a product.[14] I don't know about you, but I find it comforting to know that there's still a CEO out there who spends more time thinking about basic business priorities like actually selling his product, as opposed to grand progressive pipe dreams like eliminating hate, promoting tolerance, or saving the environment by putting fossil fuels on the blockchain. (I'm sure someone will suggest something like that at some point!)

You see, when you prioritize business concerns over political ones, everything changes. Oracle, I suspect, is unlikely to be the kind of place that would tolerate employees' threatening violence against their colleagues because of their political opinions. It wouldn't hold a crisis meeting if a senior employee decided to support a candidate whom other employees didn't like. And I doubt Ellison, unlike the wimps at Google, would choke up in tears on a stage in front of his entire company if his favorite candidate didn't win.

Naturally, many of Oracle's lower-level employees rose up in revolt at Ellison's decision to hold a Trump fund-raiser. In fact, those efforts are ongoing as I write this chapter in early 2020. But I predict that by the time this book is published, they will have gone nowhere at all.

As one left-wing Oracle employee complained, in a comment to Vox, "It signals what I and many others have always feared. Culturally, Oracle is the type of place where you'll work with many lovely people who you share common ideals with, but those ideals have to be left at the door in service of the company."[15]

Well, yes. Exactly. Leave your ideals at the door, make a good product, while the company engages with politicians of all sides on a pragmatic basis.

Pro tip for aspiring Big Tech CEOs: if you don't want to be embroiled in the kind of political controversies that have repeatedly rocked Facebook, Google, and Twitter, complaints from your most radical employees that you aren't listening to their crazy opinions are *exactly* what you want to hear.

That is not what Google, Facebook, Twitter, and other tech giants have done. Far from encouraging their employees to leave their ideals at the door, those companies encourage employees to wear them on their sleeves. Or, at least, they encourage *one* side of the political spectrum to wear them on their sleeves. The other side has to cower in the closet.

This could not be more dangerous. As we saw in the previous chapter, left-wingers are determined to control the advanced technology that will soon dominate our lives, our businesses, our culture, and our politics. The only people who might stop them (and have already helped, thanks to their numerous leaks) are the minority of conservative employees in those companies. And, as we've seen in this chapter, they are effectively silenced, unable to speak out for fear of losing their jobs. Progressive employees in Big Tech companies—except perhaps at Oracle—have a free rein to push their platforms ever further to the left. As we'll see in chapter 9, there is one Big Tech company where such efforts are particularly ominous. But before we get to that, it's time to address one other, relatively new form of censorship.

8. Financial Blacklisting

As shocking as the social media purge has been, it's only one of the ways in which Silicon Valley has clamped down on the Trump movement over the past few years. Another form of censorship, equally troubling to those who hoped the internet would return power to ordinary citizens, is financial blacklisting.

The story is similar to the history of free expression on the internet. Just as social media decentralized mass communication, the rise of online funding platforms promised to decentralize the business of political fund-raising. As we'll see in this chapter, however, activists and special interests have been able to pressure the companies that manage online transactions into censoring political viewpoints, much as they pressured social media platforms to do the same. For a while, though, it looked as if the rise of online fund-raising would revolutionize democracy in the United States.

One of the great tragedies of American politics is the enduring dominance of big-dollar donors. During election years, corporations and special interests pour hundreds of millions of dollars into campaign war chests and super PACs, drowning out the grass roots with a deluge of astroturfed (imitation grassroots activity, typically funded by special interests) messages.

In the past decade, online fund-raising has emerged as a major threat to this model—a chance for small money to beat big money. One of the best examples of this was the insurgent presidential campaigns of former congressman Ron Paul in 2008 and 2012. Much like Trump, Paul mixed skepticism of mass immigration, overseas military adventurism, and corporate-backed trade deals like NAFTA to create an antiestablishment cocktail that was poison to elites and nectar to the masses.

He never received much in the way of big donations—but the digital era allowed him to find a way around this problem. Paul's campaign was one of the first to truly recognize the power of online fund-raising to beat the big donors at their own game. Observers were shocked when, during the Republican primaries in 2007, Paul raised $6 million from small donors in a single day of online fund-raising. Not only did this outpace all his GOP rivals at the time, but the sum also beat John Kerry's single-day record of $5.7 million, which he received a day after winning the Democrat presidential nomination three years earlier.[1]

Online fund-raising would allow Paul to remain a thorn in the GOP establishment's side for many years to come, sustaining a movement that would ultimately feed into the Tea Party. In truth, it wasn't just Paul who was a thorn in the establishment's side—it was the internet, which, much in the way it disrupted establishment media, now threatened to upend the whole model of big-dollar politics.

In the years since, a plethora of online funding platforms have sprung up on the internet. Crowdfunding sites like Kickstarter, GoFundMe, and Indiegogo provided an easy means for ordinary people to contribute their money to the projects and causes they were passionate about. Subscription services like Patreon emerged, allowing people to contribute monthly sums to their favorite content creators. Platforms like YouTube and Twitch introduced tools for fans to support independent personalities. A democratic future in which small donors displaced large investors seemed to beckon.

It didn't last. Just as social media companies clamped down on alternative news sources after the 2016 election, the funding platforms also began to tighten their grip. Patreon found excuses to kick off a broad range of figures on the right, including documentary journalist Lauren Southern and the popular classical liberal Carl Benjamin. The former was banned because of a report about a boat attempting to stop illegal migrant crossings in the Mediterranean, as we covered in chapter 5. Benjamin, meanwhile, was banned for turning racist language against actual racists in the alt-right—Patreon conveniently neglected the context and banned him anyway, in a controversial move that spurred even political centrists like Sam Harris, Dave Rubin, and Jordan Peterson to boycott the platform.[2]

Platforms like GoFundMe also cracked down—even before the post-Trump panic began, it deleted the funding page for conservative commentator Jamie Glazov's "anti-Sharia" tour, which aimed to expose anti-Israel sentiments from then candidate Hillary Clinton.[3] It deleted a campaign to raise funds for a Christian-owned bakery in Oregon facing a six-figure fine for refusing to bake a cake for a same-sex wedding.[4]

Kickstarter isn't much better—the platform banned the project of a Swedish academic who aimed to expose correlations between mass immigration and sexual assault in his home country.[5] Indiegogo, Kickstarter's main competitor, hasn't to my knowledge enacted any high-profile bans yet—but its policies explicitly ban any funding project that "promotes hate," or "promotes hate symbols and/or hate terms on their website, as defined by the Anti-Defamation League."[6] The Anti-Defamation League, run by former Obama aide Jonathan Greenblatt, has labeled a host of innocuous symbols "hateful" in recent years, including anti-antifa images (images critical of the violent, far-left antifa movement) the OK hand sign, and a cartoon image of a frog.[7] That's Indiegogo's "hate" expert!

Beyond the funding platforms lies an even more dangerous threat—the banks, credit card companies, and electronic payment processors like Stripe and PayPal. In the hands of these financial giants lies the terrifying power to exclude people from the entire banking system, reducing them to the status of economic outcasts, second-class citizens.

Naturally, radical leftists are desperate for these companies to use their power. In 2017, the "racial justice" organization Color of Change began mobilizing online activists to target financial services including PayPal, Stripe, Mastercard, Visa, American Express, Discover, and Apple Pay, urging them to cut services to "hate groups." Citing atrocities like the massacre of black churchgoers by Dylann Roof, the organization's "Blood Money" campaign accused the companies of providing "the financial support white nationalist groups need to fund and organize hatred and violence against Black people and other marginalized communities."[8]

From just the front page of the campaign's website, you might think that Color of Change targets only white supremacists and neo-Nazis. This isn't the case, of course. The "hate groups" listed by the website include anti-Sharia organizations, including Pamela Geller's American Freedom Defense Initiative, Brigitte Gabriel's ACT for America, Robert Spencer's Jihad Watch, and Frank Gaffney Jr.'s Center for Security Policy. David Horowitz's Freedom Center, the socially conservative Family Research Institute, and the South Africa Project, which raises awareness about racially motivated murders of white farmers in South Africa, are also on the list. So, too, are several border security and anti-mass-immigration organizations, including American Border Patrol, Americans for Legal Immigration (ALI-PAC), and Americans for Immigration Control.

Color of Change lumped these groups in with genuine white supremacists and skinhead groups, urging financial deplatforming of them all. To be clear—even deplatforming just the true extremists would be a massive imposition of corporate censorship and a de facto undermining of the First Amendment. But the fact that groups like Color of Change are already agitating for mainstream conservative, anti-Sharia, traditionalist, and immigration-control advocates to be effectively shut out of the financial system shows us just how far they want to go.

The activist efforts are intensifying. In 2019, citing the "Blood Money" campaign, far-left activists lobbied Mastercard to propose to shareholders the creation of a "human rights committee" that would monitor and potentially cut off payments to the alleged "far right."[9]

Will the pressure campaign be successful? To its credit, Mastercard didn't, in the end, create a "human rights committee." But neither it nor Visa nor online payment systems like PayPal can boast of an unblemished track record in the matter of political deplatforming.

Mastercard, along with Visa and PayPal, cut WikiLeaks off from their services in 2011—the first modern example of politically motivated financial blacklisting in the West. Mastercard also reportedly pressured Patreon to suspend services to Jihad Watch founder Robert Spencer in August 2018. In a leaked conversation, Patreon representatives also appeared to imply that "rules" created by credit card companies may have played a role in its decision to remove Carl Benjamin from the platform.[10] None of this looks good for the future of financial access—and if the current leadership of banks, payment processors, and credit card companies isn't woke enough for the Left, it wouldn't be surprising to see internal agitation to have them replaced.

The threat of corporate rule is so severe that even moderate liberals have sounded the alarm. When I reached out about the topic to the Electronic Frontier Foundation (EFF), a liberal-leaning digital rights group, I was surprised to get not only a quick response from its spokeswoman—but an exceedingly strong one.

"EFF is deeply concerned that payment processors are making choices about which websites can and can't accept payments or process donations. We've seen examples—such as when WikiLeaks faced a banking blockade—of payment processors and other financial institutions shutting down the accounts of websites engaged in legal but unpopular speech."

Warning of a world in which "banks and payment processors turn into de facto internet censors," the EFF representative explained how actions by a few big companies could effectively exclude people from the entire financial system.

"Policies by big financial institutions like Visa and Mastercard also influence the policies of other financial intermediaries—including payment processors and crowdfunding sites. That means that speech-restrictive policies by just a handful of companies—especially Visa and Mastercard, and also PayPal to an extent—can make it difficult or impossible for some law-abiding websites to process payments or donations at all.

"These financial giants have little incentive to defend free expression online because it doesn't impact their bottom line, and it's often difficult or impossible for small websites to appeal decisions to shut down accounts or freeze payments. We need to be asking ourselves: Who should be deciding what kind of speech should be allowed to thrive online? Should it be Internet users, elected officials, or the courts? Or should it be financial intermediaries, like Visa and Mastercard?"

The Next Stage of Censorship

There are signs of resistance from some of the older financial institutions. In April 2018, following a left-wing pressure campaign aimed at stopping banks from doing business with certain firearm retailers, Wells Fargo announced that "the best way to make progress on these issues is through the political and legislative process."[11] This was a welcome pushback against progressive efforts to bypass the democratic process and use the power of corporate America to enact their agenda.

That said, there are still potential danger signs. In 2019, Chase Bank shut down the bank account of Enrique Tarrio, the Afro-Cuban chairman of the Proud Boys, a right-wing fraternity founded by Gavin McInnes. In a letter to Tarrio, Chase Bank wrote that "after careful consideration," it could "no longer support" his activities. Responding to a query from conservative author and activist Michelle Malkin, Chase denied suspending service to Tarrio for political reasons. Other right-wing figures, including combat veteran and independent journalist Joe Biggs, and Republican congressional candidate Laura Loomer, also had their Chase accounts mysteriously suspended.

An undercover sting by Project Veritas revealed what some employees of Chase Bank were "carefully considering" behind closed doors. While some inside the bank blamed "clerical errors" for Tarrio's account closure, another employee expressed confusion as to why his account was closed. "I see nothing that indicates any reason why the account should be closed," said one. Another explained to an undercover reporter that Chase is not involved with "alt-right people" and that the bank doesn't "get involved in any business relationships" with people of "no moral character."[12]

Responding to my request for comment, a Chase spokeswoman strongly denied that the accounts had been shut down for political reasons. "We have never and would never close someone's account or 'suspend service' due to their political affiliation," said the spokeswoman. "You know and I know that's a ridiculous assertion. I am not able to give out private information on any client, but they all know exactly what happened. There are dozens of really important reasons why a bank may need to suspend or close down someone's account." She did not comment on the specific remarks made by Chase employees to the undercover Project Veritas reporters.

Financial censorship is certainly the future that progressives and far-left activists seem to want. The Left, who still portray themselves as the sworn enemies of corporate power, have sought to use the private sector as a means to achieve their agenda. Whether it's pressuring banks to cut ties with certain gun retailers or demanding they cut off support to the so-called Far Right, the progressive ideology that has been repeatedly rejected by American voters at the ballot box is worming its way into corporate America.

If Republicans want to protect their grass roots, they must do something about it. Trusting the corporate sector to fix the problem on its own, and to behave in the best interests of consumers rather than radical activists, simply isn't working. Whether it's tech giants or financial services, it seems the corporate sector has a habit of taking advice from its worst enemies. And as we'll see in the next chapter, the corporate sector now has unparalleled power to manipulate democracy.

9. The World's Most Dangerous Company

Twenty years ago, if I mentioned the idea that a company might set its sights on knowing everything there is to know—about the world, about the most obscure topics—you might assume I was talking about the unthreatening folks who publish the *Encyclopedia Britannica*. But now there's Google, a company that wants to know not only everything about the world, but everything about *you*, too. This is the era of Google, whose mission statement is to "organize the world's information."

Google wants to know everything there is to know, and it has assembled the greatest surveillance network in the history of mankind in order to make it happen. Across the world today, there are 2.5 billion active Google Android devices, along with 2 billion installed Google Chrome browsers, along with 52 million Google Home devices. Add to that 1 billion Gmail users, as well as YouTube's 2 billion monthly users, and you have a tech company whose reach knows no equal. Google reads the emails you send to your friends. Its laptops and tablets know what you're working on. Its web browsers and search engine know what your interests are, allowing its algorithms to predict what they will be in the future. YouTube knows what music you listen to and what you watch for entertainment. Its Android phones know what you're texting, whom you're calling, where you are, and where you're going. It is a level of surveillance and knowledge that the former Soviet state security agency, the KGB, could only have dreamed of. Even Facebook can't really compete with Google's vast database of information about ordinary people, collected from both digital services and hardware devices. Facebook, after all, is less likely to know what website you visited recently or what questions you've asked a search engine. Google, meanwhile, knows what medical information you're searching for, what destination you're going to, and what you're emailing your boss.

Google's status as repository of the world's knowledge, as well as the all-seeing eye penetrating into all our daily lives, gives it more influence over ordinary people than any other company has had in history. If Google were just an archive of information that everyone used (which it is), that would make it influential enough—but it's more than that. Knowing almost everything about us, it also knows exactly how to get our attention, how to affect our behavior—how to manipulate us.

One person who has done more than anyone else to study the potential effects of Google's power is psychologist Dr. Robert Epstein. The former editor in chief of *Psychology Today*, Epstein has published more than fifteen books and more than three hundred articles on psychology, artificial intelligence, and a variety of other topics. A Harvard-educated liberal, Epstein became interested in researching Google after the search giant placed warning labels on his website, which had been infected with malware, in 2012.

Epstein started to investigate potential effects of search engine results on decision-making, including political decision-making. In 2013—long before left-wing bias from Big Tech companies would become a major national issue—Epstein and his colleague Ronald E. Robertson sought to demonstrate the potential political effects of a biased search engine. They took a diverse set of Americans and presented them with a choice of two political candidates. One group was given a biased set of search results, and the other was not. After viewing the search results, the study participants were asked to back one candidate or the other.

The study, which Epstein summarized in an article for *Aeon* magazine, generated a shocking result:

> All participants were first given brief descriptions of the candidates and then asked to rate them in various ways, as well as to indicate which candidate they would vote for; as you might expect, participants initially favoured neither candidate on any of the five measures we used, and the vote was evenly split in all three groups. Then the participants were given up to 15 minutes in which to conduct an online search using "Kadoodle," our mock search engine, which gave them access to five pages of search results that linked to web pages. People could move freely between search results and web pages, just as we do when using Google. When participants completed their search, we asked them to rate the candidates again, and we also asked them again who they would vote for.
>
> We predicted that the opinions and voting preferences of 2 or 3 per cent of the people in the two bias groups—the groups in which people were seeing rankings favouring one candidate—would shift toward that candidate. What we actually found was astonishing. The proportion of people favouring the search engine's top-ranked candidate increased by 48.4 per cent, and all five of our measures shifted toward that candidate. What's more, 75 per cent of the people in the bias groups seemed to have been completely unaware that they were viewing biased search rankings.[1]

Epstein and his colleagues would replicate the findings over several studies during the next two years, including in a study on real voters in the 2014 Indian elections. It found search-engine-induced shifts in voting preferences of up to 60 percent in some demographics. The results of these studies, which Epstein dubbed the "Search

Engine Manipulation Effect" (SEME), are summarized in a 2015 report for the *Proceedings of the National Academy of Sciences*.[2]

As a result of his research, Epstein has called Google the "most powerful mind-control engine ever created."[3] He believes that the vast power of search engines to alter our political preferences stems from the fact that the users of the technology don't perceive search results to be biased. In Epstein's study on the 2014 Indian elections, 99.5 percent of the participants showed no realization that the search results they saw had been altered to favor a particular candidate. Unlike partisan news or political ads, where the bias and attempts at persuasion are often obvious, seemingly neutral search results are able to bypass our natural psychological defenses against manipulation. Testifying before the Senate Judiciary Committee in 2019, Epstein called the search engine manipulation effect "one of the most powerful forms of influence ever discovered in the behavioral sciences."[4]

If Epstein's findings are even close to correct, then Google's power is far too vast to remain in unaccountable, private hands. Even if Google were a perfect company, run by politically neutral leaders, with a comprehensive system of checks and balances to ensure political bias never affects its products, the unseen power to sway elections around the world is not something that can just be given over to a private actor with no public oversight.

Unfortunately, Google *does* currently have that power, and there is no law or regulation or public body that can legally stop the company from using it. As we'll see in later chapters, politicians and regulators have been utterly paralyzed over how to respond to the danger posed by Big Tech's political bias. The only major regulatory action against the tech giants has come in the form of antitrust investigations—that's big companies being held to account by slightly smaller companies. While these efforts aren't bad per se, politicians and regulators—with the exception of a few farsighted individuals like Senator Ted Cruz (R-TX), Senator Josh Hawley (R-MO),

Representative Paul Gosar (R-AZ), and Representative Tulsi Gabbard (D-HI)—have been far less interested in defending the political rights of the citizen against Silicon Valley. For the moment, we are all stuck in a situation where companies like Google wield unimaginable political power, asking us to take it on faith that they won't misuse it.

On that point, Epstein is not optimistic. According to his research, Google has *already* helped sway elections. The psychologist, along with researchers at the American Institute for Behavioral Research and Technology, preserved more than thirteen thousand election-related search results on Google, Yahoo!, and Bing from the 2016 election. Epstein and his researchers discovered "significant" bias in Google results in favor of Hillary Clinton in "all 10 positions on the first page of search results in both blue states and red states." (Keep in mind, roughly 75 percent of Google search users don't go beyond the first page of results.)[5] Based on his findings about the search engine manipulation effect, Epstein believes this pro–Hillary Clinton bias shifted at least 2.6 million votes in her favor in 2016.

Epstein conducted another, even larger study ahead of the 2018 midterm elections. Preserving more than forty-seven thousand results from Google, Yahoo!, and Bing, with search results linking to nearly four hundred thousand web pages, he once again found significant bias in favor of Democrats in Google search results. Again applying his findings about SEME, Epstein concluded that these search results would have affected upwards of 78.2 million votes.

These numbers may sound staggering, but keep in mind that Google's search engine has a market share of over 90 percent in the United States. It processes roughly forty thousand search queries per hour, translating to an astonishing 3.5 billion searches per day, and 1.2 trillion per year.[6] When one company has that near a monopoly over our access to information, Epstein's breathtaking estimates start to make sense. It's commonly accepted that a business can live or die based on its position in Google's rankings—there's an entire cottage industry, called search engine optimization (SEO), dedicated to helping companies make the front page of key search results. If it's that important to business, why wouldn't it be similarly important to politics?

Although Epstein did discover pro-Democrat bias from Google search results, his studies still assume good faith on the part of the tech company. For example, in his analysis of the "Go Vote" reminder that Google displayed on the home page of its search engine for the 2018 midterms, Epstein notes that the message would have reached more Democrats than Republicans, simply because more Democrats than Republicans use Google. Likewise, some features of Google's search engine, like its prioritization of old, established sites that are linked to by many other sources, favors websites like Wikipedia that happen to have a strong left-wing bias. Still, Google can't have predicted that when it designed its original search algorithm. In most of his research, Epstein has been careful to avoid claiming that Google's biased search results are intentional.

So, it's somewhat strange that Google is so panicked about the psychologist's investigations. In a lengthy comment to the *Washington Post* following the publication of Epstein's findings on the 2016 election, the tech giant denounced his research as a "poorly constructed conspiracy theory.

"We have never re-ranked search results on any topic (including elections) to manipulate political sentiment," said the company in its statement to the *Post*. "Moreover, we do not make any ranking tweaks that are specific to elections or political candidates, period. We always strive to provide our users with the most accurate, relevant answers to their queries."[7]

Over the next few pages, I'll demonstrate why we should be highly skeptical of Google's assurances. From top to bottom, the company is replete with left-wing bias. Before that, though, consider what Google *could* do if its executives were really trying to sway an election. Remember, this is a company that knows more about our likes, interests, preferences, and day-to-day lives than any other entity on earth. Google knows whether you vote Republican or Democrat—as Epstein has pointed out, it would be easy for Google to send slightly more get-out-the-vote reminders to Democrats than to Republicans, in a manner that would be difficult to detect. Indeed, it could go deeper—if, for example, Google knows that certain Republicans tend to check Google between seven a.m. and nine a.m., it could make sure that it displays its turnout reminders between ten a.m. and twelve p.m. If Google knows that a swing voter is particularly concerned about blue-collar jobs, it could display news results that highlight Democratic promises to boost the blue-collar economy, while hiding news stories about the effectiveness of Trump's policies in that area. When you consider the depth of Google's knowledge and reach, the potential for manipulation seems to be without limit. It again highlights the inherent danger of allowing one company to maintain such power, without any laws or public oversight to prevent its use.

But that's enough mere imagining. Let's turn to what we actually know.

Manual Interventions

In its response to Epstein, Google said it does not make any "ranking tweaks that are specific to elections or political candidates, period." Google CEO Sundar Pichai has made even bolder statements before Congress, telling lawmakers that the tech giant does not "manually intervene" on any particular search result.

In these claims, Google's leadership faces skepticism from many conservatives, as well as from Democrat Tulsi Gabbard, who has accused the tech giant of censoring her campaign messages. But, more important, the claims of Google's leadership are also challenged by its own employees.

Pichai's assurance to Congress was challenged in an article by Mike Wacker, who worked as a software engineer at Google from 2014 until May 2019. Responding directly to Pichai's claim that the tech giant never manually intervenes in search results, Wacker bluntly wrote, "Sundar Pichai did not tell the truth when he made this statement."[8]

To make his case, Wacker cited several leaks from Google, including one involving his own internal messages that I published on Breitbart News in January 2019, in which he described the manipulation of search results on YouTube, a Google-owned platform, as a "smoking gun" proving political bias. This leak, which we will examine more closely in the chapter on YouTube, showed that Google maintains a "blacklist" (Google's word, not mine) of handpicked search terms on YouTube. When terms are added to the blacklist, search results are reordered to favor videos from "verified" sources, which are themselves handpicked by YouTube. I don't know what Sundar Pichai's definition of "manual intervention" is, but it's hard to imagine a manually edited blacklist that favors manually picked sources not falling within it.

It's one thing to examine what an organization does from the outside, but it's inside scoops like the blacklists leak that tell the real story. We can learn a lot more about a company, its culture and its hidden practices, from the way its employees talk to one another when they think no one is listening. How did Google employees react to this discussion of a blacklist? With total nonchalance. "We have tons of white- and blacklists that humans manually curate," said one employee in the leaked discussion. "Hopefully this isn't surprising or particularly controversial." In public, before Congress, Pichai assured us all that the company doesn't manually intervene in search results. Behind closed doors, his employees tell a very different story.

What about Google's response to Epstein's research, in which the company claimed it never engages in "ranking tweaks that are specific to elections"? A "ranking tweak" is, if anything, an even broader category than a manual intervention. Especially with Big Tech's post-2016 obsession with protecting "election integrity," is Google's assurance really true?

Once again, a leak from inside the company appeared to contradict its public statements. In June 2019, investigative journalists at Project Veritas published parts of YouTube's blacklist file, showing that just over a year earlier, ahead of Ireland's referendum on legalizing abortion, several terms related to the vote had been added to the blacklist. These included "repeal the 8th" (a reference to the eighth amendment of the Irish constitution, which banned abortion except in instances where the mother's life is threatened), "Irish catholic," "pro-life," and "abortion is murder."[9] To use Google's own words, this looks an awful lot like a ranking tweak specific to a democratic vote.

A highly charitable defender of Google might argue that the company's public statements referred to its main search engine, not to YouTube (although neither of the statements specified that). But this would be a weak defense—the most popular search engine in the world is Google, but the *second*-most-popular search engine in the world is YouTube. As early as 2009, search volume on YouTube outstripped Yahoo!'s by 50 percent and Bing's by 150 percent.[10] Are we supposed to be reassured that Google is reranking election-related search results only on the world's second-most-popular search engine?

What's more, other leaks from the company show that Google's main search engine is subject to manual tweaks too. When I published Mike Wacker's internal messages about YouTube's blacklist in 2019, I also published a message from a member of Google's Trust and Safety team, explaining to Wacker that, while the bar for manual interventions in searches on YouTube is lower than on Google's main search engine (hey, it's only the *second*-most-popular search engine, right?), such interventions on Google's main search engine do indeed take place.

Here is that employee's message in full:

I work in Trust and Safety and while I have no particular input as to exactly what's happening for [YouTube] I can try to explain why you'd have this kind of list and why people are finding lists like these on Code Search.

When dealing with abuse/controversial content on various mediums you have several levers to deal with problems. Two prominent levers are "Proactive" and "Reactive":

- Proactive: Usually refers to some type of algorithm/scalable solution to a general problem
  - E.g.: We don't allow straight up porn on YouTube so we create a classifier that detects porn and automatically remove or flag for review the videos the porn classifier is most certain of
- Reactive: Usually refers to a manual fix to something that has been brought to our attention that our proactive solutions don't/didn't work on and something that is clearly in the realm of bad enough to warrant a quick targeted solution (determined by pages and pages of policies worked on over many years and many teams to be fair and cover necessary scope)
  - E.g.: A website that used to be a good blog had it's [sic] domain expire and was purchased/repurposed to spam Search results with autogenerated pages full of gibberish text, scraped images, and links to boost traffic to other spammy sites. It is manually actioned for violating policy

These Organic Search policies and the consequences to violating them are public.

Manually reacting to things is not very scalable, and is not an ideal solution to most problems, so the proactive lever is really the one we all like to lean on. Ideally, our classifiers/algorithm are good at providing useful and rich results to our users while ignoring things that are not useful or not relevant. But we all know, this isn't exactly the case all the time (especially on YouTube).

From a user perspective, there are subjects that are prone to hyperbolic content, misleading information, and offensive content. Now, these words are highly subjective and no one denies that. But we can all agree generally, lines exist in many cultures about what is clearly okay vs. what is not okay. E.g. a video of a puppy playing with a toy is probably okay in almost every culture or context, even if it's not relevant to the query. But a video of someone committing suicide and begging others to follow in his/her footsteps is probably on the other side of the line for many folks.

While my second example is technically relevant to the generic query of "suicide," that doesn't mean that this is a very useful or good video to promote on the top of results for that query. So imagine a classifier that says, for any queries on a particular text file, let's pull videos using signals that we historically understand to be strong indicators of quality (I won't go into specifics here, but those signals do exist). We're not manually curating these results, we're just saying "hey, be extra careful with results for this query because many times really bad stuff can appear and lead to a bad experience for most users." Ideally the proactive lever did this for us, but in extreme cases where we need to act quickly on something that is so obviously not okay, the reactive/manual approach is sometimes necessary. And also keep in mind, that this is different for every product. ***The bar for changing classifiers or manual actions on [spam] in organic search is extremely high.*** [Emphasis mine.] However, the bar for things we let our Google Assistant say out loud might be a lot lower. If I search for "Jews run the banks"—I'll likely find anti-semitic stuff in organic search. As a Jew, I might find some of these results offensive, but they are there for people to research and view, and I understand that this is not a reflection of [how] Google feels about this issue. But if I ask Google Assistant "Why do Jews run the banks" we wouldn't be similarly accepting if it repeated and promoted conspiracy theories that likely pop up in organic search.

Whether we agree or not, user perception of our responses, results, and answers of different products and mediums can change. And I think many people are used to the fact that organic search is a place where content should be accessible no matter how offensive it might be, however, the expectation is very different on a Google Home, a Knowledge Panel, or even YouTube.

These lines are very difficult and can be very blurry, we are all well aware of this. So we've got huge teams that stay cognizant of these facts when we're crafting policies considering classifier changes, or reacting with manual actions—these decisions are not made in a vacuum, but admittedly are also not made in a highly public forum like TGIF or IndustryInfo (as you can imagine, decisions/agreement would be hard to get in such a wide list—image if all your CL's [change lists] were reviewed by every engineer across Google all the time). I hope that answers some questions and gives a better layer of transparency without going into details about our "Pepsi formula."

Best,

Daniel

As you can see from the section I highlighted, "Daniel" admits that Google does occasionally intervene in search results on its main search engine (internally referred to as "organic search"), as well as in search results on YouTube. "Daniel" also tells us that the decisions about how much "offensive" content Google should tolerate in its search results are made in secrecy, closed off to most employees at the company.

The News Blacklists

And that's just the start of Google's bias problems. In April 2019, the Daily Caller obtained evidence of something called the "deceptive news domain blacklist"—yet another Google blacklist, used to filter "problematic" news sites out of search results. The policy document obtained by the Daily Caller states that it was approved by Ben Gomes, who was then Google's head of search. As reported by the Caller, Gomes reported directly to then CEO Sundar Pichai.

"The purpose of the blacklist will be to bar the sites from surfacing in any Search feature or news product," the document said. "It will not cause a demotion in the organic search results or de-index them altogether," it added, meaning that affected sites would be banned from featured areas of Google search results, including the "top news" feature and Google's "knowledge panels," which frequently appear in the top right-hand side of search results.

Sites on the blacklist included a range of conservative blogs and news websites, including the Gateway Pundit, Conservative Tribune, the American Spectator, and the websites of conservatives Caroline Glick and Matt Walsh. Amazingly, Google responded by denying that the blacklist constituted a "manual intervention," or that the policy was an "attempt to make any judgement on the political leanings of a website."[11] Google doesn't make any judgments on a website's political leanings, you see—it *just so happens* that a host of websites marked down for "deceptive news" happened to be leading conservative sources.

Further evidence of Google's meddling with news came when Project Veritas released a batch of leaked internal files from the company in August 2019.[12] The release included a file called "news black list for site google now," described as a "manual list of sites excluded from appearing as Google Now stories." Google Now was a feature that proactively delivered information to users based on their interests and search habits—the goal behind it was to harness Google's data about you to predict the information that you would be interested in seeing. The company no longer uses the term "Google Now," but its features have been spun off into other Google products, including the Google Assistant.

The blacklist included even more prominent conservative websites than "deceptive news." The websites of conservative commentators Glenn Beck, Steven Crowder, and Rush Limbaugh were all included. So, too, were the Daily Caller, RedState, Chicks on the Right, Right Side News, Twitchy, FrontPage Magazine, and Rebel Media. A few far-left sites, including Occupy Democrats, Right Wing Watch, Feministing, and Media Matters, were also on the list. Nowhere to be found on the list: CNN, the *New York Times*, the Huffington Post, Vox, or BuzzFeed. The bias on the Google Now blacklist appears to have been in favor of mainstream, established sources and against partisan ones. That does not necessarily make it better, though—it's still Google deciding what news we should see.

In August 2018, President Trump tweeted that Google search results were "RIGGED" against him.[13] Trump cited a claim that had recently been made by a writer at conservative website PJ Media who, after analyzing several Google searches for the word "Trump," found that 96 percent of the results came from liberal-leaning news sources.[14]

The president was quickly mocked as a "conspiracy theorist" by the mainstream media (which, of course, are the beneficiaries of any pro-liberal bias from Google). And yet, in the year since then, we've seen the release of a YouTube search blacklist, a "deceptive news" blacklist, and a Google Now blacklist, all of which seem to have a disproportionate impact on conservative media. A conspiracy theory? It doesn't seem that way anymore.

Indeed, some of Google's top people have been pretty open about their goals. We've already seen, in earlier chapters, how Google executives stood up before their employees a few days after the 2016 election, denounced the election result as "offensive," and pledged to make the populist movement nothing more than a "hiccup" in history. Eric Schmidt, who was executive chairman of Google's parent company until 2017, was even more brazen—while his colleagues fumed in behind-closed-doors meetings, he went out in public to declare his intentions. The "project for the next decade," said Schmidt a few days after the election, should be "how people get their information, what they believe, what they don't."

They want to control your information, what you believe, and what you don't believe. Could a confession be any more naked? Who needs a "conspiracy theory" when the real-world supervillains are happy to tell the whole public what their plan is?

On that note, let's turn to another moment of honesty from Google—its "Good Censor" document.

"The Good Censor"

We briefly touched in chapter 2 on "The Good Censor," an extraordinary document admitting to a "shift toward censorship" on the part of Google. It's time to delve a little deeper.

The document was leaked to me in October 2018, around the same time that the mainstream media began accusing President Trump of believing "conspiracy theories" about Google's political censorship. Since I published the story on Breitbart News, it has been read by more than eight hundred thousand people and cited in a Senate hearing on Big Tech bias by Senator Ted Cruz (R-TX).

"The Good Censor" was prepared by Insight Labs, a team within Google dedicated to analyzing and explaining the company's products and services. In other words, they're the guys Google pays to understand Google. Since it doesn't appear to have been intended for the general public, there's no spin, no equivocating, and no half-truths—the document is remarkable in its honesty.

It describes the early days of Silicon Valley in which the majority of Big Tech still believed in the "utopian narrative" of unfettered free speech.

Those days, according to the document, are long gone. Today, "big tech firms [the document cites Google, Facebook, and Twitter] have gradually shifted away from unmediated free speech and towards censorship and moderation."

These companies, admits the document, "now control the majority of online communications," giving them the opportunity to reshape the internet according to their values. The researchers argue that tech companies like Google can either stick to the "American tradition" of speech, which "prioritizes free speech for democracy, not civility," or they can choose the "European tradition" of speech, which "favors dignity over liberty and civility over freedom." The brief argues that, since 2016, all major tech platforms, including Google, have shifted their approach toward the more authoritarian European ideal.

This choice, says the document, is taking tech platforms away from their original function as an "unmediated marketplace of ideas" and toward "well-ordered spaces for safety and civility," a role more closely associated with that of an "editor" or a "publisher" rather than a platform.

The document admits that this represents a sharp departure from what tech platforms initially promised their consumers. According to the document, the "free speech ideal was instilled in the DNA of the Silicon Valley startups that now control the majority of our online conversations."

What brought about this radical shift in policy? Not much, according to the document—progressives like Leslie Jones being trolled on Twitter, "Russian meddling" in the 2016 election, an offensive video from YouTube star Logan Paul that showed a suicide victim, and the rise of "far right" parties like Alternative for Germany. Apparently, all it took for Silicon Valley to abandon its lofty ideals of free speech were a few cases of offensive content on the internet, some ineffectual Russian trolls, and a political party its leaders don't like.

In fairness, the document does go into more detail, discussing the rise of "cyber harassment," "cyber racism," "hate speech," and "trolling," while neglecting to mention that block and mute buttons have long existed to deal with all of these things. That's a common feature of Silicon Valley's post-election censorship efforts; there's always a false choice—information anarchy on the one hand, and the iron fist of top-down control by the tech giants on the other. The middle ground, where users are empowered to block and filter their own content, is rarely given much thought.

The document continues its fearmongering. Internet users, it says, are "keener to transgress moral norms," especially when they can hide behind the cloak of anonymity. "The 'little guys and girls' can now be heard," something Google's researchers frame as a positive when they're "emerging talent, revolutionaries, whistleblowers and campaigners."

"But," warns the document, "'everyone else' can shout loudly too—including terrorists, racists, misogynists and oppressors. And because 'everything looks like the New York Times' on the net, it's harder to separate fact from fiction."

The document warns that the open internet has allowed *badthink* and *wrongspeech* to proliferate.

"The internet has united political activists, dissidents and like-minded communities of all shapes and sizes, including the oppressed minorities. On the flip-side, minority groups once pushed underground by public opinion of their abhorrent views have discovered a safer space in which to communicate, organise and reach-out to new sympathizers."

Naturally, the "fake-news" panic also makes an appearance, with Google's document warning that tech companies have risked placing "have-a-go commenters" on an even footing with "authoritative voices." Very little is done, of course, to define either of those terms.

"Untrustworthy sources and misinformation have thrived on tech platforms. Dubious distributors have capitalised on a lack of sense-checking and algorithms that reward sensationalist content. And rational debate is damaged when authoritative voices and 'have a go' commentators receive equal weighting."

Google sums up the pressures leading tech companies to "shift towards censorship" thusly: demands by authoritarian governments that have the power to limit its global expansion; the need to "monetize content through its organization"; and the need to "protect advertisers from controversial content, [and] increase revenues."

Censorship, conclude the researchers, isn't just a moral imperative to tackle the nasty racists—it's profitable, too!

Dumb F**ks

In September 2019, I was shown some messages on Blind, an app that allows employees of Big Tech companies to start anonymous discussions with their coworkers.

Although users of the app remain anonymous, they can be identified by their company's name. It proved to be a remarkable source of insight into the mood of Silicon Valley.

The messages I was shown included a discussion between some rather disillusioned Google employees. One of the employees complained, "I find myself switching off Google search more and more lately."

His reasons? Censorship of search results, a corresponding lack of trust in those search results, and "ads that take up the whole screen."

The latter is a common complaint about ad-driven Big Tech companies. But the first two are newer.

Some mocked his concerns. Another Google employee chimed in, not to deny that the company was censoring, but to defend the practice. "Tech companies are under a lot of pressure to prevent the spread of fake news...you can say 'people should decide on their own' and they have—and that's exactly what the anger is about."

"People are often stupid...ideally Google wouldn't have to do this, but the dumb fucks keep clicking on the bullshit news articles."

"That doesn't mean I trust Google to remove it," shot back the original employee.

Other Google employees agreed with him. "I try to use Duck-DuckGo and Brave browser as much as possible," said one.

(Brave is a competitor to Google's Chrome, the dominant web browser. DuckDuckGo is a competing search engine. The two announced in 2017 that they had partnered so that, when a Duck-DuckGo search was done using the Brave browser's private tabs, users' information would remain private.)

"I keep trying to switch to Yahoo and others," said another colleague. While he conceded that Google search results are still better, he said it still wasn't his first choice. "I try Yahoo first, if can't find, go to Google."

You know trust in a company has deteriorated when its own employees—even a small number of them—won't use its previously peerless products. Even more remarkable is the fact that some won't use Google even if they think it's better. They don't object to the quality of their company's products—they object to them *on principle*.

And what about the other side of Google, the side that sees the tech giant's users as "dumb fucks" who'll be deluded by "bullshit" fake-news articles? Is this a view held by a minority at Google, or does it go all the way to the top?

To answer this, we must go beyond Google's official statements and listen to what the company's leaders say in private.

Luckily, thanks to the video footage that was leaked to me in 2018, we know exactly what Google's upper management thinks of ordinary people.

Brin may not have gone as far as calling his users "dumb fucks," as the anonymous Google employee on Blind did, but calling half the American public "extremist" isn't much better.

Sundar Pichai didn't call ordinary people dumb either—he just strongly implied it! After an employee asked what the company plans to do about "low-information voters" who had been allegedly deluded by "misinformation" during the election, Pichai promised "investments in machine learning and AI" to stop the "problem" from recurring. Pichai also promised the company would work toward "correcting" its role in the creation of ideological "filter bubbles"— a technical term for political partisans seeking out information that supports their views.

See, there's no need to describe as "dumb fucks" those users who click on "bullshit"—calling them "low-information voter[s]" who click on "misinformation" is much more polite!

Does it matter that America's largest and most powerful tech unicorn, de facto gatekeeper of the world's information, appears to have total uniformity of political views in its leadership team? Well, that depends on whether you trust Google.

I contacted the company shortly before publishing the video. A Google spokeswoman quickly responded, stating that the political biases of its executives would never influence the company's products.

"Nothing was said at that meeting, or any other meeting, to suggest that any political bias ever influences the way we build or operate our products...we design them with extraordinary care to be a trustworthy source of information for everyone, without regard to political viewpoint," she said.

Even from the leaked video, we can judge Google's official statement as spin—for the executives onstage went beyond statements of personal grief about Trump's election. Pichai promised to deploy machine learning and AI to combat the alleged rise of "low-information voters." Brin referenced Google's antiextremism tools in a discussion about the alleged "extremism" of Trump supporters. CFO Ruth Porat pledged the "great strength and resources and reach" of Google to advance the company's political causes. Chief legal officer Kent Walker wished to make the populist movement a "hiccup" in history.

This was more than a company-wide group hug; it was a planning session to save the world from what Google's leaders clearly believed then—and appear to continue to believe—is a grave threat to its values: President Trump and the populist movement. And with so much unchecked, unmonitored power in Google's hands, the company isn't just the greatest threat the populist movement has ever faced—it's the greatest threat that democracy has ever faced. It is, without a doubt, the world's most dangerous company.

10. Censorship Kills the YouTube Star

In politics and culture, it is hard to overstate the importance of You-Tube, the Google-owned tech giant that dominates online video. Millennials and Generation Z do not watch cable news—they watch their favorite YouTuber.

Watching a YouTube video is not like sharing a tweet or hitting "like" on a Facebook post. Even if you don't watch a video to the end, you have to click on it, press play, and begin watching. The investment is far greater than retweeting a post that flicks across your newsfeed for an instant.

In contrast to many other social media giants, YouTube is a platform that thrives on long-form, in-depth content. Because of that, it plays a central role in developing the values and mind-set of younger generations. As a result, leftists and the media are more terrified of YouTube than they are of perhaps any other platform.

In addition, YouTube viewers' demographics are terrifying to the mainstream media.

Consider this: in 2017, according to TV raters Nielsen, the median age of Fox News and MSNBC viewers was sixty-five, while CNN's was only slightly younger at fifty-nine. The average cable news viewer, then, is an aging baby boomer at worst or an early Gen Xer at best.

Compared to YouTube, the difference is staggering. Felix Kjell-berg (better known as "PewDiePie"), the Swedish independent content creator whose channel was the most popular on the platform from 2013 until 2019, revealed in 2018 that just 1 percent of his viewers were over fifty-five. The largest segment of his audience was the eighteen to twenty-four demographic, which made up 44 percent of his audience, and the second-largest was the twenty-five to thirty-four demographic, with 28 percent.[1]

Surveys of young people also support the picture of YouTube displacing the mainstream media. A survey commissioned by *Variety* in 2014 found that American teenagers rated YouTube personalities far higher than they rated traditional celebrities on a range of factors, including relatability, authenticity, and other factors that marketers have identified as sources of influence. Of the five celebrities who topped the survey, all—including comedy duo Smosh, the YouTuber KSI, and PewDiePie—were online stars. Leonardo DiCaprio, a Hollywood megastar of the 1990s and early 2000s, languished at twentieth.[2] In other words, an online celebrity who tells his millions of young viewers that the "gender pay gap" is a myth (yes, PewDiePie did do that)[3] has completely eclipsed a traditional movie star who lectures his dwindling fan base about the importance of ditching plastic straws from the luxury of his private jet.[4]

Purely political channels don't, generally, rise to the same level of popularity as PewDiePie, who was born in 1989 and generally puts entertainment first and politics perhaps a distant third. Still, the YouTubers who focus on politics and current affairs shouldn't be underestimated—in raw numbers, they are snapping at the heels of the mainstream broadcasters, and, like PewDiePie's, their demographics are far better for advertisers.

YouTube, then, has both depth and breadth. A subscriber to a YouTube channel is, by virtue of the platform's nature, more invested in the content than a Twitter follower who sees new content virtually every second. But the YouTubers also enjoy a massive breadth, frequently reaching hundreds of thousands or millions of viewers with each video. And YouTube's devotees are far younger than the established broadcasters'. If demographics are destiny, the mainstream media is heading for the grave.

The Panic Hits YouTube

It wasn't long before the mainstream media realized that something had to be done about YouTube. They began with a hatchet job against PewDiePie, who was then the platform's biggest independent star. And they did it in the classic journalist-as-inquisitor style—by taking an offensive joke out of context and calling him a racist.

The joke the media focused on was in a now-deleted video that Kjellberg uploaded on January 11, 2017. The video shows the YouTuber testing the limits of cash-for-jobs site Fiverr by asking its freelancers to perform ridiculous or outrageous tasks. Kjellberg's requests were refused by many of the freelancers, including a mathematician who was asked by the YouTuber to draw a mathematical graph in the shape of a penis. However, two Indian video promoters did agree to hold up a sign saying "death to all Jews" while performing their signature stunt of dancing in the jungle and urging viewers to subscribe to a competing YouTube channel, KeemStar.

Kjellberg, who often films his reactions live on-camera, was visibly shocked when he discovered that the freelancers had delivered on the outrageous video. He immediately stressed that the stunt was not meant to be taken seriously and should be viewed in the context of his video, which, according to Kjellberg, aimed to highlight the absurdity of an online cottage industry that incentivizes people to perform the most outlandish of tasks for as little as $5. Kjellberg even said that he "felt bad" that the freelancers had agreed to his absurd request.

The media paid little attention to the nuance of Kjellberg's reaction and instead barraged him with negative press that ultimately led corporate sponsors to sever their ties with the YouTuber. Disney quickly pulled the plug on its professional relationship with Kjellberg, while YouTube itself canceled a reality show starring the YouTuber, which had been scheduled to launch on the platform's premium service. The platform also removed him from a list of channels approved for preferential advertising.

The *Sun*, a News Corp–owned British tabloid, led the coverage, starting with a story claiming there had been "outrage" over the video, despite the fact that the video's like-to-dislike ratio showed a largely positive reaction. A headline in Wired branded Kjellberg a "racist" and "hero to Nazis," although this headline was subsequently changed.[5] The normally respectable *Wall Street Journal* made the biggest effort to destroy Kjellberg. Three *Wall Street Journal* writers trawled through hundreds of his videos for offensive content, coming up with nine out-of-context examples that they spliced together into a video. In addition to the clips, the *Wall Street Journal* added scary background music and quotes from the Southern Poverty Law Center (SPLC) warning about normalizing "hatred."[6]

While the media succeeded in cutting PewDiePie off from some of his corporate sponsors, the skirmish did not go entirely in the mainstream media's favor. A string of prominent YouTube personalities, including Philip DeFranco (who had 5 million subscribers and 1.8 billion channel views at the time) and Ethan Klein (3.4 million subscribers; 484,000 views) rallied to PewDiePie's defense, slamming the *Wall Street Journal* and other mainstream media outlets for their smear campaign. Collectively, they reached an audience several times larger than the *Wall Street Journal*'s digital subscriber base of 1.7 million. With PewDiePie's response video alone gaining more than 10 million viewers, the *Wall Street Journal* decisively lost the battle for public support.

But who needs public support when you can bully a Silicon Valley giant into doing your bidding? After the PewDiePie skirmish, the mainstream media's next salvo against YouTube would trigger a decisive shift in the platform's policies.

News Corp would once again lead the charge against YouTube. In an article published in February 2017, the *Times* of London's head of investigations, Alexi Mostrous, declared that "some of the world's biggest brands are unwittingly funding Islamic extremists, white supremacists and pornographers" through advertisements on YouTube. Mostrous revealed how ads from major companies like Mercedes-Benz and Honda were appearing next to neo-Nazi skinhead videos and propaganda videos produced by ISIS, the terrorist group.[7] He also contacted several prominent British politicians who condemned YouTube's tolerance of extremist content.[8]

Unlike the *Wall Street Journal*'s clumsy, Pyrrhic campaign against PewDiePie over tasteless jokes, the *Times*' hit against YouTube was well-timed, perfectly executed, and devastating. The videos that Mostrous had uncovered were genuinely extremist and hugely embarrassing for both YouTube and the brands whose advertisements had run alongside them. As YouTube scrambled to find a solution to the crisis, major advertisers began a mass boycott of the platform, in what could come to be known as the "YouTube adpocalypse." By the end of March, less than two months after the story broke, financial technology analysts predicted that YouTube would lose potential revenue of up to $750 million—three-quarters of a billion dollars—as a result of the boycott.[9]

YouTube would never be the same again. The platform swiftly moved to strengthen a preexisting system that checked whether its creators' videos were "advertiser-friendly" before assigning them any ads. Before the adpocalypse, YouTube had been remarkably laissez-faire about such matters when compared with competing platforms like Twitter and Facebook. No longer. Never again would ads be sent to channels without going through YouTube's process of checks and double-checks. The phrase "demonetization" entered popular usage, as channels were stripped of ad revenue left, right, and center. YouTube's system, which relies on algorithms to sort through the platform's vast quantity of new videos, was hastily built and clumsily implemented. Keep in mind, YouTube is the same platform whose "hate speech" algorithm accidentally banned history teachers for uploading archival footage of the Nazi era (see chapter 6, "Robot Censors"). Even before the adpocalypse, YouTube's monetization algorithm had come under fire for its clumsiness, which led to the removal of ad revenue from suicide-prevention videos.[10]

Post-adpocalypse, the problem only got worse. In June 2017, Google's Kent Walker (the "make populism a blip in history" guy) announced a series of measures aimed at tackling "extremism" on YouTube. Walker announced that the platform had expanded its "trusted flagger" program, a network of NGOs and "experts" the platform relied on to flag offensive content. It would later emerge that one of these "trusted flaggers" was the far-left SPLC.[11] Walker also revealed that the platform would demonetize videos that contained "inflammatory religious or supremacist content," even if the videos didn't breach YouTube's rules. "We think this strikes the right balance between free expression and access to information without promoting extremely offensive viewpoints," wrote Walker in an official blog post.[12]

It wasn't long before this crackdown on "extremism" started to affect mainstream conservatives. This may have all started with a *Times* of London report about ISIS propaganda videos, but when YouTube's response is to take advice from the SPLC, it shouldn't be a surprise that the "extremists" targeted by the platform are suddenly not just Middle Eastern terrorists but mainstream conservatives as well. Have I told you yet about how the Left likes to manipulate the meaning of words?

By August, just a few months after Walker's announcement, YouTube was removing ad revenue from videos by former Republican presidential candidate Ron Paul that criticized America's Afghanistan policy.[13] By September, videos from classical liberal Dave Rubin featuring interviews with conservatives like Christina Hoff Sommers and Steven Crowder and Islam critic Ayaan Hirsi Ali had also been demonetized.[14] In its ham-fisted effort to tackle "extremism," YouTube had undertaken a massive overcorrection—which was no doubt exactly what many of its critics in the mainstream media had hoped for.

The Smoking Gun

As bad as the demonetizations were, it would take leaks from inside YouTube for us to understand the true depths of the platform's post-adpocalypse capitulation to the mainstream media.

In late 2019, I was contacted by a whistle-blower inside Google, YouTube's parent company, who claimed he had a "smoking gun" proving the company's political bias. He had discovered the existence of a file, called "youtube controversial query blacklist," which allowed the platform to adjust the top search results for any given term to favor a set of "verified" channels that had the platform's stamp of approval. By adding a term to the blacklist, YouTube could wipe videos from nonverified channels off the top search results, burying them down the page, where Google, the world's leading expert on search habits, knew only a small percentage of users would ever bother to look.

Did YouTube use this blacklist sparingly? Did it target only highly specific search terms where genuinely extremist videos, like Islamist propaganda, could be found? Not at all—my source revealed that search terms for mainstream political topics like abortion had been added to the blacklist, as had searches for the names of certain political figures, like far-left antigun activist David Hogg and Representative Maxine Waters (D-CA). By adding these terms to the blacklist, YouTube ensures that the first thing people see when searching for them is a string of results from "verified" channels—mostly the pro-Democratic, pro-Left mainstream media.

Try searching YouTube for videos about Maxine Waters—the top results are, as of this writing in early 2020, from the following "verified" channels: NBC, NBC, CNN, NBC, C-SPAN, PBS, *The View*, CNN, MSNBC.[15] What an unbiased set of sources!

When I asked YouTube to comment on the record about the blacklist, the answer I got was classic plausible deniability: "Over the last year we've described how we are working to better surface news sources across our site for news-related searches and topical information. We've improved our search and discovery algorithms, built new features that clearly label and prominently surface news sources on our home page and search pages, and introduced information panels to help give users more authoritative sources where they can fact check information for themselves."

By saying they want to surface "news sources" in search results and give users "more authoritative sources," YouTube can claim to the world that its blacklist is politically unbiased. Yet when searches for a controversial Democratic politician return a string of videos from CNN and NBC, it's easy to conclude otherwise.

The story of how the term "abortion" ended up on YouTube's blacklist is even crazier.

My source told me that the term was added on December 14, 2018, at 3:17 p.m. That date is significant because it was the same day that a far-left, pro-abortion writer for *Slate* had contacted the company to complain about the prominence of pro-life videos in the search results. YouTube altered its search results for one of the most politically fraught topics in America because of a single complaint from a single journalist.

Naturally, once "abortion" was added to the blacklist, the search results changed dramatically. Before the change, the top ten videos included congressional testimony from Dr. Anthony Levatino, a former abortion doctor turned pro-life activist, as well as a video from pro-life conservative Ben Shapiro. Most egregiously, a nonpolitical video featuring a woman's personal story about regretting an abortion after being persuaded to undergo one also disappeared from the top results.[16] In their place came videos from BuzzFeed, Vice, CNN, and *Last Week Tonight with John Oliver*.[17] YouTube viewers who search for "abortion" are now confronted with a stream of pro-abortion propaganda from the mainstream media. All this because *one* left-wing writer complained.

My source later revealed that the same thing had happened a year prior. In September 2018, left-wing MSNBC host Chris Hayes took to Twitter to criticize YouTube for surfacing antiestablishment videos in its search results.

"My favorite example of how informationally toxic YouTube's algorithm is [is] this," said Hayes. "Imagine you're a high school freshman and got a school assignment about the Federal Reserve."

Hayes went on to highlight several anti-Fed videos that appeared in the top ten search results, including a video called "Century of Enslavement," which criticized the Federal Reserve system. Hayes also drew attention to a video from the John Birch Society, a mainstream paleoconservative society that has recently hosted speakers ranging from Representative Thomas Massie (R-KY), to acting White House chief of staff Mick Mulvaney. Hayes called the John Birch Society video "conspirational quackery."

Web archives from 2017 show that "Century of Enslavement" was indeed one of the top YouTube search results for "Federal Reserve," as was an animated video from an anarcho-capitalist channel critiquing the Fed. A *New York Times* news item about the Fed was also in the top ten results, as well as a neutral "explainer" video from Crash Course Economics, indicating that the top ten results were actually quite balanced. But left-wingers like Hayes don't want their views to be equally represented. They want them to be dominant.

Hayes got what he wanted. On the same day that he posted his tweets, the blacklist file was amended to include the term "Federal Reserve." The anti-Fed videos that Hayes complained about disappeared from the top ten search results.

Perhaps it's because of the devastating adpocalypse, but it

certainly seems that when journalists ask YouTube to jump, the Google-owned platform asks, "How high?"

This is a disaster for democracy. As we saw in chapter 5, YouTube has gone further than any other platform in censoring the Trump campaign, taking down more than three hundred of the president's videos. Leaks from Project Veritas also show that the platform has interfered in democratic votes overseas as well, deploying its blacklist file to control search results for terms related to the 2018 referendum on the legalization of abortion in Ireland.[18] It's extraordinary that some people in the establishment are still concerned with "Russian interference" when unaccountable tech giants are meddling in democratic votes before our very eyes.

It is also a disaster for society. When you consider the fact that the YouTube search function is often the first port of call for millennials and zoomers seeking new information about a topic, the shameful reduction of search results on controversial topics to a string of anodyne reports from preapproved mainstream sources is a travesty. On matters as important and life changing as abortion, people searching for information will most likely find only mainstream opinion, the narrowest of viewpoints politically acceptable to the mainstream.

And what about YouTube's independent creators? Some are "verified" by YouTube, meaning they won't be affected by the blacklist. But others, especially newer channels, are not. For a platform that was once the gold standard for independent voices trying to find an audience, the path for new channels becomes ever steeper, ever more difficult to follow. As if the multimillion-dollar budgets of mainstream news channels weren't enough to compete with, YouTube is giving them favored treatment in its search algorithm as well. If you're an independent journalist or political commentator, why even bother creating a YouTube account? The platform has made it clear that it's going to elevate the big broadcast networks while suppressing you. Increasingly, it looks like YouTube will become cable 2.0.

In 2019, two of the biggest critics of leftism on YouTube, Carl

"Sargon of Akkad" Benjamin and Mark "Count Dankula" Meechan, had their channels fully demonetized by YouTube. This meant they were permanently banned from using the platform to earn a living. For both men, YouTube was their primary platform, where they had developed an audience and turned commentary into a full-time career. It was an example of how, with a little effort, ordinary people could accumulate followings to rival those enjoyed by anchors for CNN and MSNBC. In 2019, YouTube told the world—not anymore!

This sad story is remarkably similar to the way Facebook pulled the rug out from under its ecosystem of independent publishers. A platform that once welcomed the creation of independent media had suddenly turned hostile. With no legal recourse and no rights, there was nothing those independent creators could do except look for alternative platforms. The journalists had won, again.

11. The Defamation Engine

In the last two chapters, we looked at Google. Now it's time to look at the website that appears most often at the top of search results—Wikipedia.

Few examples of Big Tech's leftist bias are more obvious than Wikipedia, the online encyclopedia that misleadingly brands itself as open for "anyone to edit." It is, of course, nothing of the sort. Anyone can *try* to edit it, but a cursory glance at the pages of prominent political figures should tell you all you need to know about whose edits get accepted into the record of history, and whose do not.

Let's start with the Wikipedia entry for conservative Fox News personality Sean Hannity, the most-watched cable news host in 2017, 2018, and 2019.

In the very first paragraph, Wikipedia once alleged that the Fox host is not a true journalist—instead, it said, Hannity hosts an "opinionative, non-journalistic, pseudo-conspiracy program."[1] After two short paragraphs, Wikipedia again insisted that Hannity has "promoted conspiracy theories" and "falsehoods," including "untrue accounts about Hillary Clinton's health."

And that's just the *introduction* of Hannity's Wikipedia entry. I could go through the remaining 90 percent of Hannity's page and catalogue the other smears, but that would fill a whole chapter. Instead, let's turn to a comparable figure on the left: MSNBC host Rachel Maddow.

Maddow, like Hannity, is a highly opinionated host who has had her fair share of controversies. She once speculated, on-air, that Russian president Vladimir Putin might have been blackmailing President Trump into withdrawing troops from Syria by using secret video footage of Trump in a compromising situation.[2] This, of course, had no basis in fact. She once falsely claimed a Republican governor, the oh-so-radical John Kasich of Ohio, had signed a bill into law that required women seeking an abortion to undergo a "mandatory vaginal probe." Even the left-leaning fact-checker PolitiFact said Maddow's claim was "about as far as can be from the truth."[3]

Given the standards applied to Hannity, surely we can expect Maddow to receive similar treatment? Surely, Wikipedia will tell us that she's promoted "falsehoods" about Ohio abortion laws and spread "conspiracy theories" about Vladimir Putin blackmailing an American president?

Of course not! The most controversial thing we learn from the introduction of Maddow's Wikipedia entry is that she's a liberal. Two paragraphs in, Wikipedia allows Maddow to define herself: "I'm undoubtedly a liberal, which means that I'm in almost total agreement with the Eisenhower-era Republican party platform."

Weird—why don't the Wikipedia editors include Hannity's self-description of his role and beliefs in his page's introduction? He's been on television more than two decades—I'm sure they could find a self-description somewhere!

We can only assume that they didn't want to.

Wikipedia entries for websites follow the same predictable pattern. The entry for Breitbart News is awash with smears—again, right at the top of the page, where the maximum number of visitors will see it. Wikipedia falsely claimed that Breitbart has published "lies, conspiracy theories, and intentionally misleading stories."[4] You may wonder why no Wikipedia editor added links to some of Breitbart's own stories about itself—that might be because Wikipedians have decided Breitbart links can't be used as a "reliable source."[5]

The page falsely claims that Breitbart "aligned with the alt-right" under Steve Bannon, even though both Breitbart and Bannon rejected the label when it became co-opted by white supremacists. Breitbart, says Wikipedia, "has been called misogynistic, xenophobic, and racist."

Sure, it's been *called* that. But you'll have to search far and wide for a Wikipedia page about a left-wing website that reels off the worst allegations about it from its critics in the very first paragraph.

For example, look at the Wikipedia page for the Daily Beast, one of the leading left-wing news and opinion websites.

Does Wikipedia tell us that the Daily Beast regularly publishes blatantly racist headlines about white people? (Examples include "Have White People Lost Their Minds?," a headline telling white people to "Pipe Down and Listen," and "The Unbearable Whiteness of Congress.")[6]

Wikipedia does not tell us that.

Does Wikipedia tell us that the Daily Beast spread smears about conservative kids from Covington Catholic High School, falsely claiming they were "terrorizing and mocking an old and presumably weak man"? (The "weak old man" was a radical activist who deliberately antagonized the kids for wearing MAGA hats—and the kids did nothing in response but stand around looking sheepish.)

Wikipedia does not tell us that.

Unlike the case with Breitbart News, we read only positive or neutral things about the Daily Beast on its Wikipedia page. We are told that it's an "American news and opinion website focused on politics and pop culture." Similar to Maddow's Wikipedia page, the Daily Beast's page is given the privilege of describing itself. Its editor in chief is quoted as saying the site's focus is on "scoops, scandals, and stories about secret worlds."

Not until the very bottom of the Daily Beast's page do we learn about one of the worst things the site has done—its doxing of a black forklift driver, Shawn Brooks, for the apparently shocking act of creating a video mocking Democratic Speaker of the House Nancy Pelosi.

I'm willing to bet that if the Daily Beast were a conservative publication, its Wikipedia introduction would include something along the lines of, "The Daily Beast has spread personally identifying information about an African American forklift driver over stories of questionable newsworthiness."

But it isn't. So, it doesn't.

I've saved the best example for last—politicians.

Justin Trudeau is the prime minister of Canada. He was reelected in 2019 after his left-wing Liberal Party won the most seats in the election.

You'll find all of this information right at the top of his Wikipedia page, as well as the fact that he is the second-youngest prime minister in Canadian history, and that he achieved the largest-ever increase in a party's parliamentary seats when he was first elected in 2015. If you're interested, the introduction also tells you that he previously worked as a camp counselor, a nightclub bouncer, and a snowboard instructor.

What the introduction *doesn't* tell you is that Justin Trudeau was once a fan of wearing blackface. He didn't do it just once. He did it *multiple times*. During the run-up to the 2019 vote, no fewer than three instances of the Canadian prime minister wearing blackface were uncovered—and Trudeau told reporters he "doesn't know" how often he's done it.[7]

On Wikipedia, the blackface scandal is buried way down on Trudeau's page. It doesn't even get its own category—it's instead shoved into a subsection about the 2019 elections. You can bet your bottom dollar that if a right-wing politician had been involved in a similar controversy, it would be displayed far more prominently on their Wikipedia page.

For example, let's look at Donald Trump's.

"Trump has made many false or misleading statements during

his campaign and presidency," says Wikipedia, no later than the *third paragraph* of the page's introduction. "Many of his comments and actions have also been characterized as racially charged or racist."

Two more paragraphs down—and we still haven't left the introduction—we're told all about the corruption allegations made against Trump. We're told that Trump "welcomed and encouraged Russian foreign interference in the 2016 presidential election," an allegation strongly disputed by conservative commentators.

Interesting! Let's skip back to Trudeau for a moment. Have you heard of the SNC-Lavalin affair? It was a corruption scandal that rocked the Trudeau government. In 2019, after a series of bombshell revelations in the press, and the resignation of the Canadian minister of justice, the ethics commissioner of the Parliament of Canada found that Trudeau's office had breached the Conflict of Interest Act by pressuring that minister of justice to intervene in a criminal case involving the Quebec-based international construction company SNC-Lavalin. The investigation that Trudeau allegedly intervened in concerned payments of C$48 million in alleged bribes made from SNC-Lavalin to the son of late Libyan dictator Muammar Gaddhafi from 2001 through the government's downfall in 2011.[8] If convicted, the company could be banned from Canadian government contracts for ten years.

Sounds like a big scandal, right? It was—the story dominated the Canadian media for months. And yet, like the blackface scandal, it's buried in a subsection on Wikipedia. The topic isn't even linked in the page contents, a hyperlinked list of key items that appears directly below the introduction of every detailed Wikipedia page. Unlike the scandal-ridden introduction to Trump's page, the most radical things we learn from Trudeau's are that he successfully won two elections, is comparatively young, and used to be a nightclub bouncer.

Whether it's describing politicians, personalities, or news outlets, Wikipedia displays a bias that is blindingly obvious. The question is:

Why does it matter? High school teachers still tell their students never to cite Wikipedia as a source, right? Doesn't everyone know you can't trust it?

Maybe everyone knows that, but it doesn't remove its influence. Wikipedia, by a long shot, has the most powerful search engine ranking of any website in existence. On virtually any Google search for a major topic, you're likely to see a Wikipedia link among the top three results, if not at the very top. A study of one thousand randomly generated Google search terms in 2012 found that Wikipedia accounted for an astonishing 56 percent of top results, 24 percent of second results, and 9 percent of third results.[9] If Google is Frankenstein's monster, Wikipedia is its bride.

This is only partly due to favoritism from Google. Most of the reason is because Wikipedia enjoys a truly colossal amount of links from other websites, a factor that most search engines see as a good sign—if many sites are linking to you, it's considered a mark of authoritativeness. On this, it's hard to compete with Wikipedia—the site had accumulated a staggering 1.7 *billion* external backlinks as of 2016.[10]

Wikipedia is also helped by its age. It was founded in 2001, long before Facebook, Twitter, and many other well-known websites. This is also a good sign to search engines—in the eyes of their automated web crawlers, an established website is less likely to be a scam site and is less likely to disappear overnight. Of course, this is a pretty weak basis for trust. Some websites have been around since forever, but they are still untrustworthy. Just look at Snopes!

Like most other sites, Wikipedia is at the mercy of Google. A single algorithm change could cause the encyclopedia to go the way of the dodo. That said, Wikipedia seems to have little to fear from the all-powerful search engine. Google-owned YouTube uses Wikipedia entries to fact-check videos it deems to be "conspiracy theories."[11] And Google itself uses content from Wikipedia in its "knowledge panels," the Google-approved snippets of information that sometimes appear to the right of search results. In 2019, Google again gave Wikipedia a signal of its approval, with a $3.1 million donation to the encyclopedia's parent company, the Wikimedia Foundation.[12]

In other words, there's little chance that Wikipedia will run afoul of Google's efforts to include only "authoritative sources" in its top search results. Unlike the average high school teacher, Google seems to have considerable faith in Wikipedia's authoritativeness. Wikipedia's status as the top dog on most search results is secure, for now.

This has huge implications for our online reputations. For most internet-connected people, the first thing we'll encounter when we look for information about a new topic is a set of Google results. And one of the first things we'll see on those Google results is a Wikipedia link. Whether we're an individual, an organization, or a political movement, we are all at the mercy of Wikipedia, its rules, its institutional biases, and its editors—almost all of whom are anonymous and unaccountable.

That should frighten everyone, but it should especially frighten people who are right of center. Wikipedia—and the first page of Google results, with which it is closely intertwined—are two major end points of what I call the defamation engine. It's a production line of smears, churning out character assassinations day after day, with all the efficiency of Henry Ford's factories. It begins with partisan advocacy organizations, left-wing "media watchdogs," and journalists who cover the "Far Right." It ends with Wikipedia and the top results on Google searches, from which the finished products are rarely, if ever, removed.

Wikipedia editors—and the Wikimedia Foundation—feign neutrality by pointing to their set of rules, which stipulate that only claims backed up by "reliable sources" can remain on a Wikipedia page. It's not *Wikipedia* falsely labeling you a racist, see, it's the *reliable sources*.

This ham-fisted variation of "just following orders" is, of course, a sleight of hand. It's Wikipedia editors, after all, who make and enforce the rules. They decide what counts as a "reliable source," and they've chosen to systematically purge any source that offers an effective counternarrative to left-wing and establishment smears. Breitbart News, the Daily Caller, and the Gateway Pundit—three of the biggest news websites that make a point of countering left-wing smear tactics—are all on Wikipedia's list of "deprecated sources," meaning editors are discouraged from citing them to back up (or challenge!) factual claims. Two prominent right-leaning British tabloid newspapers, the *Daily Mail* and the *Sun*, are also on the list.[13] And after Breitbart was added to that list, the editors went a step further by banning any citation of the site as a "reliable source."

In other words, if the *Washington Post* declares you are a bigot (as it did, falsely, to the high school kids from Covington Catholic), and Breitbart News or the Daily Caller points out that the allegation is a bunch of baloney, only the *Washington Post*'s version of reality will appear on Wikipedia. How convenient!

New depths of absurdity are reached when the "reliable sources" contradict what the subject of a Wikipedia article says about itself. Take the claim that Breitbart News is a "platform for the alt-right," for example. It's an old smear, based on a single out-of-context statement from former executive director Steve Bannon, made at a time when the "alt-right" had yet to be captured by the neo-Nazis and white supremacists who have come to dominate it. The movement has since been repudiated numerous times by Breitbart, by Breitbart writers, and by Bannon himself. The idea that a company that was founded in Israel, by Jews, that once operated a section called "Breitbart Jerusalem" and has a staff more diverse than that of many liberal publications, is secretly in league with white supremacist anti-Semites is self-evidently absurd to anyone who spends more than a moment thinking about it.

None of that matters on Wikipedia, though, because the forces attempting to label Breitbart (and the whole of the Trump-supporting Right) as crypto-Nazis are "reliable sources," and Breitbart is not.

That's not the whole picture, though. Wikipedia editors do a whole lot more than just parrot what the "reliable sources" tell them. They're active participants in the smear machine. They don't just cite the smears that come out of the mainstream media. They refine them, amplify them, and strategically ignore anything that diminishes them—all to help the misleading information achieve maximum effect.

If Wikipedia editors wanted to use "reliable sources" to challenge the false "alt-right" association on Breitbart's page, they could. A collaborative study between Harvard and the Massachusetts Institute of Technology, published in 2017, concluded that Breitbart News is definitively *not* part of the alt-right, and employs a style that is clearly distinct from white supremacist websites like the Daily Stormer. The author of the study, Yochai Benkler, told the *New York Times Magazine* in 2017 that "Breitbart News is not the alt-right."

Wikipedia's own rules identify academic studies as the peak of reliability.[14] And of course, there's no questioning Harvard's or MIT's credentials, especially if you value prestige and reputation as highly as Wikipedia does. The study's author spoke to the *New York Times*—another "reliable source" normally considered unimpeachable by Wikipedia editors. And yet, three years after it was published, the study is not cited in the Wikipedia article's introduction. What does this tell us? It's not simply a problem of Wikipedia relying too heavily on the mainstream media. It's a problem with Wikipedia's editors themselves, who carefully cherry-pick the "reliable sources" to make the Trump-supporting Right seem as evil as possible.

Renegade Editors

Wikipedia tries to fool you with its promise that "anyone can edit" its pages. And sure enough, in the top left-hand corner of every topic, you will indeed find an "edit" button. You can click on it and begin editing pages, without even signing up for an account. It has all the appearances of an open door. But don't let yourself be tricked—behind it is a brick wall.

One person familiar with the rigged system is a former Wikipedian who edited the site under the pseudonym "The Devil's Advocate"—we'll call him TDA for short. It was an apt nickname, he explained, because he had a habit of challenging the prevailing consensus of other editors—a tendency that would eventually see him banned from the site. His story reveals the lie behind Wikipedia's "Anyone Can Edit" slogan—in reality, the only edits with any staying power are those made by the site's ruling clique of established editors. They'll quickly reverse any edits you make that challenge their worldview, even if your edits are meticulously researched. Cross them often enough, as TDA did, and you'll simply be banned. Try it! Pick a controversial subject, find a Wikipedia page about it, and try to include cited sources to facts that the Left doesn't like. Then watch how quickly you get shown the door.

In our conversation, TDA explained what happens if a new Wikipedia user, trusting the site's pledge of openness, decides to make an unwelcome edit:

> If the edit was unsourced, they will reject it for that reason. Should it have a source, they may question its reliability, which can mean a source "deprecated" or banned from use as a reliable source or sources the editor just doesn't like that aren't widely recognized as solid sources. Even if the sources meet Wikipedia's "reliability" test, the editors may still get [them] removed by arguing it is "undue" information (i.e., there need to be more sources). Usually, restoring the edit leads to an "edit war" where the senior editors remove it each time. On occasion other editors step in and, because editors are limited to only undoing an edit three times in a day, the newbie will often get blocked after a warning. Unless other senior editors show up to support the newbie, the advantage nearly

always goes to the senior editors opposing the edit, regardless of merit.

Why does the advantage nearly always go to the senior editors? Because, explained TDA, on Wikipedia the truth is determined by committee. If enough editors disagree with a fact, regardless of how many "reliable sources" may back it up, it is no longer a fact. The mainstream commentators who constantly howl about how the internet has ushered in a "post-truth" age would do well to look closely at Wikipedia's system.

Keep in mind that almost all Wikipedia editors are anonymous. Having the truth determined by "experts" is hardly an infallible system, but Wikipedia doesn't even demand expertise from its editors. The truth is determined by anyone who can cobble together support from a majority of editors who happen to be interested in a topic. Who those editors are, their level of knowledge, and their biases are irrelevant. The result is that the "facts" on a Wikipedia page are determined by whichever editors happened to take an interest in the topic. And who do you suppose is most interested in Sean Hannity's page or Donald Trump's page? The editors who want to smear them, of course!

That's not to say that there are no dissident editors who will challenge the consensus, but their efforts typically prove futile and can lead to vendettas against them. TDA said his opponents on the site misrepresented what he had done in order to get him banned—and because everything on Wikipedia is determined by consensus, it wasn't long before they were successful.

I had a habit, consistent with my username, of challenging the prevailing view on any given dispute when I saw flaws. While I generally stayed civil and followed the rules, editors at times lied about my conduct or went after me over any technical breach they could identify. They usually behaved way worse than me, but they had the advantage of being in the majority. A bunch of sanctions against me got notched up as a result. They didn't need especially strong evidence of misconduct to put me on the path to a full ban, though they still managed to cite some shoddy evidence.

Even for TDA, who spent eight years editing the site prior to his ban, challenging Wikipedia's groupthink proved to be a suicide mission. If a veteran like TDA couldn't safely question the consensus, even after years of familiarizing himself with the site's labyrinthine set of rules and regulations, what chance does a newbie have?

Arming yourself with "reliable sources" makes little difference when facing down the Wikipedia clique. As TDA explained, the site's established clique will ensure you struggle to get your edits accepted, whether you have reliable sources or not. Wikipedia editors cherry-pick from reliable sources to push their narrative—that's why, despite numerous Wikipedia-approved sources noting that Breitbart News is not an "alt-right" website, the insinuation remains at the top of its Wikipedia page.

TDA has catalogued numerous cases where Wikipedia editors clubbed together to remove reliable sources that contradicted left-wing narratives. Since 2016, TDA said, the tendency among editors has been to cite reliable sources that feature the "most inflammatory characterizations of Trump and his associates and their actions," while disregarding or downplaying those that take a contrary approach.

One such example is the Wikipedia article "CNN Controversies." The title is self-explanatory—it's about controversies involving CNN, of which there are many. Many more, in fact, than Wikipedia editors would like you to know about.

TDA has chronicled how, in 2017, editors with a history of favoring left-wing positions invaded the page and gutted the article.[15] The editors removed nearly a third of the page—"reliable" sources included. One editor removed a section about a CNN producer making a joke about President Trump's plane crashing. Another editor removed several references to criticism of former CNN contributor Kathy Griffin, who posed in a mocked-up photo featuring a beheaded president Trump. The editor even removed a reference to criticism of Griffin from one of CNN's own hosts, Jake Tapper. The fact that these incidents had been reported on by Wikipedia-approved "reliable" sources didn't matter—they were removed anyway.

There are many such cases. TDA cited the article "Gamergate Controversy" as a notorious example that predated the Trump era, and one of the first instances in which the biases of Wikipedia editors became apparent. The article, about an online standoff between left-wing video game critics and ordinary video game fans who objected to the intrusion of political correctness into their hobby, became a battleground of partisan editing. Left-wing editors attempted—and largely succeeded—in branding the movement as bigoted and sexist. It was because of his efforts to counter the biases of his colleagues in this edit war that TDA found himself banned from the site.

Other examples mentioned by TDA included the Wikipedia article on alleged Russian interference in the 2016 election, in which left-wing editors called for a "purge" of all material that criticized the allegations, even if the criticism was backed by Wikipedia-approved "reliable" sources. In a separate edit war, many of the same editors argued that reporting from the Hill's John Solomon and from Politico about alleged Ukrainian interference in the 2016 election—the widely reported allegation that the Ukrainian government worked with the Democratic National Committee and Hillary Clinton to tie Trump and his former campaign consultant Paul Manafort to Russia—be labeled a "conspiracy theory."

Conservative personalities and organizations are, as should now be apparent, the number one victims of Wikipedia's maelstrom of bias. You can rely on Wikipedia to remind you about all the smears and half-truths about virtually any major name of the Center-Right.

President Trump "welcomed and encouraged" Russian interference in the 2016 election. Breitbart News "aligned with the alt-right." The Daily Caller publishes "fake stories" and "deceptively edited videos." Fox Business Network anchor Lou Dobbs and Sean Hannity are "conspiracy theorists." Popular millennial conservative Paul Joseph Watson is a "far right conspiracy theorist." Activist and political candidate Laura Loomer is a "far right conspiracy theorist." Comedian and media entrepreneur Gavin McInnes is "far right" and founded a "neo-fascist men's group." Retired conservative journalist Lauren Southern has been "described as alt-right" and "white nationalist." Campus conservatives' Turning Point USA is "accused of racist practices" and "potentially illegal involvement in the 2016 election." British journalist Toby Young is called out for "misogynistic and homophobic tweets." British conservative prime minister Boris Johnson has been accused of using "racist, sexist, and homophobic language." Katie Hopkins, another British conservative, has "frequently been described as far right." Islam critic and female genital mutilation survivor Ayaan Hirsi Ali has been accused by critics of "having built her career on denigrating Muslims." The Rebel Media, a Canadian conservative media organization, is a "platform for anti-Muslim ideology" and "described as being part of the alt-right movement."

It goes on and on. Wikipedia's characterization of the modern Center-Right, cobbled together from the least charitable "reliable sources" its left-wing editors could find, is little more than a progressive fever dream. A Wikipedia article about a conservative should be taken in much the same way as a Huffington Post or a Salon article about a conservative—with a large dose of skepticism.

License to Lie

Wikipedia, of course, did not invent character assassination. Painting your political opponents as villains is a tactic as old as time—you'll struggle to find a politician who hasn't tried it. Journalists, too, delight in hatchet jobs. For many in the field, misrepresenting ideological opponents as bigots or lunatics is a kind of sport. The modern-day Left is particularly good at this. It has a host of well-funded organizations, including the Southern Poverty Law Center, the Anti-Defamation League, Right Wing Watch, and Media Matters, whose sole apparent purpose is to discredit the progressive movement's critics. In a world where Google and Wikipedia didn't exist, the wheels of the smear machine would, no doubt, continue to turn.

What Wikipedia and Google have done is make the problem a whole lot worse. In the predigital era, when a left-wing pundit on CNN called a Republican a racist, a right-wing pundit on Fox would call them a liar, and that would be that. Five minutes of television, easily forgotten. On the internet, though, nothing is forgotten. Minor stories written by no-name writers at second-tier publications that might otherwise dwindle in obscurity can now end up on your Wikipedia page and in your Google results forever. All it takes is for a sufficiently motivated editor to deem the source "reliable" and worthy of citation.

This is to say nothing of the fact that today, there's more material to cite in a Wikipedia article than ever before. Before the internet really took off, a newspaper would publish a morning edition and an evening edition. Today, a newspaper aims to pump out new stories for its website twenty-four hours a day, seven days a week. Writers need to meet quotas and generate clicks, and there are few easier ways to do so than by trawling the Twitter posting histories of your ideological opponents, looking for material for a shocking hatchet job. If you're a writer who works for the Daily Beast, the Huffington Post, or BuzzFeed, you'll likely be considered "reliable" enough for your two-minute hate to be cited on the web's leading encyclopedia.

That's what makes Wikipedia such a crucial part of the defamation engine. Absent Wikipedia, its smears might be forgotten to history. With it, they are permanently etched onto the digital record, just a quick Google search away.

So, what happens when an obviously false claim about you appears on your Wikipedia page and then ends up on the front page of Google search results for your name? Is there any legal recourse? Can you do anything, other than fruitlessly complain about how unfair it is?

That's precisely what happened to the California Republican Party. After a rogue editor changed the party's Wikipedia entry to include "Nazism" as one of its official ideologies, the smear was automatically published on Google's "knowledge panel" in searches for the California GOP. Google eventually intervened to remove the label, but only after conservative journalists and House GOP leader Kevin McCarthy called attention to it. Who knows how many people read the smear before the correction was made?

If Google and Wikipedia were publishers, the California GOP probably would have sued them. But like all tech companies, they're protected by the iron shield of Section 230, which grants them wide-ranging legal immunities. As for the individual editor who added the "Nazism" smear, they can't be held accountable either, because they're anonymous.

Shockingly, the same is true for most edits on Wikipedia— perhaps nobody but the editors themselves knows who's responsible for the vast majority of the site's content. Almost all Wikipedia editors operate under pseudonyms. I'm usually the first to defend the virtues of anonymity, but people who have the power to annihilate your online reputation are the last people who should get a pass from accountability. We don't know who they are; we don't know what agenda they have; we don't know what special interests they serve. If they make a mistake, large or small, they suffer no consequences.

Like Facebook and Twitter, Wikipedia insists that it is a neutral *platform*, not a publisher that would be legally liable for trafficking in smears. According to the Wikimedia Foundation, the encyclopedia is simply a conduit for content created by other people, like a telegraph cable, a phone line, or a typewriter.

I call bullshit.

If the material your website publishes is burned into the top of Google, seemingly for all time, you are not just a publisher—*you're the most powerful publisher in the world*. Given that Wikipedia wields such a staggering level of influence over the reputations of virtually every business, organization, and prominent individual, it's insane that it can't be held accountable for what its editors write.

If you're defamed by the *Washington Post*—today a far less influential publication than Wikipedia, despite its storied history—then you can sue the *Washington Post*. Oftentimes, the mere threat of a lawsuit is enough for a traditional publisher to retract obviously false claims about individuals or organizations.

For Wikipedia, there's no such obligation. Safe behind Section 230, as well as their own anonymity, the site's editors can lie, smear, omit, twist, and misrepresent at will.

That's one of the big reasons why character assassination is so much easier today than it was just a few decades ago. In the golden age of the tabloids, the same lowbrow newspapers disparaged by Wikipedians as "unreliable sources," at least there was still some need for editorial responsibility.

I'm sympathetic to social media companies' argument that they need Section 230, or some form of it, to guarantee free speech on their platforms. If Facebook were held liable for its billions upon billions of user-generated posts, it couldn't function as a business. Ditto Twitter, YouTube, Instagram, and Reddit.

Wikipedia is not like those companies. In the course of a single day, there's an average of 500 million new tweets on Twitter, 720,000 new hours of video footage on YouTube, and 4.75 billion new pieces of content shared on Facebook. On Wikipedia, by comparison, an average of just seven hundred new pages are added every day. Compared with the social networks, that's a drop in the ocean. Facebook can convincingly argue that it cannot possibly impose editorial oversight on its daily deluge of user-generated content. The same is simply not true of Wikipedia.

Wikipedia, more than other tech companies, neither needs nor deserves the protections of Section 230. It is simply unacceptable that the most powerful publisher on earth is exempt from the legal obligations of other, less influential publishers. It is time for Congress to act to remove its privileges. Given the large number of Wikipedia articles, lawmakers should consider giving the site a grace period to correct problematic pages and implement new systems of editorial control before its legal protections are stripped, but stripped they must be. If Wikipedia wants to allow its editors to remain anonymous, that's also fine—but if the Wikimedia Foundation doesn't step in to correct any smears that arise as a result of this, it should prepare for lawsuits. Don't feel too bad for them—the Wikimedia Foundation had more than $100 million in revenue as of 2017. They can deal with it!

There's no doubt that if Wikipedia were tamed, it would deal a serious blow to the defamation engine. Wikipedia would have to think twice before it allows dodgy factual claims from mainstream sources to be amplified, or even enhanced. The ability to seek legal damages would give individuals and organizations more power over their online reputations. The first page of your Google search results would become a little less terrifying and a little easier to change.

Sadly, though, that won't be the end of the defamation engine, because the problems go far deeper than just Wikipedia. As we'll see in the next chapter, the World Wide Web is starting to resemble a spiderweb—something you get stuck in before you're eaten alive.

12. The World Wide Honeypot

Conservatism, wrote the late philosopher Sir Roger Scruton, blossoms from the realization that "we have collectively inherited good things that we must strive to keep." Central to the conservative instinct, according to Scruton, is "a sentiment that all mature people can readily share: the sentiment that good things are easily destroyed, but not easily created."[1]

The conservative instinct is most alive during times of upheaval, when old traditions and lifestyles are under threat. It is perhaps no surprise that populist conservative movements have soared to success in various countries around the world at the very moment when globalization and technological disruption have reached a zenith. More and more of us feel a sense of unease, an instinctive awareness that the tectonic forces of change sweeping through our society threaten to sweep away cherished elements of our way of life along with them.

In this chapter, I will focus on four important social goods that are deeply threatened by technological change, and that conservatives should endeavor to protect. They are privacy, forgetfulness, forgiveness, and liberty. All four are, of course, intimately connected. Without privacy, every detail of our lives, including likes, dislikes, virtues, and vices, is subject to censure and judgment by the rest of society—which often changes its mind about what constitutes a virtue or a vice. Without forgetfulness, that censure and judgment can become permanent. The fleeting opinions, momentary lapses in judgment, and occasional failures that we all experience in life become permanently attached to our names and reputations. This in turn creates a lack of forgiveness; with too much knowledge about the vices of our fellow citizens, an atmosphere of condemnation—what has become known as "cancel culture"—reigns. All three, in turn, lead to a loss of liberty. Being always watched by an increasingly unforgiving society that never forgets can create a sense of lingering terror that cannot coexist with true liberty. Who can really feel free when the eyes of a vengeful mob are peering over one's shoulder?

Here is how Kate Eichhorn, author of *The End of Forgetting*, described the frightening world of digital permanence that confronts us:

> Until the end of the 20th century, most young people could take one thing for granted: their embarrassing behavior would eventually be forgotten. It might be a bad haircut, or it might be getting drunk and throwing up at a party, but in an analog era, even if the faux pas were documented in a photograph, the likelihood of its being reproduced and widely circulated for years was minimal. The same held true for stupid or offensive remarks. Once you went off to college, there was no reason to assume that embarrassing moments from your high school years would ever resurface.
>
> Not anymore. Today, people enter adulthood with much of their childhood and adolescence still up for scrutiny.[2]

Later in the chapter, we'll look at how technology companies have made it nearly impossible to keep our private affairs truly private—even when we're trying. Yet, in many cases, we don't try. Millennials and zoomers have grown up in a world where oversharing is highly incentivized, and where they receive no warnings about the potential ramifications of such behavior. As the baby boomers relentlessly remind us, younger generations are glued to their phones. They chase likes, retweets, upvotes, shares. They want to increase their followers on Twitter, their friends on Facebook, their subscribers on YouTube and Instagram, their karma on Reddit, their followers on TikTok, their subscribers on Twitch. With the promise of fame, attention, and even wealth, these platforms encourage us to make our lives an open book.

The addictiveness of social media is by design. This isn't necessarily shocking—every creator of a product or service, after all, wants to get consumers hooked on it. But it's still important to know. From the "infinite scroll" provided by platforms like Twitter and Facebook, which allows users to scroll through a never-ending stream of content, to the personal-data-driven algorithms that ensure that everything we see is hypertailored to our interests, to the confidence boosts we get when strangers on the internet like or retweet our posts, social media give us a constant chain of dopamine hits.

"It's as if they're taking behavioral cocaine and just sprinkling it all over your interface and that's the thing that keeps you like coming back and back and back," a former Mozilla employee told BBC's *Panorama* in 2018.

"Behind every screen on your phone, there are generally like literally a thousand engineers that have worked on this thing to try to make it maximally addicting."

The employee explained that social media companies must show investors a constant uptick in user growth and user activity in order to secure new rounds of funding and a higher stock price.

"When you put that much pressure on that one number, you're going to start trying to invent new ways of getting people to stay hooked."

The BBC even managed to get the coinventor of Facebook's "like" button, Leah Pearlman, to talk about the addictive power of her creation.

"When I need validation—I go to check Facebook," she said. "I'm feeling lonely, 'Let me check my phone.' I'm feeling insecure, 'Let me check my phone.'

"Suddenly, I thought I'm actually also kind of addicted to the feedback."[3]

The Digital Pillory

What are the potential consequences of social media addiction? Mainstream journalists have focused on the mental health implications of this trend, pointing out that for some individuals, heavy social media use is associated with anxiety, depression, loneliness, and hyperactivity.

I have no doubt that this is a problem for some people. But there's also a bigger problem, one that is less immediately apparent than the mental effects of social media. That is its role in the defamation engine.

If Google and Wikipedia make up the machinery of the defamation engine, our propensity to share everything about ourselves on social media is the fuel that keeps the wheels turning. In a world where we've been duped into committing all our thoughts, feelings, and experiences to an immutable digital record, we've all become complicit in creating our own *kompromat*, a cache of compromising information that can be used against us.

As the digital generation grows older, this grim reality has started to dawn on many of them. That drunken college photo you posted on Facebook ten years ago can be seen by a potential employer today. That politically incorrect tweet you posted at age sixteen becomes the weapon to bring down your career at age thirty. Indeed, it may not even have qualified as "politically incorrect" when you posted it—the boundaries of that term expand by the year. Imagine even a liberal in 2005 thinking that fifteen years in the future, it would be controversial to say that there are only two genders and that biological men are not women.

Sure, you could go back and delete everything—but how do you know it hasn't already been screengrabbed, or archived in a dozen hidden databases you don't even know about? On the internet, you never truly know if something is gone forever.

In the *kompromat* wars, members of the Left have an advantage. They dominate the mainstream media; they dominate Wikipedia; they influence Google and Facebook. In the battle for control of the digital-historical record, they are clearly winning. But even they are not safe.

In August 2018, a new member of the *New York Times* editorial board, tech writer Sarah Jeong, discovered that the hard way. Hours after her position at the *New York Times* was announced, some of her old tweets resurfaced, showcasing what can only be described as mind-boggling racism.

> *"Dumbass fucking white people marking up the internet with their opinions like dogs pissing on fire hydrants"*
>
> *"Are white people genetically predisposed to burn faster in the sun, thus logically being only fit to live underground like groveling goblins"*
>
> *"Oh man it's kind of sick how much joy I get out of being cruel to old white men"*
>
> *"#CancelWhitePeople"*

Jeong didn't bother to delete these four-year-old tweets. Why would she? As soon as they entered the public record, they existed forever.

Some of Jeong's colleagues at the *Times* would experience the same fate. In 2019, a number of offensive tweets from senior staff editor Tom Wright-Piersanti were unearthed, including one containing the phrase "crappy Jew year."[4] A fact-checker at the newspaper, Gina Cherelus, was revealed to have posted tweets using the words "dyke" and "faggot."[5] An associate editor was outed for tweeting "no new white friends 2k15" and "yes, Jews are indeed good with money."[6]

Don't feel too sorry for the *New York Times*. After all, nothing really happened to people like Jeong. Journalists are a protected class. What's more, this is a publication that joined in the frenzied shaming of the Covington Catholic High School kids (see chapter 5, "Deleted"), and ran a piece defending the Daily Beast's decision to unmask a black working-class forklift driver for the "crime" of creating a meme video mocking House Speaker Nancy Pelosi.[7] While the *Times* is by no means the worst newspaper engaged in online public shaming, the spotlighting of its employees' embarrassing Twitter histories certainly falls into the category of journalists getting a taste of their own medicine.

Indeed, I would go further—I would say that the entire profession of online journalism is largely responsible for the rise of "cancel culture." As written journalism transformed from the morning-edition, noon-edition, night-edition cycle of print newspapers to the twenty-four-hour, click-chasing cycle of online media, new media journalists suddenly had a lot more work on their hands. And, with the added competition from bloggers, YouTubers, and big social media accounts, journalists needed to develop new tactics to attract attention.

The tactic they settled on was to whip up social, racial, and gender-based tensions. This was starkly demonstrated by Zach Goldberg, a PhD candidate at Georgia State University. Using LexisNexis, Goldberg discovered that the number of news articles using the language of intersectional race theorists had increased massively during the rise of social media. Between 2013 and 2018, *New York Times* articles mentioning "white privilege" went from fewer than 500 per year to more than 2,500 per year—an increase of more than 400 percent. Articles mentioning "whiteness" went from around 500 per year in 2011 to more than 2,000 per year in 2017. Articles using the term "people of color" surged from fewer than 200 in 2015 to more than 800 in 2018. "Racism" went from fewer than 500 in 2013 to 2,500 in 2017.

"Intersectionality" went from fewer than 500 to more than 1,500 in the same period. "Unconscious bias," "diversity and inclusion," "systemic racism," "discrimination," "marginalized," "white supremacy"—Goldberg's research found that all these terms enjoyed similarly massive spikes in usage, all during the same time period.[8]

What this tells us is that as print publications moved online, editors began accepting articles that reveled in whipping up racial and other social schisms, at an exponentially higher rate than during the pre-Twitter era. There are many potential explanations for this: one is that media publications needed to stand out in a competitive market, so their editors encouraged reporters to write stories that would generate the most outrage. Another is that a younger generation of irony-impaired left-wing writers grew up in an online environment that included politically incorrect message boards like 4chan and thus perceived the threat of racism and other forms of discrimination to be much higher than it actually was.

Whatever the reason, these race-baiting online journalists have contributed heavily to cancel culture. They've created a world in which past mistakes are not to be forgotten, but rather held up as "teachable moments" for all of society. In the absence of genuine racial discrimination, those who are determined to talk about the issue must find other grist for their mill—like offensive tweets and jokes.

The seminal example of this was Justine Sacco, a communications executive with 170 Twitter followers, who, in 2013, tweeted an ill-judged joke about the AIDS/HIV crisis in Africa ("Going to Africa. Hope I don't get AIDS. Just kidding. I'm white!"). After Gawker Media writer Sam Biddle discovered the tweet, he blogged about it, kicking off an internet firestorm. When Sacco posted the tweet, she was about to catch an international flight to South Africa. By the time her plane landed, she had been fired from her job.

In telegraphing Sacco's dumb joke to an audience of millions, Biddle was engaging in a role that has become increasingly common in the social media age: journalist-as-inquisitor. The Gawker writer later said he regretted ruining Sacco's life, calling the results of his work a "48-hour paroxysm of fury, an eruption of internet vindictiveness." Interestingly, though, Biddle said that only after he himself had been the target of an internet mob. Maybe that's the solution—publicly shame the public shamers, cancel the cancelers, and disavow the disavowers, so that they think twice before doing it to other people.

You may think you're safe if you've never posted an offensive joke on social media, but when everyone around you has access to a computer or a smartphone, you may not be so lucky. A coder had the misfortune to discover this in 2013, at a programming conference called PyCon. The coder, who went by the name "Hank" (not his real name) in subsequent media interviews, was overheard making a nerdy innuendo about wireless "dongles" to one of his friends at the conference, in what he described as "[not] even conversation-level volume." Sadly for him, the person who overheard him was a feminist activist called Adria Richards, who had apparently dedicated her life to being a hall monitor. Richards snapped a picture of Hank and his friend, uploaded it to Twitter, and reported it to the conference organizers. An internet mob of feminists quickly formed and went after Hank and his friend, and Hank was fired from his job the next day. For making a joke about dongles. In private. To a friend. At a volume below conversation level.

We all had a good laugh at Prince Harry and Meghan Markle when they complained that they received too much media scrutiny. You would think they would both understand that if you're going to be multimillionaire celebrities and members of a hereditary monarchy, public scrutiny is to be expected. It's possible to feel a little sympathy for Harry, who didn't ask to be born a royal. But Markle, who chose first to be an actress and then to marry a prince, seems a little entitled.

But the truth is, like Justine Sacco and "Hank," you don't need to be a member of a royal household to have your privacy taken away from you. Indeed, royals might be more fortunate—their main problem is the paparazzi, who must at least follow a set of professional rules. For ordinary people, all it takes to destroy your privacy is one jealous colleague, vengeful ex, or militant activist with access to a computer. If they have sufficient details about your private life, no code of journalistic ethics and no law will protect you. In the world of social media, all of us—princesses and peasants alike—are at the mercy of the masses.

This is the true consequence of the internet's destruction of privacy. With a few clicks and a few strokes of a keypad, everyone in the world now has the power to ruin someone's life forever. It doesn't even need to be your old tweets. It could be a rumor that goes viral, a false allegation, or just plain slander. With the whole world as a potential audience, you can be sure that *someone* will believe it.

This, too, is the true cost of "misinformation." Not in elections, which have always been fraught with lying and half-truths, and where politicians have few expectations of privacy anyway, but in our everyday lives. Anyone can take an old tweet out of context, highlight an old, embarrassing picture, or tell an old, embarrassing story. Anyone can lie about us, at any time, to an audience of millions. And not everyone can afford to hire a defamation lawyer. Mainstream commentators are so laser focused on the alleged role of "misinformation" in Donald Trump's election that they've failed to grasp how the same problem can affect ordinary people. It's almost as if the establishment doesn't care about the average Joe!

And if the destruction of privacy weren't bad enough, alongside it comes the destruction of forgetfulness. In the predigital era, to learn about a scandal in someone's past, at the very least you would have to pull up newspaper archives and official records—that's if they'd been famous enough for their misdeeds to be committed to record. Today, every mistake we've made, our entire personal histories, all of our ups and downs, are potentially just a click away. And, today, it's not just public figures who have to deal with it—it's everyone.

Assuming you don't have the poor luck of "Hank," though, aren't there still ways to remain private and anonymous on the internet? Can't you use time-tested tactics like pseudonyms, throwaway emails, and Virtual Private Networks (VPNs) to keep your identity detached from your online activity?

Unfortunately, it's not as simple as that.

You Are (Not) Anonymous

In the spring of 2013, *Harry Potter* author J. K. Rowling published a novel for adults, *The Cuckoo's Calling*. But she didn't publish the book, a crime fiction story, under her own name—instead, she opted for a pseudonym, Robert Galbraith.

Bestselling authors often use pseudonyms. Other examples include Stephen King (pseudonym "Richard Bachman"); Isaac Asimov ("Paul French"); and C. S. Lewis ("Clive Hamilton," "N. W. Clerk"). There are many reasons for doing so. For some authors, it offers the chance to mitigate the biases and expectations that critics and readers may have accumulated toward them over the course of their career. For others—like crime author Agatha Christie, who wrote several romance novels under "Mary Westmacott"—it allows them to branch out into a new genre without having their new writing compared with their previous work.

Sadly for Rowling, her ruse didn't last very long. After rumors emerged on social media that Galbraith and Rowling were the same person, the *Sunday Times* sent her crime novel to Patrick Juola, a computer science professor at Duquesne University, who ran it through a software program he had developed to analyze language patterns. The program looks at common word usage, sequences of words and characters, word length, and other factors to identify an author's unique writing style. Using the program to compare *The Cuckoo's Calling* to other Rowling works as well as those of unrelated authors, Juola concluded that Rowling was the most likely author. This was enough for the *Sunday Times* to secure a reluctant confession from Rowling. Thanks to the power of technology, the author's foray into pseudonymity had lasted fewer than three months.

The technology used by Juola is called "natural language processing." It is a field that trains computers to read and understand large volumes of human speech. In identifying pseudonymous and anonymous authors, it is an example of an area in which computers are a lot more efficient than humans. Human analysts would have required years to identify and analyze the telltale stylistic quirks that linked "Galbraith" to Rowling. They would have had to pore over sentences and word sequences on hundreds of pages in multiple books, looking for patterns. In all likelihood, they wouldn't have managed to do it at all.

Juola's computer did it in about half an hour.

So, no more pseudonymity for bestselling authors? Quite possibly. But no more pseudonymity (or anonymity) for *you*, either. The same kind of technology used to identify Rowling has advanced enormously in the past decade and is at this very minute being deployed to analyze online speech. Do you think that edgy, career-destroying post you made anonymously on 4chan is never going to be tied to you? Think again!

I spoke to someone who works in computer science and the ad-tech industry, which increasingly use natural language processing analyses to increase the value of anonymous data to advertisers. What she said will scare anyone who values their privacy—and especially those who think they are safe behind VPNs, encryption, https, and other technologies designed to safeguard users' privacy. While those technologies certainly don't hurt, they won't stop natural language processing from identifying you.

Advertisers are interested in the anonymous posts people make on the internet, in part because they provide data about an internet user's likes and interests. Because of this, even content posted anonymously or pseudonymously is most likely harvested from the public areas of the internet (a process known as "scraping") and stored in databases.

"Anyone can scrape any content displayed in a browser," explained my source. "There have been controversies around scraping marketplaces and social media sites, as those contain semipublic information (e.g., LinkedIn or Tinder profiles, or anything displayed only to registered users).

"It's a gray area to what degree scraping is legal," said my source, who cited a trial that concluded LinkedIn scraping was legal because results from the semipublic site show up in Google searches. None of the safeguards established by social media sites prevent "thousands of companies and developers from scraping everything that has ever appeared online," my source said.

Once your anonymous (or pseudonymous) posts have been "scraped," my source added, the game is on for companies to tie those posts to real people and user profiles, something that can increase the value of that data to advertisers.

"Once a company has a bunch of 'base profiles' of people (e.g., a commenter with a username, an email address from a [customer database], a phone number from a form), they can pass these 'base profiles' to so-called identity matching services," my source said.

"Some examples are Stirista, AcquireWeb, GoLeads, People Data Labs. Others, like Demographics Pro, can tell you all about the audience of any YouTube or Twitter page (like the income of commenters, schools, nuanced interests, everything, but on an aggregate level).

"The biggest player in matching is Facebook," my source said. "Anyone can upload CRM [customer relationship management] data (emails, phone numbers, etc.) and Facebook will match those to users internally."

And what about identifying users who haven't linked their online content to an email address or other identifier? Or people who use throwaway email accounts and dummy phone numbers? That, said my source, is where "digital footprints" come in—something that includes the same kind of natural language analysis that outed J. K. Rowling, but also goes far beyond it.

"Digital footprints are unique identifiers, and the entire [ad-tech] industry is working together to create a 360-degree profile of each person," my source warned. "Even without personally identifiable information (like name, email, address, Social Security numbers), often each individual is unique enough for some companies to figure out who they are.

"A language model for an individual means we have a frequency distribution of terms and grammatical characteristics that we extracted from text you've written," said my source, who went on to explain that ad-tech companies and the services they rely on are now going even deeper than language analysis.

"It's surprisingly nuanced." My source said that the same types of methods for detecting unique signals in text can be used to detect other kinds of unique signals, including "mouse movements" and the "velocity of keyboard strokes.

"I used to work for a cybersecurity firm where we built authentication systems based on digital footprints, so your bank would know if it's you logging in based on how you type, among other data about your device—screen size and a bunch of other things."

Yes, you read that correctly. Mouse movements. Typing velocity. There really is *nowhere* to hide.

Even if you were to throw your phone and laptop into the trash, fly to Outer Mongolia, buy a new laptop, sign up for a new email address, and make an anonymous post from behind seven proxies... it would *still* be possible to find out who you are. If your unique writing style doesn't identify you, your mouse movements and typing velocity will. Anonymous posters of the internet, beware—you may not have been aware of it until now, but your masks are being pulled off.

The Privacy Arms Race

What can be done? The scale of the challenge for those who think privacy is of precious value to the human experience is immense. First of all, as my source explained, we don't know which companies are tracking us, or how deep their analyses go. "If an app had 100 million users, and they kept logs of everyone's device IDs, info, words, unique language models, topics, interests, clicks, keyboard strokes, and mouse movements, they could certainly tell if two users are likely the same (even if the two accounts change some of those things).

"But it's impossible to tell what companies keep track of, so you don't know what to even mask. This is referred to as an arms race in cybersecurity—each time hackers figure out what companies will monitor to spot bots, they make the bots a bit more unique."

The good news is that not all is lost. The same language-analysis software that is used to detect the author of an anonymous post can also be used to warn that author, and even recommend changes (almost like an autocorrect feature) to mask their unique style. Masking mouse movements and keyboard strokes is more of a challenge, but remember that these are just inputs—signals received by a computer. It's not impossible to imagine software that mixes false inputs with genuine ones to mask writing speed and mouse movements.

However, as far as I know, no such privacy-protecting technology currently exists. If hackers and cybersecurity experts are in an "arms race," it's time for anonymity defenders to get serious about the privacy arms race—because the bad guys are currently way ahead of them.

13. The "Free Speech Wing of the Free Speech Party"

If you were to poll Twitter users and ask them what feature they'd most like to see on the platform, I'd bet $100 that the most popular response would be "an edit button."

Instead of giving users what they want, Twitter has, since 2016, prioritized a different set of features. Features that "shadowban" users—hiding their tweets from searches, or downranking them in the public areas of Twitter without their knowledge. Features that deliberately limit engagement on tweets, like the ability to ban replies. Crackdowns against the nonthreat of "Russian bots." Expansion of the "Trust and Safety" team of professional censors, along with the establishment of an external Trust and Safety Council that included some of the most far-left intersectional social justice warriors you could imagine.

Silicon Valley loves using cutting-edge business jargon like "synergy" and "disrupt," but Twitter seems to have forgotten another one—"opportunity cost." All the time they've spent developing advanced tools of censorship is time they could have spent improving the user experience. Remember, this is a platform whose own CEO had trouble using its "Twitter threads" feature, admitting that it was "confusing" to use the feature in an interview with a journalist.[1] But, hey—on the bright side, at least we got night mode!

Twitter isn't as big as other Silicon Valley companies. It doesn't hoover up as much data as Facebook or Google, because it doesn't have the same kind of reach. Its value to news sites is limited—my own editors at Breitbart regard it as relatively lackluster for boosting traffic. For a long time, the world of finance concurred—after peaking at $69 per share shortly after going public, Twitter's stock price consistently hemorrhaged, bottoming out at $14.02 in June 2016. Speaking to the *Wall Street Journal* in 2015, a number of major advertisers expressed skepticism about Twitter's value to the industry.[2] Although its stock price has since improved, Twitter for a long time was the sick man of Silicon Valley—the social media giant that, more than others, struggled to turn a decent profit.

Despite its comparative smallness and rocky financial history, however, Twitter has had an outsize impact on political culture. Twitter in 2020 might as well be renamed "Trumper"—the president has excelled at harnessing the platform, using it to bypass the media and take his messages directly to his supporters (or at least, to the ones who haven't been banned from the platform). The president even credited the platform with helping him win in 2016: "When somebody says something about me, I am able to go bing, bing, bing and I take care of it. The other way, I would never get the word out," said Trump in an interview. "I doubt I would be here if it weren't for social media, to be honest with you."[3]

How does Twitter repay this praise from the president? By allowing tweets calling for his assassination to stay up, sometimes for days, sometimes for weeks. A report from Mashable published shortly after the president's inauguration found more than twelve thousand tweets containing the phrase "assassinate Trump."

"We asked several users about their recent 'assassinate Trump' posts, all of them said they hadn't been contacted by anyone about their post and they all remain up," wrote Mashable.[4]

These kinds of double standards are, naturally, par for the course with Twitter. As we saw in chapter 5, Twitter let violent threats against the kids from Covington Catholic High School remain on the platform for days and did not even remove the "verified" checkmarks from the accounts that tweeted them, much less ban them. Racial abuse against white people from *New York Times* writer Sarah Jeong was allowed to remain on the platform, too, with no repercussions against her account (which was soon also verified). This hypocrisy was apparent even before the election—the Hill reported in June 2016 that death threats against Republican senators were allowed to remain on Twitter for more than two weeks before being taken down.[5] And in the same year, Twitter did nothing to punish the rapper Talib Kweli Greene after he repeatedly called Breitbart's Jerome Hudson a "coon" for being a black conservative.[6]

In 2018, Twitter gave itself the authority to ban users for bad "off-site behavior." It later appeared to use this far-reaching power to ban Infowars founder Alex Jones for calling CNN senior media reporter Oliver Darcy an "anti-American, anti–free speech coward." Jones didn't say it on Twitter, but in a hallway on Capitol Hill—Twitter banned him anyway, after he tweeted a video of the interaction.

But if Twitter were consistent in its application of the "off-site behavior" rule, it would have to ban far more people than Jones. It would have to ban Madonna, who mused about "blowing up the White House" in 2017. It would have to ban actor Johnny Depp, who joked about assassinating the president. It would have to ban actor Robert De Niro, who said he'd like to punch Trump in the face. But Twitter is a platform that seems to think Sarah Jeong's comparing white people to "dogs pissing on fire hydrants" isn't a violation of its hate-speech policies, so why should we expect any consistency?

Twitter told me that "per our policy on terrorism and violent extremism[, it] examines a group's activities both on and off Twitter," but that "for individual accounts, although context matters, we primarily take action purely on the basis of the content they [post] on the service."

By the way, Madonna later said her comment about bombing the White House was just a metaphor. But Twitter isn't so understanding about metaphors when they come from right-wingers. The first major right-wing figure who was banned from the platform—the "patient zero" of Twitter censorship, if you will—was former journalist, author, and business owner Chuck Johnson. Twitter banned him, permanently, because he had promised to "take out" Black Lives Matter activist DeRay McKesson, which Twitter interpreted as a violent threat. But Johnson, at the time, was running a crowdfunded news project called GotNews. His threat to "take out" McKesson was, he says, his way of promising to dig up dirt on the activist. Even Amanda Hess, a left-wing journalist at *Slate*, accepted Johnson's explanation and linked to an article by one of her colleagues at *Slate* that used the same metaphor.[7]

Since then, conservatives have experienced widespread censorship from Twitter, for similarly spurious reasons. Whether it's activist and politician Laura Loomer, who was permanently banned after criticizing a Democratic politician, Ilhan Omar, as "pro-Sharia" and "anti-Jewish," or Alex Jones, banned after insulting a CNN reporter, the pattern is very much the same. As we saw in chapter 5 in the case of Andy Ngo, Twitter will ban right-wingers simply for posting facts. To outside observers, it seems as if the platform will avail itself of any excuse to punish conservatives, and any excuse to forgive left-wingers.

"Conversational Health"

During the transition period between social media platforms' original commitments to free speech and their new role as gatekeepers of information, it was long rumored that the tech giants—Twitter in particular—were using "shadowbanning" as well as overt censorship.

Originally developed to tackle spambots, a "shadowban" is a covert ban rather than an overt one. Shadowbanned accounts are allowed to continue posting, but the platform limits or even fully suppresses the reach of their posts. This is a way to censor accounts without letting the account holders know that they are being censored. Unlike the subjects of overt bans and suspensions, which are frequently publicized and protested, shadowbanned users are unaware that they have been shadowbanned, which leaves them with no opportunity to appeal or protest. It is the most dangerous form of censorship—the hidden kind. As the name implies, users are standing in the shadows, shouting into the void, and wondering why no one is replying.

After years of unconfirmed reports about covert censorship from Twitter, Project Veritas was able to capture undercover footage of a former engineer at the company, Abhinav Vadrevu, appearing to admit that Twitter used the practice. In the video, Vadrevu references shadowbanning, stating that "in the past, people have been really, really pissed off about that," and adding that he wasn't sure if "Twitter does this anymore."[8]

Several months later, an investigation by Vice confirmed that the accounts of several high-profile Republican politicians had been covertly hidden from the public areas of Twitter. The report also found that Democrats "were not being 'Shadow Banned' in the same way."[9]

In a since-deleted tweet, Axios reporter Jonathan Swan conceded that conservatives who had long complained about covert censorship may have had a point. "Must admit that when some [Republican] sources have complained about this to me I mocked them to their face as conspiracy theorists," Swan said. "This Vice article makes me rethink that, and response from Twitter is inadequate."

In the end, Twitter had no choice but to go public about its previously hidden practices. Spinning the covert censorship as an effort to create "conversational health," the company made a series of public blog posts over the course of 2018 explaining the practice. In one, Twitter explained that it was going to restrict the spread of "troll-like" content:

In March, we introduced our new approach to improve the health of the public conversation on Twitter. One important issue we've been working to address is what some might refer to as "trolls." Some troll-like behavior is fun, good, and humorous. What we're talking about today are troll-like behaviors that distort and detract from the public conversation on Twitter, particularly in communal areas like conversations and search. Some of these accounts and Tweets violate our policies, and, in those cases, we take action on them. Others don't but are behaving in ways that distort the conversation.

———

Because this content doesn't violate our policies, it will remain on Twitter, and will be available if you click on "Show more replies" or choose to see everything in your search setting. The result is that people contributing to the healthy conversation will be more visible in conversations and search.[10]

Strip away the corporate jargon, and what Twitter is admitting to is shadowbanning. It admitted that it will covertly suppress content that meets certain "signals." It admitted that the content being suppressed doesn't necessarily violate its policies. It made no indication that users who have been categorized as "troll-like" will be notified of their new status (and it appears that no one has ever reported being categorized as such). Twitter spokespeople have consistently denied that this practice, or any other, constitutes "shadowbanning." But if it walks like a duck and quacks like a duck, it's probably a duck.

As of January 2020, Twitter has made covert censorship part of its official terms of service. A report that month noted that the platform's terms of service had been updated to give the company the power to "remove or refuse to distribute any Content on the Services" and "limit distribution or visibility of any Content on the service." Twitter made no mention of how and to what extent allegedly "unhealthy" content would be "limited" in distribution or visibility.

Should we praise Twitter for finally being transparent? After all, it's a lot better than Google, whose search blacklists had to leak before the company acknowledged their existence. And it's a lot better than Facebook, which kept secret its "hate agents review" list and its "deboosting" algorithm, the latter of which was allegedly used to covertly suppress the reach of live video from conservative content creators.[11] Still, I don't think Twitter should get any praise for transparency, because covert censorship is one of the shadiest, sneakiest, least-transparent practices you can imagine a tech company engaging in. Not only have they given themselves the power to censor you— they've given themselves the power to censor you without even telling you about it. Whenever your tweet impressions inexplicably drop, or whenever you start to hemorrhage followers despite maintaining your activity, you'll wonder whether you've suddenly become unpopular, or whether you've been shadowbanned—and you'll never be fully sure of the true answer. Remember, the people who run social media platforms are the world's foremost experts at creating engagement and creating an environment for the viral spread of content. As such, they're also the world's foremost experts on *stopping* you from going viral. With no law or election regulation to stop them, do you really think they won't use that power?

Consider the implications of this. Twitter can't ban President Trump, despite the longing of many of its left-wing employees that it do so (extraordinarily, one Twitter employee, a Muslim immigrant living in Germany, was once able to briefly delete Trump's entire account before higher-ups noticed and restored it).[12] But, even if it can't ban the president, it can absolutely censor his supporters, covertly or otherwise.

This may not seem like a big deal if you compare Twitter's reach to that of Google, Facebook, YouTube, or even Instagram, but it is important when you consider Twitter's influence on the political culture. Twitter, more than any other platform, is the place where grassroots activists, journalists, and members of the intelligentsia meet, organize, and grow their movements. Movements from the Left and the Right, in America and beyond, have used Twitter to leap into the national discourse at a rate far faster than they had been able to do before Twitter existed.

There are examples on the left: #BlackLivesMatter was, initially, just a Twitter hashtag used by black Americans who wanted to speak out against alleged abuses of power by the police. The hashtag had staying power and, over time, evolved into the established movement of the Far Left that we see today.

There are examples on the right: #StopTheSteal was a hashtag that Republican activists used in the 2018 election to mobilize supporters and draw scrutiny to alleged malpractices by Florida vote counters in the state's Senate and gubernatorial races.

There are examples of cross-partisan consumer movements: #Gamergate was an alliance of left-libertarian, moderate, and conservative video game consumers speaking out against the encroachment of political correctness and far-left intersectional ideologies into their hobby. The movement, built around nothing more than a Twitter hashtag, sustained itself for well over a year, encompassing email-writing campaigns, real-world meetups, and the growth of new voices on the center and culturally libertarian left.

And then there are the non-American movements, the most famous of which was the Arab Spring. A study by a team of researchers at the University of Washington involving an analysis of millions of tweets as well as content from other social media platforms found that "social media carried a cascade of messages about freedom and democracy across North Africa and the Middle East, and helped raise expectations for the success of political uprising."[13] Around the same time, the phrase "Twitter revolution" emerged as a term used frequently by commentators.

That was the early 2010s—the golden age of free speech on social media, when observers believed the power of unrestricted internet free speech could topple dictatorships around the world. At the height of the Egypt protests in January 2011, the government of Hosni Mubarak shut down access to both Twitter and Facebook across the country, leading to an immediate call by then president Barack Obama that he restore access to the services. At that time, American officials were even training activists in developing countries to use Twitter and other platforms to mobilize movements—it looked like social media would become an arm of the American deep state, toppling unhelpful dictators around the world.

A close friend of mine who works for a U.S. government agency (albeit not for an agency focused on foreign policy) follows the topic of internet censorship closely. He said that during the early 2010s, the U.S. establishment was the world's most powerful champion of internet freedom.

"They formed NGOs—the National Endowment for Democracy, the McCain Leadership Institute," he said. "There was a network of State Department–funded NGOs that would go into Tunisia, Egypt, Lebanon and start Facebook/Twitter groups...create these soft human rights violations campaigns against these regimes for not having an open internet."

Hillary Clinton's State Department, said my source, "realized the internet can be used for regime change at an unheard-of speed."

But, he concluded, all of that enthusiasm dissipated in 2016, when the Western political establishment realized that the same technologies they had used to bring about regime change around the world could be used at home to regime-change the establishment. To that establishment, the passage of Brexit and the rises of Trump, Italy's Matteo Salvini, Brazil's Jair Bolsonaro, Britain's Jeremy Corbyn, and Vermont's Senator Bernie Sanders all were signs of the internet's malign influence. The big panic, of course, was the idea that a foreign power—namely, Russia—could manipulate internet technologies against Western elites. At the time of the Arab Spring, my source said, the Western foreign policy establishment was the "number one champion of internet freedom" because it saw it as a tool of regime change. By 2016, that mentality had done a complete one-eighty, and a more common position was "Oh no, Russia can use it to regime-change us!"

Hangover at the Free-Speech Party

The trajectory of Twitter's enthusiasm for unfettered free speech has largely followed that of the political establishment. In 2012, the general manager of Twitter in the United Kingdom, Tony Wang, famously referred to the platform as the "free speech wing of the free speech party."[14] His comments were later echoed by then CEO Dick Costolo.[15]

That was then; this is now. Twitter's current CEO, Jack Dorsey, has claimed the "free speech wing" comment was never serious. "Certainly, this quote around 'free-speech wing of the free-speech party' was never a mission of the company," said Dorsey in 2018. "It was never a descriptor of the company that we gave ourselves. It was a joke, because of how people found themselves in the spectrum."[16]

Maybe he thinks it's just a joke, but to ordinary people—the majority of whom value free speech—it's Twitter itself that has become the joke.

We shouldn't be too hasty to lay all the blame at Jack Dorsey's doorstep. Current and former employees of the company have told me that Dorsey, although he is a progressive, is nowhere near as progressive as the people directly below him. One former employee identified Del Harvey, head of Twitter's Trust and Safety team, as the real left-wing menace inside the company. "She's a hard-core SJW [social justice warrior] and has a vindictive streak," the source told me in 2018. This is a pattern we see at other tech companies, too—as noted in other chapters in this book, Mark Zuckerberg regularly comes under criticism from his own left-wing employees on a range of issues, including outreach to conservatives and failures to tackle "fake news." Google faces similar problems—left-wingers at the company have revolted on more than one occasion over the company's outreach to conservatives, including its funding of the Conservative Political Action Conference in 2017 and its decision to include the president of the Heritage Foundation on its now-canceled AI ethics advisory council.

Regardless of who may be responsible, however, it's clear that Twitter has strayed far from its early position as the "free speech wing of the free speech party." Since 2016, Twitter has developed increasingly elaborate methods of controlling the flow of information on its platform, hidden behind Orwellian terms like "conversational health." The cradle of grassroots movements has become a nest of censors and commissars. Say something that rubs Twitter (or its algorithms) the wrong way, and you'll be censored without even realizing you've been censored. Those of us who do not work for Twitter have no idea how extensive this is, but it's clear that the potential for antiestablishment movements to grow on the platform is much diminished. The message is clear—if you want to build an online grassroots political movement . . . avoid Twitter!

14. When Facebook Kills Your Business

Joe Speiser, an enterprising New York City millennial, is that most American of breeds—an entrepreneur. In 2014, he founded a start-up called LittleThings. Speiser noticed that, though the website was originally intended to sell pet products, its feel-good posts about pets were attracting oodles of traffic. Like any good entrepreneur, he leaned in—and within a couple of years, LittleThings was a media powerhouse. Millions of Facebook users clicked on its cutesy stories about pets, home, and family. In an industry famous for clickbait that would have once filled the pages of tabloids and gossip magazines, LittleThings hit the big time offering harmless content that could improve the day of almost anyone. In short, Speiser did exactly what the system had told him to do—work hard, build something people want, and achieve the American dream.

Unfortunately for Speiser, he built his dream on digital sand—sand on a private beach owned by Mark Zuckerberg. And so, in January 2018, due to a decision made thousands of miles away in Palo Alto, California, Speiser's business would wash away with the tide. So, too, did its one hundred employees, without so much as an apology from the Silicon Valley behemoth that, virtually overnight, had terminated their livelihoods.

Their jobs were lost in large part because of a change to the News Feed algorithm, which determines what posts Facebook users see as they scroll down their home page. The change, which kicked in on January 18, 2018, shifted the focus of the News Feed away from "businesses, brands, and media" and toward posts from friends and family. Naturally, Facebook users were not given a chance to opt out of the new system—like most Silicon Valley power moves, it was imposed on them from above.

For publishers like LittleThings, which relied on Facebook for much of its traffic, the result was disaster. Just over a month after Facebook announced its change, LittleThings announced that it had lost 75 percent of its traffic and would be shutting down. A despairing COO of the company told DigiDay that until earlier in the month, the site's editorial approach "was working." And then, suddenly, it wasn't. A thriving business was shut down, and one hundred employees were laid off, allegedly because of an algorithm change that neither they nor Facebook's billions of users seem to have been consulted on.

The LittleThings story is not uncommon. Whether it's an algorithm change or a ban, Facebook has displayed little remorse for the actions it has taken that, with the push of a button, have destroyed businesses and careers.

In October 2018, Brian Kolfage, a decorated U.S. Air Force veteran who sacrificed three limbs for the United States in Iraq, became another Facebook target. Not only did it take down his conservative news site, Right Wing News, but it also took down the page for his coffee company, Military Grade Coffee. Facebook offered only a vague explanation as to why it had torpedoed a disabled veteran's coffee company, saying only that he had been warned to stop engaging in "behavior that violated our policies." Kolfage said he had invested around $300,000 in Facebook ads for the pages he managed before Facebook took them down.[1]

You can argue that the news sites run by Kolfage were clickbait sites, no doubt—but Facebook's sudden turn against clickbait in 2017–18 is just another example of how the social network suddenly switches its rules in response to pressure, leaving publishers with little time to adjust their behavior to the new system. Facebook had tempted publishers with the promise of easy money through clickbait stories, only to suddenly pull the rug out from under them. It was Facebook that had created an incentive for clickbait before 2016, but it wasn't Facebook that suffered for its reversal—it was the very businesses that Facebook had incentivized.

Even if you're a serious journalist running a serious news site, you aren't safe on Facebook. In 2018, Ken LaCorte, an executive at Fox News, left the network to start his own news website, LaCorte News. To assist with the project, he recruited John Moody, a fellow Fox executive who was senior VP for news editorial at the network. The site intended to produce serious journalism about politics, the media, and Silicon Valley.

Unfortunately for LaCorte, as is the case with all online news websites, he was forced to build a heavy presence on Facebook to promote his new site. As it had for LittleThings and Right Wing News, everything went well initially—until it didn't. In November 2019, Facebook erased LaCorte's Facebook presence, citing violations of its policy on "spam and misrepresentation." The ban occurred shortly after LaCorte had published the name of alleged government whistleblower Eric Ciaramella. (Other conservative media organizations, including Breitbart News, faced censorship on Facebook for doing the same.)

"First Facebook temporarily suspended us for reporting the whistleblower's name," Ken LaCorte told me at the time. "We complied, and the suspension was lifted. Shortly after we posted an image about the blackout—with the whistleblower's name obscured—the company wiped out all of our pages on Facebook, Instagram and the personal accounts of me and a number of the company's writers and editors."[2]

It's possible that Facebook has a case against Kolfage and LaCorte, but given the company's unwillingness to provide any more than a vague explanation for its bans, it's impossible to know for sure.

Even if Facebook did have a case, there's still the matter of a fair trial. A commercial landlord who evicts a business from his property because it refuses to pay the bills may also have a case, but he must still obtain a court order before throwing anyone out. That's because society has recognized that eviction causes massive disruption, to both businesses and individuals, and that there needs to be some level of due process involved, adjudicated by an impartial court of law.

No such luck on Facebook—there's no eviction notice, no time to prepare, and no impartial due process. Thanks to the legal immunities tech companies secured from Congress in the 1990s, it's nearly impossible to take them to court and win. No matter how much time or how many thousands of dollars you've invested in promoting your business on Facebook, no matter how many jobs you've created, and no matter if you've done nothing wrong, Mark Zuckerberg can take it all away with a snap of his fingers.

Ironically, the same man who has extinguished the hopes of so many new media entrepreneurs over the past two years has also been held up as the pinnacle of the American dream. It was a point well noted by *Slate*, a left-wing magazine with which I usually disagree. Here is how its writer, Will Oremus, described the way Republican politicians treated Zuckerberg when he testified before both houses of Congress in April 2018: "When addressing a veteran or active-duty member of the U.S. military, it's common for government officials to begin by thanking them for their service. And when Republicans address an American business tycoon, it's apparently good form to congratulate them on their massive riches before attempting any sort of critique of the harm they've wrought in society."[3]

"Mr. Zuckerberg, in many ways you and the company that you

created, the story that you've created, represents the American Dream," said Senator John Thune, a Republican. "Many are incredibly inspired by what you've done."

Representative Greg Walden, another Republican and then chairman of the House Commerce Committee, wasted precious minutes of the hearing praising Zuckerberg for the "quintessentially American entrepreneurial spirit" and for starting a company "from your dorm room." With that kind of fanboying, it's little wonder that Republicans made no attempt to remove the legal privileges that allow tech giants like Facebook to censor at will.

The "American dream" narrative is, as Joe Biden would put it, a load of malarkey. Sure, Zuckerberg did start Facebook in his dorm room—at *Harvard University*, the most elite campus in America. Before that, he attended Phillips Exeter Academy, a private school that counts U.S. senators, Pulitzer Prize winners, one president, and two presidents' sons among its alumni. Never mind the fact that Zuckerberg is credibly accused of ripping off the idea for Facebook from two other Harvard entrepreneurs, the Winklevoss twins—the Facebook founder's tale is hardly an inspiring rags-to-riches story. Even if someone with as privileged a background as Zuckerberg could be said to represent the American dream, he now represents its dark side—the all-powerful tycoon, master of a monopolistic empire that crushes smaller companies underfoot.

Facebook can get away with terminating whole businesses without warning because it and other tech companies are shielded by Section 230 of the Communications Decency Act—that's the law that Republicans like Thune and Walden failed to amend when they had the opportunity. Chapter 15 will cover the details of this law, along with efforts to reform it. For the purposes of this chapter, we'll use a briefer explanation: it allows tech companies to argue in court that they have a right to censor whatever they want, whenever they want, and for whatever reason they choose. It doesn't matter if you've invested a thousand dollars or a million dollars in growing a business on Facebook—if the platform decides to kick you off, you have less due process than a corner hot-dog stand fighting an eviction notice.

It's easy to criticize businesses that make Facebook a central part of their model, but especially in the case of publishers, they don't really have a choice. A full 43 percent of American adults now get their news from Facebook, the largest margin of any tech platform. Next in line are YouTube, with 21 percent, and Twitter, with 12 percent[4]—two other tech platforms that can also kick you off without giving you any legal recourse. In the modern world, a publisher without access to Facebook is like a fish without access to water. And in the world of conservative media, there are a growing number of suffocating fishes.

The Panic Hits Facebook

Facebook didn't overhaul its News Feed because it had a vendetta against cutesy clickbait sites like LittleThings. The shuttering of that website was collateral damage in a digital carpet-bombing campaign aimed primarily at conservative media, conservative politicians, and conservative online influencers. It happened because Facebook, for an entire year beforehand, had borne the brunt of progressive rage over the outcome of the 2016 election. All tech companies were affected by the fake-news panic we covered in chapter 3, but Facebook was perhaps the highest-priority target. As the most influential platform for publishers, its influence over news and politics was rivaled only by Google. Facebook, more than any other platform, had become the internet's primary means of disseminating news. Progressives, stung from the loss of the White House, became determined to bully the platform into favoring them.

Soon after the 2016 election, fingers of blame quickly pointed at Facebook. "Facebook is battling questions over whether, as a rapidly growing platform for sharing news and views, it had undue influence over the election of Donald Trump," reported the *Financial Times*, six days after the election. The article went on to cite data from Social-Flow, a social media optimization firm, that said Facebook users spent almost three times as much time reading stories about Donald Trump on the platform as they did reading stories about Hillary Clinton.[5]

The second half of the article discussed the problem of "fake news" and "hoaxes" on Facebook—issues that had been barely reported on before Trump's win. It concluded with a classic media trick, an "expert" conveying an opinion in an allegedly straight news report—the expert, of course, said that Zuckerberg needed to "take more responsibility for what is published on the platform," including hiring human editors.

This narrative, born from the BuzzFeed report on "fake news" that we covered in chapter 3, would be repeated endlessly by the mainstream media over the next year. The words were different, but the message was always the same:

"Facebook elected Donald Trump."

"It was because fake news tricked American voters."

"Mark Zuckerberg must take responsibility."

In December, a month before Trump was inaugurated, the *Guardian* published an end-of-year feature: "2016: The Year Facebook Became the Bad Guy."[6]

"With Trump's election, Facebook wrestles with the power of fake news," was the headline at CBS, five days after the election.[7]

"Here's Why Facebook Is Partly to Blame for the Rise of Donald Trump"—*Fortune*, November 10, 2016. Four days after the election.

The *Washington Post* was more creative, tracking down an actual purveyor of fake news and asking him if he had helped elect Trump. His answers ranged from "I think I helped it," to "I don't know, I don't know if I did or not." Naturally, the *Post* ignored his "don't knows" and ran with the headline "Facebook Fake-News Writer: 'I Think Donald Trump Is in the White House Because of Me.'"[8]

The media's campaign against Facebook wasn't a passing fad. Throughout the year, the negative headlines kept on coming.

"Facebook Struggles to Purge Fake News"
> —*Financial Times*, May 1, 2017

"Facebook Promised to Tackle Fake News. But the Evidence Shows It's Not Working"
> —*Guardian*, May 17, 2017

"Facebook's Role in Trump's Win Is Clear, No Matter What Mark Zuckerberg Says"
> —*Washington Post*, September 8, 2017

"Obama Tried to Give Zuckerberg a Wake-up Call over Fake News on Facebook"
> —*Washington Post*, September 24, 2017

Even for the vigilant observer, it may be difficult to determine if there was a bigger rush from Democrats and the media to blame Mark Zuckerberg for Trump's election, or to start planning Trump's impeachment.

At the end of the year, the media rushed to spotlight former Facebook executives who were criticizing the company. Ex-president Sean Parker's warning that Facebook's addictive products were addling the minds of children was promptly blasted out in headlines across the web.[9] So was the contention from former user-growth VP Chamath Palihapitiya that Facebook built tools to destroy "the social fabric of how society works."[10]

The media's motivations are made all the more obvious when compared with the way they behaved when President Trump's predecessor, Barack Obama, used Facebook to help him win.

In those elections, the media also noted the growing importance of Facebook in determining the outcome of presidential races. Indeed, the former president considered the social network to be so important that, in 2011, he became the first sitting head of state to visit the company's headquarters, where he palled around with Mark Zuckerberg in a company town hall. But because the Democrat won, the difference in coverage was like night and day. There were no headlines about the dangers to democracy back then, and no yearlong panic. A *Guardian* article penned after Obama's 2012 victory lovingly ascribed his victory to "Facebook and the power of friendship."[11]

Another useful comparison can be found in the way the media talked about Facebook's woeful track record on privacy. When news emerged, in 2018, that the British data analytics firm Cambridge Analytica had exploited Facebook's lax privacy protections to accumulate data on the habits of its users, and subsequently deployed that data on behalf of the Trump campaign, the media turned it into a massive scandal that raged for months. In fact, it was the Cambridge Analytica "scandal" that spurred Zuckerberg's appearance before a highly unusual committee hearing of both houses of Congress. And this was when both houses were controlled *by Republicans.*

But when Obama's former analytics director Carol Davidsen admitted that their campaign had engaged in far worse behavior ahead of the 2012 election, there was silence. Davidsen admitted that Facebook had allowed them to collect the "entire social graph" (meaning information on all its users). Here's the real shocker, though—she also revealed that Facebook staffers went to the Obama campaign offices shortly after the election and admitted that "they allowed us to do things they wouldn't have allowed someone else to do because they were on our side."

Here was a naked admission, from one of Obama's senior campaign staffers, that the platform relaxed its own privacy standards to help a Democratic president get elected. And there was no scandal. No outrage. No congressional hearing. (Did I mention that Republicans were in control of Congress at the time?)

A good rule of thumb is to remember that the media never actually care about what they say they care about. Their yearlong tantrum against Facebook had nothing to do with concerns about hoaxes or misinformation, and the Cambridge Analytica "scandal" had nothing to do with concerns about user privacy. The media cared about just one thing: they believed Facebook had put a populist Republican in the Oval Office.

The media's relentless shaming campaign against Facebook was intended to send the company a message: do what we want, or the beatings will continue. You helped elect Trump. You made it harder to push our narratives. You stopped us from anointing an establishment Democrat. *Don't do it again.*

Make the World More Closed

It wasn't long before Facebook caved in to the pressure campaign. In late 2017, as the panic was still in full swing, a Facebook insider gave me a glimpse of what was to come. Like most of my Silicon Valley sources, he chose to remain anonymous to avoid potential industry blacklisting—so we'll simply refer to him as the insider.

The insider told me of Facebook's plans to harness its vast trove of data on the behavior of its users to craft and shape their political opinions.

"The plan for polarization is to get people to move closer to the center," said the Facebook insider. "We have thousands of people on the platform who have gone from far right to center in the past year, so we can build a model from those people and try to make everyone else on the right follow the same path."

In just a few words, the insider had confirmed one of the worst fears that society has about tech companies—that they will use their vast amount of information on our lives and behavior, combined with their vast amount of control over our attention, to effectively brainwash us.

In 2014, it was revealed—to the considerable dismay of observers—that Facebook had conducted an experiment to control the emotions of huge numbers of its users. Facebook's researchers unashamedly published the results of its experiment in a scientific journal, announcing to the world its ability to manipulate the mood of its users based on the posts delivered to their News Feeds. Depending on what it put in front of them, Facebook could make people happier or sadder, more expressive or less expressive. And it could all be done without their knowledge.[12]

According to the insider, Facebook would use similar tactics to control the political ideology of its users—by adjusting what they saw on their News Feed, its executives hoped to create a centrist majority on its platform.

"Let's say hypothetically that everyone who goes from far right to center watched video XYZ," explained the insider. "Then maybe we adjust the priority of video XYZ in the feed. But it probably isn't going to be so clear and we will build some black box model that does who-knows-what... but the inspiration will be a list of people who we know moved to the left."

When I first heard this story, I was worried about how to confirm it—the source hadn't given me his name, and I couldn't find a second source to corroborate his claims. It turned out that neither of these things mattered, because it wasn't long before Facebook openly admitted its plans to manipulate our political opinions from the top down.

Facebook hinted at its new agenda during a company summit in June 2017, when it threw out its old mission statement, "Making the World More Open and Connected." In its place came a slogan that sent a subtle signal about the company's new priority to control its users' allegedly polarized opinions: "Bring the World Closer Together." Simply giving people the ability to talk to one another was no longer enough. In the grand progressive tradition of group hugs and hate-speech laws, Facebook's new mission was to make everyone like each other—or else.

Speaking at the summit, Zuckerberg summed up the company's new, proactive vision: "Look around and our society is still so divided. We have a responsibility to do more, not just to connect the world but to bring the world closer together." An article in TechCrunch speculated about whether this meant Facebook was willing to "[alienate] some of its more intolerant users" or "prioritize its mission over its business."[13]

Casual suggestions from the mainstream media have a habit of making their way into the policy books of Silicon Valley companies, so frightened are they of negative coverage, and several months later, TechCrunch got its answer.

In his announcement about Facebook's fateful January 2018 News Feed change, Mark Zuckerberg said that he expected the change would cause the amount of time that people spent using Facebook to "go down" (making the company less profitable in the process), but that he was okay with that.[14] Sure enough, as markets opened the day after Facebook's announcement, the company's stock value fell by 4 percent.[15] Zuckerberg's own personal net worth dropped by an eye-popping $3.3 billion.[16] Had Zuckerberg really made a decision that he knew would hit both his company and himself in the wallet, for as whimsical and noncommercial a reason as, to quote his Facebook post, the "well-being and happiness" of his platform's users?

Of course not. God does not play dice, and neither does Mark Zuckerberg. "Making users happier" was the Silicon Valley branding for a change that took power away from publishers in general, and from conservative publishers in particular. What Facebook lost in stock price, its executives likely hoped to make up for in political capital—it should not go unnoticed that the company made its announcement just two months after Democrats gained control of the House of Representatives.

The politically uneven results of Facebook's change quickly became apparent. On the face of it, it was politically neutral—Zuckerberg's statement said that "brands, businesses, and media" would be hit by the change. But a closer look at the types of pages that saw their traffic tumble paints a stark picture of political bias.

Just over a month after the change, I investigated the impact for Breitbart News, using analytics from NewsWhip, a social media monitoring company. The Breitbart investigation found that engagement on President Trump's official page had declined by 45 percent—almost half—in the month since Facebook introduced its change. Engagement on his individual posts dropped by 38 percent over the same period.[17]

Conservative media also felt the squeeze, with virtually no sites going unaffected. In the months following the News Feed change, Breitbart News fell from ninth in the Facebook rankings to twenty-first. The Facebook traffic of Western Journal, another conservative website, fell by almost half. The Gateway Pundit, a site that had soared in popularity during the election, experienced a 55 percent drop in Facebook traffic after the change. PragerU, the giant of conservative online video, saw a 32 percent reduction in its Facebook traffic, despite the fact that it published 18 percent *more* content in the month following the News Feed change.[18]

Although Facebook said that all brands and businesses could expect to see a drop in their traffic, establishment publishers appeared to be unaffected by the changes. As the numbers of conservative publishers plummeted, the numbers of mainstream media soared. Just over two months after the News Feed change, the top two publishers on Facebook were CNN and NBC, with the *New York Times* and the Huffington Post also in the top five. Only one conservative broadcaster, Fox News, made the top five. Was the rapid success of the mainstream media, just a few months after the News Feed change, an accident? Facebook made no attempt to conceal its motives—in June, it announced plans to launch a set of "fully funded" news shows on its platform, including shows from CNN, ABC, and Univision.[19] This was no secret plan hatched in a smoke-filled room—Facebook would wear its favoritism for the mainstream media on its sleeve.

According to my insider, this is no accident. He said that the January 2018 News Feed change was the result of a year's work by people who were rabidly anti-Trump. Think about the initiatives trumpeted by Facebook after the election—protecting "election integrity," combating "misinformation," preventing "polarization"—my insider said that all of those initiatives were driven by the company's anti-Trump elements.

"Immediately after the election, GSM [Global Sales and Marketing] folks, folks in other areas of Facebook, and even executives were very outspoken about their feelings," said my insider. "It was easy to notice that the most outspoken Trump antagonists were soon working in, and leading, the efforts to combat fake news, misinformation, and polarization.

"These efforts were never presented as a referee system (which would have dissuaded those antagonists from joining) but instead as a way to invoke positive social change. The well was poisoned from the start."

According to my insider, Facebook held post-election meetings that resembled Google's—with a clear focus on how to make elections "better."

"In the integrity kickoff meeting shortly after the election, employees fantasized about how they could improve elections here and abroad," said my source. "Many non-citizen tech workers were upset that they could not vote in the U.S. election when they saw the results. Some saw Facebook's election efforts as a gateway to [influence] the vote without needing a vote. Facebook is fighting foreign influence with its own foreign influence."

At no point did Facebook's top brass appear to pause and consider how it would look to outsiders that the company suddenly prioritized the "improvement" of elections just days after a candidate they didn't like was voted into office. Mark Zuckerberg has said he was fascinated with the Roman emperor Augustus Caesar, whose reign marked an end to the supremacy of the Roman Senate. It seems appropriate, given the contempt that many inside Facebook apparently have for the will of the people.

Hate Agents

Facebook's efforts didn't solely focus on algorithmic tweaks to elevate the mainstream media. In the manner of politicians, tycoons, and gangsters since time immemorial, the tech giant also created an old-fashioned enemies list. Called the "Hate Agents Policy Review" spreadsheet, it was leaked to me in 2018, after which I published its contents on Breitbart News. The leak exposed the extent of Facebook's efforts to control political speech on its platform. When I first saw the "hate agents" document, which was sent to me by an anonymous source inside Facebook, I knew it was a bombshell of the same caliber as Google's "Good Censor" or YouTube's "smoking gun" blacklist. Facebook was creating a program to label high-profile political individuals as potential "hate agents," and a framework to monitor their every step, on *and* off the platform, to find excuses to blacklist them.

Even more alarmingly, the document showed that Facebook wishes to extend its influence over people's opinions beyond its own platform. Examples of potential "hate speech" that took place off Facebook were also logged on the document, next to people's names. One Australian politician, former senator Fraser Anning, was dinged by Facebook for attending a rally where members of far-right groups were present—a rally that took place in the real world, not on a Facebook server. In another example, the designation of Paul Joseph Watson as a "hate agent" was justified in part by his decision to interview British right-wing activist Tommy Robinson on his YouTube channel—but YouTube isn't under the jurisdiction of Facebook, any more than a real-life rally is. What's more, the idea of banning someone because of who they interview is patently absurd: are they also going to ban the Vice journalists who interviewed ISIS members?

In other words, Facebook doesn't merely want to control what you say on its platform—it wants to control what you say, what you think, and what you do *everywhere*. If you want access to the world's most important social network, you aren't allowed to have your own political opinions—they must meet Facebook-approved standards. Not satisfied with regulating the digital public square, it now appears to want to regulate physical public squares too. A Facebook spokesman told me that the company goes through a "rigorous review process" to determine if a group or person should be banned under its "dangerous individuals" policy, and that "this requires more than just attending one event to be banned." The spokesman did not deny that Facebook monitors off-site behavior.

The "hate agents" list appears to have been made to be continually updated. The version I received was from the spring of 2018—who knows how many more individuals have been added to the list since then?

At the time, the majority of names on the list were right-wingers. They included Paul Joseph Watson, Laura Loomer, Milo Yiannopoulos, Carl Benjamin, Fraser Anning, Lauren Southern, Alex Jones, Brigitte Gabriel, conservative commentator Candace Owens, the German politician Lutz Bachmann, Italian politician Alessandra Mussolini, French author Renaud Camus, British politicians Anne-Marie Waters and Jim Dowson, and Slovak far-right figures Marian Kotleba and Milan Mazurek.

The reasons for their inclusion on the "hate agents" review list are even more troubling. Many of the "violations" cited by the document concern interviewing or associating with someone who has been banned by Facebook. As mentioned, a violation was added to Paul Joseph Watson's entry due to his interview with Tommy Robinson, who had previously been designated a "hate agent" and banned by Facebook. An entry next to Laura Loomer's name, meanwhile, censures her for "associating with Gavin McInnes," another conservative figure who had been banned prior to the document's leak. Perhaps the most shocking "violation" cited by Facebook is the one next to the name of Carl Benjamin, the British YouTuber also known as "Sargon of Akkad." Facebook notes, as a potential violation, that Benjamin "neutrally represented" a member of the Proud Boys on his show, and that the Proud Boys are a banned organization.

Responding to my questions for this book, Facebook said that for "people who have not taken such extreme measures like calling for violence or are not a member of an organized hate group, but still meet our criteria for designation as dangerous individuals, we think the right thing to do is to prevent them from using our services, but not restrict the speech of other people who might praise them for any reason at all." Facebook confirmed that it will allow people to post content that speaks positively of or praises Alex Jones, Paul Nehlen,

Laura Loomer, Milo Yiannopoulos, or Paul Joseph Watson. However, Facebook also confirmed that Paul Joseph Watson's praise of Tommy Robinson was one of the "signals" that contributed to the former's ban—so the company's leniency seemingly doesn't extend to perhaps the most influential critic of radical Islam in Britain. It's hard to overstate how draconian this is. Facebook is effectively forcing the Right to de-network itself, both online and offline. Merely associating with the wrong people, by attending the same rally that they are attending, interviewing them on your show, or speaking about them in neutral terms is enough for Facebook to push you toward a ban. This means that every major conservative influencer must dissociate from whomever Facebook brands with its scarlet letter, or else lose access to its 2 billion users. Facebook is wielding its immense power not just to ban wrongthinkers from its platform, but to cut them off from society as a whole—even from people who might sympathize with them. This is corporate totalitarianism, imposed by a tech elite who want you to fear their wrath, to have their speech codes in the back of your mind whether you're on their platform or off it. Controlling you while you use the platform is not ambitious enough for Facebook. If you want to use the platform, they want to control you *everywhere*.

Far-left progressives who delight in the thought of the totalitarian suppression of their adversaries might be enthused by Facebook's extreme form of censorship. But even they should take pause, because one of the notable things about the "hate agents" list is that it includes figures of the Far Left.

Women's March cofounder Linda Sarsour appears on the list, with a number of "borderline" statements logged next to her name. "Borderline" statements, as defined by Big Tech companies, are statements that brush up against a policy violation—in Sarsour's case, the violation was "hate speech."

In one such "borderline" case, Facebook noted that in 2018, Sarsour "made a statement referring to Israel as 'the oppressor' and says that 'humanizing' the oppressor is a problem." In another statement in 2018, Sarsour "made anti-semitic statements which question Jewish Americans' loyalty to America." Facebook nonetheless concluded that the anti-Semitic statement did not "violate our policies or meet our signals." Facebook also investigated Sarsour's defense of the Palestinian terrorist Rasmea Odeh but ultimately did not log it as a policy violation because Odeh is "not on our Terrorist Figure list." A Facebook spokesman told me in April 2020 that the company "routinely" reviews individuals and groups against its "dangerous individuals and organizations" policy, but that the company has "no further update" on whether anyone "does or does not violate this policy at this time."

Linda Sarsour's fellow Women's March cofounder and frequent collaborator, Tamika Mallory, was also on Facebook's list in 2018 because of her numerous associations with the anti-Semitic black nationalist Louis Farrakhan. Facebook noted that in February 2018, Mallory lent support to Farrakhan by attending a Nation of Islam rally at which he was present, and that in May 2017, she posted an image with Farrakhan, calling him the "GOAT (Greatest Of All Time)." Facebook noted these cases as "not currently a violation" of its policies against hate. However, this was before Farrakhan himself had been banned from the platform—if Mallory wants to keep her Facebook account, she should probably think twice before attending any more Nation of Islam rallies.

Other leftists who appeared on Facebook's "hate agents" list include the antifa activist Joseph Alcoff, who was arrested in 2019 in connection with an assault against two U.S. Marines in Philadelphia. So, too, was Dwayne Dixon, an antifa leader and teaching assistant at the University of North Carolina at Chapel Hill. Neither Alcoff nor Dixon had any policy violations attached to their names at the time the list was leaked to me but were instead placed in a category marked for future investigation.

Several black nationalists were also on the list. These included Louis Farrakhan, who was later banned by Facebook; the convicted child trafficker and black nationalist Dwight D. York; and the former chairman of the New Black Panther Party, Malik Zulu Shabazz.

We shouldn't get ahead of ourselves—as Facebook's attitude to Linda Sarsour's anti-Semitic comments shows, the company is treating far leftists with kid gloves. Figures from the Right are being banned for hosting the "wrong" guests on their YouTube channels, while Sarsour's questioning of Jewish Americans' loyalty to the United States isn't logged as even a policy violation.

That said, it is significant that Facebook is watching these people—and, as with figures on the right, it is watching not just their online activity but their offline behavior as well. If members of the Far Left believe Facebook will never come for them, they should think again. Remember—it's the *leaders* of the Democratic Party that Facebook listens to, and those people aren't exactly huge fans of the likes of Sarsour and Mallory.

Conservatives and Trump supporters should also refrain from cheering Facebook's investigation of the Women's March radicals. This isn't just because it's woefully limp-wristed compared to their crackdowns against right-wingers—it's also because neither the Far Left nor the Far Right should have to worry about their social media accounts disappearing because of constitutionally protected speech. Facebook is the largest public square in the world, which means it has a duty to protect all legal speech on the platform—even controversial, offensive, hateful speech. As we all know, Facebook and other Big Tech companies will never uphold that duty until regulators force them to, but in the meantime, conservatives shouldn't cheer the potential censorship of their opponents, tempting though it may be.

If you want to tell them "I told you so," though—be my guest!

In the aftermath of the 2016 election, the media and left-wing advocacy groups begged Facebook to become the global referee of publishers. They got what they wanted, and now Facebook is flexing its muscles—first against the political Right, obviously, but I predict it'll soon turn against the antiestablishment Left, too. It already monitors them. Soon, it'll start censoring them, too.

Globalist neoliberals who long for the days when the most radical thing the Democratic Party could produce was Barack Obama might enjoy this, but no one else has cause to celebrate here. Toppling the establishment requires left-wing political insurgents as well as right-wing ones, and unchecked censorship on Facebook and other platforms poses a grave risk to both. At Facebook, political interference is now an open conspiracy—the company's executives have admitted they want to control the flow of news, and they've admitted they want to manipulate our political opinions (framing it as a campaign against "polarization" doesn't make it any less manipulative). This is the world created by the mainstream Left, which demanded that the previously freewheeling rules of social media had to be changed when they realized they could no longer win at them.

Beyond politics, it's an affront to the rights of the consumers and businesses that depend upon Facebook. As the platform takes more control over the information it pushes to users, and the sources that it bans from the platform, consumers slowly lose choice over what content they can see.

For businesses, the situation is even more dire. Facebook can decide, with the push of a "ban" button or the change of an algorithm, whether they fail or prosper. Business owners who rely on Facebook know that the fate of their employees is determined not just by producing a good product, but also by the whims of Mark Zuckerberg.

How did this crazy situation arise? How can someone invest years of time and millions of dollars into a business and not have any rights over it? How can there be no due process for throwing a business, with employees who depend on it and consumers who enjoy it, off the platform on which it depends for survival? How do Facebook and other platforms get away with it?

As we'll see in the coming chapter, it's because America's politicians let it happen. The power of Silicon Valley is inextricably tied to another center of wealth and corruption.

15. When Silicon Valley Met Washington

As we've learned in the years since 2016, Congress has struggled to implement President Trump's promised border wall. Immensely popular with at least half of the country, the project would cost approximately $21.6 billion, according to estimates from the Department of Homeland Security. This is a tiny sum compared to other policies funded by Congress, such as the $5.6 trillion approved since 2001 for highly unpopular regime-change wars.[1] Yet Congress, even when both houses were controlled by Republicans, failed to fund the project. It's almost as if they don't have the best interests of Americans at heart!

I feel the same when I think about the special perks that America's "public servants" have given to Silicon Valley. One handout in particular stands out—it's a law that enabled Big Tech companies to ride roughshod over the rights of the consumers and small businesses that depend on them, not to mention Americans' long-standing political rights to freedom of speech, association, and assembly. This giveaway of giveaways, infamous to critics of the cozy relationship between Big Tech and Big Government, is called Section 230 of the Communications Decency Act. It is the impregnable wall that prevents the tech giants from suffering any legal repercussions for trampling on the rights of their users. And, unlike Trump's wall, it enjoys maximum support in Washington.

Free-market libertarians (many of whom are in the pay of Big Tech) like to argue that Section 230 protects free speech online. The full title of the law, as it appears in U.S.C. 47, should disabuse you of that notion. The stated purpose of the law, passed in 1996, is to provide "protection for private blocking and screening of offensive material."[2]

In other words, the libertarians are wrong—Section 230 is a censorship law. That has always been its primary purpose. Indeed, one paragraph in the law specifically protects tech companies from lawsuits over restricting speech—whether or not the speech is constitutionally protected. Here is what it says: "No provider or user of an interactive computer service shall be held liable on account of any action voluntarily taken in good faith to restrict access to or availability of material that the provider or user considers to be obscene, lewd, lascivious, filthy, excessively violent, harassing, or otherwise objectionable, whether or not such material is constitutionally protected."[3]

Whether or not such material is constitutionally protected—what a line!

That's the law that America's "public servants" established, and it's the law they still protect to this day. Let that sink in.

What this means is that on a social media platform, you have no rights to due process. You can invest millions of dollars into building a business on Facebook or YouTube. You could have thousands of employees who depend on it, and millions who consume its content, services, or products. You could have spent years, decades, building it up from nothing. Yet under Section 230, Facebook or YouTube or any other platform you may depend on could take it all away whenever they feel like it.

Even a tenant renting a $1,000-a-month apartment in a sketchy part of town has more due-process rights than that. In many states, landlords must first obtain a court order before evicting a tenant. Yet someone who sets up shop on Facebook or YouTube's digital property has no such rights, regardless of how much the platform has profited from them, or how much of their own prosperity depends on it. Digital landlords can evict you with impunity.

This violates basic principles of justice that have been widely accepted since the eighteenth century—before the United States was even founded.

In drafting the Declaration of Independence, the Constitution, and the Bill of Rights, the founders drew a great deal of inspiration from the work of the English Enlightenment philosopher John Locke. To the Americans who had been taxed without representation, and whose property had been appropriated by British colonial troops, Locke's theory of the right to property was especially compelling. Locke argued that an individual's natural right to property arose at least in part from his labor.

"Labour makes the far greatest part of the value of things we enjoy in this world," wrote Locke in his *Second Treatise on Government.* "Labour being the unquestionable property of the labourer, no man but he can have a right to what that is once joined to, at least where there is enough and as good left in common for others."

Locke believed that once you've invested your time and resources into something, you have some level of ownership over it. He would no doubt be horrified at the fact that legislators in the country founded on his principles have given people no ownership over their social media accounts, no matter how much labor they may have invested in them.

I'm not one of those people who think Enlightenment philosophers were right about everything. But there's a reason the values they created have had such enduring appeal—there is a basic principle of fairness behind Locke's argument. If you've invested long hours, days, weeks, even years of labor into something, people shouldn't be able to rip it away from you on a whim. That's the perverse "right" that tech companies claim for themselves under Section 230, and it is monstrously unfair.

The libertarians who defend Section 230 aren't wholly wrong— there are parts of the law that are supposed to protect free speech. In particular, subsection c(1) states that online platforms will not be "treated as the publisher or speaker of any information provided by another information content provider."[4]

In non-legalese, that means Twitter will not be held legally responsible for material posted by Twitter users, YouTube will not be held legally responsible for material posted by YouTube users, and Facebook will not be held legally responsible for material posted by Facebook users. The same applies to any platform or website that brands itself as a platform for user-generated content. To use more familiar terms, Facebook is in the same legal category as a newsstand. If the *New York Times* defames you, you can sue the *New York Times*, but you can't sue the retailer that supplied it. They didn't print the words, nor did they edit them, so they're not responsible.

Without this protection—or something like it—free speech on the internet wouldn't be possible. Even Facebook, with its vast resources, would not be able to legally vet the billions of posts produced by its users every day. Its business model would cease to function.

The same goes for YouTube, Instagram, Twitter, Reddit, and virtually every other platform for online speech. For free speech to exist on websites, discussion boards, and social media platforms, the law needs to make it clear (as Section 230 seemingly does) that users, not the platforms that host them, are responsible for their speech.

However, while subsection c(1) is *supposed* to protect free speech, it actually does the opposite. Tech companies have twisted the meaning of the clause to give themselves all the rights of a publisher with none of the responsibilities.

You'd think that tech companies would be eager to avoid the "publisher" label, given that the legal immunities of Section 230 are meant to apply only to platforms. But they haven't just avoided it— they've *embraced* it. In one court case after another, tech giants have argued that they have the editorial rights of a publisher, with none of the legal liabilities that come with those rights.

When PragerU, the educational nonprofit set up by conservative Dennis Prager, sued Google for restricting the spread of its videos on YouTube, the tech giant used Section 230 to defeat the case. Google's legal team argued that limiting its ability to censor would "impose liability on YouTube as a publisher." Google also argued that it had a right to censor Prager if it wished, because "First Amendment protection for a *publisher's* editorial judgements encompasses the choice of how to present, or even whether to present, particular content"[5] (emphasis mine).

Google could have just relied on subsection c(2) to make its case. But then Prager's lawyers could have argued that the clause only enables Google to restrict content that is "obscene, lewd, lascivious, filthy, excessively violent, harassing or otherwise objectionable"— and Prager's content is, of course, none of those things. It's far better for the company to have a publisher's right to censor for whatever reason they choose.

Other tech platforms have adopted this strategy, too. In two separate cases, Facebook has argued that it has a publisher's right to censor anything it chooses—not the limited Section 230 right to censor only "objectionable" material.

When conservative activist and Republican political candidate Laura Loomer was booted off the platform in 2018, Facebook used the same arguments Google did to have the case dismissed. In its legal filings, Facebook stated, "Under well-established law, neither Facebook nor any other *publisher* can be liable for failing to publish someone else's message"[6] (emphasis mine).

In a separate case, earlier in the year, Facebook's lawyers made the same argument: "The publisher discretion is a free-speech right irrespective of what technological means is used. A newspaper has a publisher function whether they are doing it on their website, in a printed copy or through the news alerts."[7] In both cases, the courts ruled in favor of Facebook.

When Twitter was taken to court by the Canadian feminist Meghan Murphy, who was banned from Twitter for referring to the transgender provocateur Jessica Yaniv as a "him," the tech platform did the same thing. Its lawyers argued that Murphy's lawsuit, if successful, challenged "a publisher's traditional editorial functions."

Twitter executives, like those at Facebook and Google, believe the platform is a publisher, with the right to accept or reject content for whatever reason it chooses.

In a separate case, from American Renaissance editor Jared Taylor, Twitter's lawyers went even further. Pressed by the presiding judge on whether Twitter lawyers believed the platform had the right to deny service to its users "for any reason whatsoever," the lawyers somehow ended up arguing that it had the right to ban people from the platform because of their race, gender, or sexual orientation.

No, that's not an exaggeration—Twitter, one of the wokest companies in the world, literally argued in court that it had a right to implement racist, homophobic, or sexist policies if it wished to.

I've copied the full exchange between the judge and Twitter's lawyer, Patrick J. Carome, over the next pages—not least because it is highly amusing! But beyond the comedy, you'll also see the staggering breadth of censorship rights that tech platforms claim for themselves.

> **THE COURT:** Sir, let me, just to be really candid with you: You are way overstating the law. Does Twitter have the right to take somebody off its platform if—it does so because it doesn't like the fact that the person is a woman? Or gay? Or would be in violation of Title 7? Or would be in violation of the age discrimination laws, or the disability discrimination laws? Of course not. And this provision says, "for any reason or no reason." I mean—
>
> **MR. CAROME:** Certainly, Your Honor—
>
> **THE COURT:** Give me a break. Your position—your absolutist position doesn't fly, at least in a setting such as a demurrer.
>
> **MR. CAROME:** Your Honor, I—I think this is a question of law; it's not a question of fact.
>
> **THE COURT:** So what is the answer?
>
> **MR. CAROME:** And, in fact, as to Your Honor's question about could a First Amendment speaker choose by gender, or age,

or something like that, in fact—I mean Twitter would never, ever, ever do that; it's totally contrary to everything it does. But, in fact, the First Amendment would give Twitter the right, just like it would give a newspaper the right, to choose not to run an op-ed page from someone because she happens to be a woman. Would Twitter ever do that? Absolutely not, not in a million years. Does the First Amendment provide that protection? Absolutely it does.

THE COURT: What case says that?

MR. CAROME: That is—

THE COURT: What case says that [an] entity like Twitter can discriminate on the basis of religion, or gender, or sexual preference, or physical disability, or mental disability?

MR. CAROME: With respect to the content that it distributes?

THE COURT: With respect to whether the person can have an account or not.

MR. CAROME: This is a question about—this is not a business relationship; this is a question about whose speech am I required to distribute?

THE COURT: Again, mistaken. It is—the allegation is as to a relationship with a licensee that can be terminated pursuant to the terms of service, for any reason or no reason. That's the allegation.[8]

Tech companies have lawyered the clauses of Section 230 beyond recognition. They've given themselves unlimited powers to editorialize their users' content, while avoiding any legal responsibility for the results of that editorializing. Twitter, as we've just seen, believes it even has the right to censor you on the basis of race, gender, or sexual orientation.

Section 230's preamble states that the law's purpose is "to encourage the development of technologies which maximize user control over what information is received." The exact opposite has happened—users have no control whatsoever. All the power is in the hands of the tech companies. The only question remaining is, given that Section 230 is such a broken piece of legislation, why hasn't it been amended?

Silicon Valley's Swamp Creatures

You would think that conservatives would be the first in line to demand Section 230 reform. After all, haven't they been hit hardest by Silicon Valley censorship? And aren't they supposed to be the biggest opponents of the government's handing out of special privileges to big business, at the expense of small businesses and consumers?

Sadly, many of Washington's resolute foes of big government are willfully blind on the issue of Section 230. For many years, Big Tech companies have learned how to play the game of Washington by spending their way to influence with advocacy groups, think tanks, and politicians from across the political spectrum. In 2017 and 2018, Google was the top-spending corporate lobbyist in Washington, beating out Boeing and AT&T, with Amazon and Facebook not far behind.[9]

Despite the protestations of far-left tech employees who want their companies to have zero contact with the Right, the Beltway think tanks, politicians, and columnists that make up "Conservative Inc." have been big winners in Silicon Valley's push for political influence. In the years since Trump took office, evidence of deepening financial and lobbying ties between Big Tech and Big Conservatism has continued to emerge.

Take a look at Google's disclosures on spending to third-party organizations, and you'll see some familiar names. The American Conservative Union, which hosts the annual Conservative Political Action Conference, is a recipient of Google money.[10] So, too, is the Cato Institute, the most prominent free-market think tank in Washington. The Heritage Foundation, one of the oldest voices of social conservatism in Washington, is also included. The American Enterprise Institute, the Competitive Enterprise Institute, the National Review Institute, the Atlantic Council, the Federalist Society, Heritage Action, R Street Institute, the National Taxpayers Union, the Ripon Society, the Republican Governors Association, the Republican Legislative Campaign Committee, the Republican Attorneys General Association—you can find them all on Google's "nice" list (as for their "naughty" list, I suspect I'm near the top of it). It might be faster to list the conservative institutions that *aren't* on the take from Google.

In fairness to Conservative Inc., not all of them have let their Google funding stop them from criticizing Big Tech. CPAC hosted a panel featuring fired Google engineer James Damore in the same year that it received Google funding, and it hosted prominent critics of Big Tech on its main stage the year after that. Google spreading its cash around also failed to prevent Republican attorneys general from launching an antitrust investigation into the company—although whether any of them will pull their punches in the course of that investigation remains to be seen.

Still, it's mind-boggling that any conservative group thinks it's a good idea to take money from the same people censoring the most prominent voices on the right out of the digital town square. In the new world of conservative politics, taking money from Silicon Valley is about as toxic to your reputation as taking money from Planned Parenthood would be.

A word of advice to Turning Point USA, which to its credit has not yet taken any money from Big Tech: don't! Also, ditch the placards that praise "capitalism" for producing tech giants.[11] Praising the system for creating deceptive, censorious, culturally far-left tech giants that flood Washington with money to buy special privileges is not going to make conservatives—especially young conservatives—fall in love with capitalism.

Google's senior executives are pretty brash about their reasons for funding conservatives. In audio recordings from 2018 that were leaked to the press, Google's then senior director of public policy, Adam Kovacevich, can be heard admitting that Google funds conservatives so that it can achieve its ideological and political goals. In the recording, Kovacevich linked Google's "deep relationship" with the American Enterprise Institute and the Competitive Enterprise Institute (both recipients of Google funding) to the fact that one of its members authored a piece defending the tech giant against arguments that it should be broken up.[12] The op-ed was published in *National Review*, whose linked think tank, the National Review Institute, also took money from Google. In further comments, Kovacevich discussed his hopes that the company's funding of conservatives would help "steer" the conservative movement "away from nationalistic and incendiary comments."[13]

The author of the *National Review* piece insisted that Google's funding had nothing to do with his decision to write it, but who will believe him? With so much Big Tech money floating around Washington, it's hard to take any of Conservative Inc.'s defenses of Silicon Valley in good faith. Not least because, while their arguments usually rest on the idea that competition is the best solution to bad corporate behavior, in the same breath they defend Section 230—which is a government handout!

The Senate's youngest member, Josh Hawley of Missouri, quickly encountered this Conservative Inc. doublespeak when he attempted to roll back that handout. As Republican attorney general for Missouri, Hawley—who was born in 1979—had already taken on Google with an antitrust investigation. Once in the Senate, he set his sights on Section 230, the company's all-important legal shield.

Criticizing Section 230 as a "sweetheart deal that no other industry enjoys," the senator's solution is the "Ending Support for Internet Censorship Act," which he introduced to the upper chamber in June 2019. The proposed law would amend Section 230 so that large tech companies seeking immunity for user-generated content would first have to provide the Federal Trade Commission (FTC) with "clear and convincing evidence that their algorithms and content-removal practices are politically neutral." The FTC would then approve or reject the company's application for immunity based on a supermajority vote.[14]

Hawley's proposal is actually quite moderate. It doesn't impose full First Amendment standards on tech companies, and it still allows tech companies to editorialize their users' content—it simply requires them to do so in a politically neutral manner. Moreover, the provisions of the bill apply only to large tech companies—platforms with more than 30 million monthly active users in the United States, 300 million monthly active users worldwide, or $500 million in global annual revenue. Small start-ups and medium-size businesses would receive the same Section 230 protections as before—the only companies affected by the regulation would be those that already have the resources to audit themselves for bias. Politically, this was a very clever addition to the bill—it sidesteps the reflexive libertarian argument against regulation, namely, that it is more burdensome to small businesses than to large ones. Under the provisions of Hawley's bill, small businesses wouldn't be affected at all.

Naturally, that didn't stop Silicon Valley's surrogates in Washington from throwing a hissy fit. "Josh Hawley's internet censorship bill is an unwise, unconstitutional mess," thundered one of the icons of conserve-nothing conservativism, National Review's David French. French argued that it would be impossible for large tech companies to prove their products aren't designed to discriminate against any political viewpoint. Of course, this isn't true—as leaks like the YouTube search blacklist show, once you peek under the hood of technology companies, it's not hard to see who is being favored and who isn't. French argued that the best way to ensure free speech on large technology platforms was "persuasion, not coercion."[15]

Surprisingly for a man supposedly enamored with market capitalism,

French does not seem to understand the concept of incentives—namely, that if tech companies believe their Section 230 privileges are being put at risk by their political discrimination, they are far less likely to engage in it. It's hard to believe that a man of French's intelligence would deploy such feeble arguments on purpose. And, as with the magazine's piece opposing the breakup of Big Tech companies, it's hard to forget that the National Review Institute has taken money from Google.

Another recipient of Silicon Valley cash, the Heritage Foundation, also attacked Hawley's bill. This was particularly galling because, earlier in the year, the esteemed conservative think tank had been subjected to utter humiliation by one of its Big Tech benefactors. As we covered earlier in the book, in April 2019, Google shut down a planned AI advisory board after its far-left employees revolted at the fact that its members included Heritage Foundation president Kay Coles James. Breitbart News obtained and published the internal conversation at Google, in which left-wing employees accused James, an African American woman, of being an "outspoken bigot" who considers LGBT people to be "sub-human."[16] Not only did Google's management apparently fail to challenge these smears of their conservative ally in Washington, but they also effectively caved in to them by shutting down the planned advisory council.

Still, later in the year, the Heritage Foundation was continuing to earn its Google paychecks, attacking Senator Hawley's bill as a reincarnation of the 1980s Fairness Doctrine. In a November 2019 article, foundation researcher Diane Katz declared that "systemic bias against any group" on social media has "not been proven" (apparently they missed the YouTube blacklists, the Facebook "deboosting," the digital erasing of alternative media, and the algorithm changes that conveniently cut traffic to conservative websites by up to 90 percent).

Katz went on to argue that "deregulation benefits underdogs," even though Hawley's bill specifically excepts "underdogs" from its provisions...unless Katz believes that a company making

$500 million in global annual revenue is somehow still an "underdog"! She warns that stripping Section 230 protections from tech companies would force them to block "all but the blandest content" or "refrain from caution altogether and subject the public to the extremes of human depravity."

The obvious third option—tech companies providing their users with tools to develop their own customized blocks and filters—does not seem to have occurred to Katz. Then again, the whole purpose of the Heritage Foundation's position on Big Tech seems to be the deliberate avoidance of such obvious solutions.

The Heritage Foundation, like the National Review Institute and the Competitive Enterprise Institute and all the other fixtures of Conservative Inc. that have been accused of paid shilling for Big Tech, insists that its knee-jerk defense of tech corporations against any and all proposed regulation has nothing to do with the fact that they are partly funded by those corporations. Responding to Fox News host Tucker Carlson, who pointed out those financial ties, the Heritage Foundation insisted that its political positions were not "influenced by donations or outside political pressure" and drew attention to its criticism of Google on matters such as Project Dragonfly, its abortive censored Chinese search app.

The Competitive Enterprise Institute issued a similar statement, declaring that its views were simply a result of its long-standing opposition to "government regulations that interfere with property rights, free flowing prices, and consumer choices in the market."

Should we believe these protestations? Maybe. Maybe these groups actually do drink their own Kool-Aid and really believe that a minor change to an obscenely overreaching legal privilege will somehow lead to the end of the internet. Maybe they do believe that "consumer choice" is maximized when a decision to follow Alex Jones on Twitter is abruptly overridden by a faceless executive a thousand miles away, at the demand of a Democrat politician. Maybe they think that "property rights" are upheld when I can invest ten years and

$1 million into building a business on a tech platform, but have zero legal protections against that platform suddenly taking it away—for no reason or any reason, as Twitter's lawyers seem to believe. Maybe they do believe all of that, and their Big Tech money has nothing to do with it. Although, really, I'm not sure why so-called think tanks would prefer to be seen as stupid rather than malicious.

Net Neutrality Nothingburger

The frustrating positions of Conservative Inc. notwithstanding, liberals and progressives haven't been much better. In the early days of the Trump administration, their attention was stuck on an issue that isn't particularly important to consumers—net neutrality.

Net neutrality was the crowning jewel of President Obama's internet policy; aptly for a president known for his rhetorical chicanery, the phrase is itself a trick. In much the same way that the 2001 "Patriot Act" implied its critics were against patriotism, Obama's net neutrality implied that its opponents were against a "neutral" internet.

Nothing could be further from the truth. Net neutrality, like Section 230, was another freebie for Silicon Valley tech giants. It imposed a set of regulations on internet service providers (ISPs) like AT&T and Verizon, prohibiting them from charging more money to deliver costlier forms of internet content. In other words, under net neutrality, AT&T could not ask Netflix or YouTube to pay extra for fast delivery of data-heavy HD video streaming. Moreover, competitors to Netflix who could not match the streaming giant's library of content could not compete on streaming speed or data costs either, because ISPs were forced to treat everything the same.[17] In short, it was a law that benefited companies like Facebook, Netflix, and YouTube. Consumers didn't lose a great deal from it, but they didn't gain much either.

When the Trump-appointed Federal Communications Commission (FCC) chairman Ajit Pai announced he would repeal the Obama-era rules in 2018, all hell broke loose on the liberal left. Liberal and progressive commentators—many of whom really believed the Obama administration's hype about preserving a "neutral" internet, went into meltdown.

"This is an egregious attack on our democracy," declared Bernie Sanders. "The end of #NetNeutrality protections means that the internet will be for sale to the highest bidder."[18]

"The End of the Internet as We Know It," screamed a CNN headline—even though net neutrality had been in effect for two years before then. "Trump's FCC repeals Obama-era net neutrality regulations intended to keep the web open and fair."[19]

The identitarians of the Left offered particularly amusing predictions of doom. "The repeal of net neutrality is an attack on the LGBTQ community," warned the gay advocacy group GLAAD. "The internet is a lifeline for LGBTQ people to build community support networks and access LGBTQ resources on history, suicide prevention, and health—allowing broadband providers to regulate access is a direct and unconscionable attack on freedom of expression."[20]

"Imagine a world where a woman searches the internet but can find no information on how to access an abortion," hypothesized the pro–abortion rights group NARAL. "Imagine trying to call your representative, but you can't get through, because the phone company is being paid to limit the number of phone calls to Congress."[21]

While the identitarians may have won on hysteria, the tech giants beat them on hypocrisy. "Net neutrality is the idea that the internet should be free and open for everyone," wrote Mark Zuckerberg, whose company would put an algorithmic boot on the neck of publishers mere months later. "If a service provider can block you from seeing certain content or can make you pay extra for it, that hurts all of us and we should have rules against it."[22]

It's hard to disagree with Zuckerberg—if a corporate giant can "block you from seeing certain content," that is indeed a problem. But the ISPs generally don't do that, while Facebook does it all the time! So, what's the bigger problem?

Google made similar appeals. "Thanks in part to net neutrality, the open internet has grown to become an unrivaled source of choice, competition, innovation, free expression, and opportunity," wrote the search giant, in a message urging its users to petition the FCC to preserve net neutrality.[23] This, from the same company whose researchers admit that they embarked on a "shift towards censorship" after 2016!

Of course, none of these doom-laden predictions came to pass. AT&T, Verizon, and Comcast did not suddenly begin censoring websites or throttling service to competitors once net neutrality was repealed. The phone companies did not limit the number of phone calls to Congress. Gays were not banned from the internet, and women were not prevented from finding abortion websites. The only censorship of content came from platforms like Facebook, Twitter, and YouTube, which were never bound by net neutrality in the first place. There's nothing wrong with laws and regulations that prevent corporate censorship—but next time, why don't we aim them at the companies that actually do it?

Heroes and Villains

When it comes to tech regulation, the political terrain is not a pretty sight. Conservative Inc., flush with cash from Silicon Valley, tries to persuade you that removing Big Tech's special legal privileges is somehow an attack on the free market, or a return to the 1980s Fairness Doctrine, which required the holders of broadcast licenses to include opposing viewpoints on controversial topics. Progressives and liberals, meanwhile, want to convince you that AT&T and Verizon are planning to censor us, while saying nothing of the fact that Facebook, Twitter, and Google are *actually* censoring us, right now.

Some people get it. On the right, a small but growing group of Republican legislators has held Big Tech's feet to the fire on censorship and is moving to reform Section 230. In the Senate, Josh Hawley,

Ted Cruz, and Marsha Blackburn of Tennessee all stand out for their bold moves and tough statements on the issue.

In the House, Representatives Louie Gohmert (R-TX), Jim Banks (R-IN), Jim Jordan (R-OH), Markwayne Mullin (R-OK), Matt Gaetz (R-FL), Billy Long (R-MO), and Paul Gosar (R-AZ) have demonstrated a keen understanding of the issue. Some, like Gohmert and Hawley, have introduced legislation to address it. Whether they can overcome the establishment wing of their party remains to be seen, but their efforts are backed by the grass roots, while the establishment is not.

Prominent conservative voices have also rejected the Conservative Inc. line on Big Tech. Tucker Carlson, activist James O'Keefe, Michelle Malkin, author Ann Coulter—these are just a few of the conservative stars who reject the laissez-faire approach for Silicon Valley. Even Turning Point USA founder Charlie Kirk, normally several steps behind Carlson when it comes to skepticism about big business, has said Section 230 protections should be stripped from tech companies that don't behave in a politically neutral manner—the same principle behind Senator Hawley's bill.[24]

The voices that criticize the censorship from the Left are fewer, but they do exist. It was a Bernie Sanders–supporting leftist, Tim Pool, who famously gave Twitter's CEO a dressing-down over censorship during an episode of Joe Rogan's podcast.[25]

Glenn Greenwald, a cofounding editor of the Intercept, also stands out, condemning his fellow leftists for "beg[ging] Silicon Valley giants to become roving parents of the internet...we're now inundated with an endless ritual of journalists & politicians tattling on people they dislike to Principal Jack & Prince Zuck: pleading that they be given detention or time-outs."[26]

"One of the greatest & most exciting promises of the early internet was its unparalleled freedom of expression, action & exploration unconstrained by [government] & corporate control," wrote Greenwald in another comment. "Just two decades later, it's about begging a handful of tech giants about who should & shouldn't be heard."[27]

In Congress, the situation on the left is bleaker. Straying far from their purported role as the critics of big business's power, Democratic lawmakers today spend more time demanding corporate censorship than denouncing it. It was pressure from Democrats that preceded the blanket ban of Alex Jones and Infowars from virtually every major tech platform in 2018.[28] No less a figure than the Democrat who coauthored Section 230 in the 1990s, Senator Ron Wyden of Oregon, has called for legislation to ensure content from "bad actors" who violate "the bounds of common decency" is swiftly taken down by tech platforms.[29] The Democratic National Committee, meanwhile, has called on Facebook to censor political ads from President Trump, on the grounds of alleged "misinformation."[30]

Democratic presidential candidate and Hawaii congresswoman Tulsi Gabbard is her party's honorable exception. After Google failed to run her ads during a post-debate surge of interest in her candidacy, she sued the tech giant. She has repeatedly condemned Big Tech for censoring political voices across the spectrum, accusing Silicon Valley of "throwing free speech out the window."[31] Her actions and statements contrast favorably with those of her presidential primary opponent, Senator Elizabeth Warren of Massachusetts, who has condemned tech censorship when it affects her own messages but demands more of it against her political opponents.[32]

And what of Trump? The president seems to understand the issue, condemning Google, Twitter, and Facebook for engaging in censorship.[33] He even used a speech at the United Nations to call attention to the issue.[34]

In spring 2020, the president acted, issuing an executive order that aims to narrow Section 230's scope. The order also seeks federal investigations of tech bias as a potential deceptive business practice. But the president has not been well served by his advisers. The U.S.-Mexico-Canada Agreement, the president's flagship trade bill, actually strengthens the Section 230 provisions that allow tech giants to suppress content, giving them even more leeway to censor "objectionable" material without any legal repercussions. As with many issues, President Trump has the right instincts, but White House bureaucrats appear to work overtime to thwart them. His online supporters, meanwhile, are dropping like flies. If Trump wants to have a functioning digital grass roots at the next election, he needs to do more than just tweet about the problem.

On this issue, like many others, Washington is still a corrupt morass—it's the swamp. If consumers don't want to live under the boot of tech companies, and if business owners want to protect their digital property from arbitrary termination by a Silicon Valley executive, nothing less than sustained, organized action from the grass roots will cure the disease.

We should take heart from the saga over the Stop Online Piracy Act and the PROTECT IP Act, the online privacy bills that lawmakers tried to pass at the beginning of the decade. The laws, which would have given entertainment companies massive powers to censor the internet, were originally set to sail through Congress with bipartisan support. But a massive grassroots effort—encouraged, for self-serving reasons, by the tech companies themselves—forced lawmakers to change course. Politicians were flooded with emails and phone calls from constituents worried that the free, open internet was about to be snuffed out. The pressure from below worked—the legislation failed to pass.

We are at a similar moment. The internet has been seized by a handful of all-powerful tech lords who now determine whose voices are heard in the digital public square, whose causes are suppressed and whose are promoted, and whose businesses thrive and fail. Eventually, Silicon Valley will even determine who wins elections and who loses them. This cannot continue—and only a massive shout from the citizens of America will make Washington take action.

16. "Just Build Your Own"

One of the most frustrating things you will encounter in the debate on Big Tech censorship is the argument that dissatisfied conservatives should simply "build their own" alternatives to the major platforms.

It is a tempting proposition, designed to appeal to the best instincts of free-market conservatives. The solution to a private company behaving badly is to build a different private company that behaves better; so goes the argument. Just let the invisible hand of capitalism work its magic, and all will be well.

Unfortunately, it's not as simple as that. As we'll see in this chapter, those who *have* built alternatives to the established tech platforms have to contend with the fact that access to the market is tightly controlled by their Big Tech competitors. They must also deal with political bias from payment processors, internet hosting providers, internet security providers, and other essential services that they need in order to exist as viable businesses. And in case that wasn't enough of a challenge, alternative tech platforms like Gab and 8chan enjoy little to no support from the straitlaced free-market conservatives who claim to support small competitors.

Before we get into that, though, a much more basic point has to be made: even if competing platforms are built, that doesn't affect the case for better industry-wide standards. On the contrary, it makes the need for such standards even more pressing.

Let's say a competitor to Twitter emerges and is adopted by

millions of eager Americans keen to avoid censorship at the hands of Jack Dorsey's goons. Users of this new platform might spend months, even years, building from scratch their audience on the new platform. They might pay social media managers to help them. They might buy ads. They might do all the things that they would have otherwise done on Facebook, Instagram, Twitter, or YouTube.

Let's say they do all that, investing their time and money into the new platform, which prospers and attracts a wide audience. What's to stop a new CEO from taking over the platform and deciding to ban them? Moreover, what's to stop Facebook or Twitter from acquiring the platform, as they have done many others? Users of the new platform would be no better off than before. That's what happens when you don't have proper industry-wide standards—the small guys are always at risk.

No matter how much the "build your own" conservatives repeat their mantra, there is no escaping the fact that tech platforms, big and small, currently have the legal right to ban you for virtually any reason they can think of. Competition is not the point: the fact that thousands of landlords exist in America doesn't make it acceptable for one of those landlords to evict you because he or she doesn't like the color of your T-shirt. No amount of competition would make that state of affairs acceptable.

Yet that is the kind of power that social media platforms currently wield. No platform, from Facebook and Twitter to Parler and Gab, should be allowed to maintain such an imbalanced relationship with its users. Even if the company is benevolent and never abuses its power, users should not be forced to build their social media accounts—their connection points to the wider world—on such uncertain and risky foundations.

The "build your own" conservatives also present the movement with a false choice—political solutions versus alt-tech solutions. But, as the internet meme says, why not both? Section 230 needs to be replaced with better, industry-wide standards that impose fair due process on tech platforms that wish to suspend service to a user. But it's also clear that competing tech platforms are essential and must be encouraged.

Weirdly, the people who are most reluctant to take away Big Tech's congressionally granted perks (see the previous chapter) seem reluctant to promote the most viable competitors to those platforms.

"We see senators and congressmen whining about Big Tech bias for years now with absolutely nothing being done about it," said Andrew Torba, founder of the free-speech platform Gab, in an interview for this book.

"These senators and congressmen could easily join Gab and start promoting their content and ideas on our site. They call themselves 'free market conservatives,' but when the free market provides [a solution] they opt instead to whine about the problem. Ironically on Twitter."

Through Gab, Torba created what is perhaps the first viable free-speech alternative to Twitter and Facebook to gain significant traction. With more than 1 million registered users, Gab is easily the most active social media platform that was purpose-built for overcoming Silicon Valley censorship. Torba and his team have also built other products aimed at circumventing censorship, including Dissenter, a browser add-on that attaches an uncensored comments section to every website.

However, the story of Gab is also a story of why the "build your own" argument is not as simple as it seems. Despite a ceaseless stream of innovative, free-speech-friendly products from the team at Gab, Big Tech companies like Google and Apple have consistently erected obstacles to prevent those products from reaching a mass market.

First, there's the censorship of app marketplaces. Apple and Google dominate the market for smartphone operating systems—a whopping 99 percent of mobile devices around the world use either Google's Android OS or Apple's iOS.[1] This means that in order to easily reach smartphone consumers, Gab and other apps must have access to the Apple App Store and Google's Play Store.

Both of those have banned Gab, citing the site's tolerance for "hate speech." Moreover, Google and Mozilla, which control a dominant share of web browsers, have banned the Dissenter add-on. Gab responded by building its own web browser, also called Dissenter—and then Apple banned that from the App Store! Even though a browser can't possibly host "hate speech," Apple sought to justify the decision by arguing that Gab's other products contained "objectionable content." It's like banning Boeing 747s because the completely different 737 MAX turned out to be faulty.

Needless to say, there are huge double standards in play. As Torba explained to me, "Big Tech platforms like Facebook, Reddit, and Twitter have human traffickers, child exploitation, livestreamed murders, and even more horrific content. They also have plenty of 'hate speech,' especially against white people, Christians, men, and minorities who support President Trump. All of these platforms are allowed to remain on both app stores. They haven't been no-platformed by any service providers. No advertisers are boycotting their platforms. There is no media outrage about them at all.

"By any reasonable measure, the content and behavior on Big Tech platforms is objectively worse than the 'mean words' a small subset of Gab users post on our platform," continued Torba. "Yet Gab is the great boogeyman of the internet for some reason. The double standards and hypocrisy are glaring for anyone paying attention."

Torba is correct. The massacre of Muslims at a mosque in Christchurch, New Zealand, was livestreamed on Facebook. The murderous group ISIS, for many years, employed a network of Twitter accounts that numbered in the tens of thousands. On any given day on any of the main social media platforms, you can find an abundance of violent threats and "hate speech"—even by those companies' own definitions of the term. Yet it won't take you long to find the apps of YouTube, Twitter, Instagram, and Facebook on either Apple's or Google's marketplaces.

Think back to the prologue, in which the fictional mailman mused that a delivery service that carried mail containing "hate speech" might find itself banned from using the roads. This is the modern-day equivalent. "Compete with us!" say the tech giants. "Build your own!" say their shills in the conservative movement.

Meanwhile, Big Tech controls all the access points to the consumer—web browsers, app marketplaces, and of course the social media platforms themselves. In the dissemination of apps and browser plug-ins, Big Tech is both player and referee.

This is, of course, nakedly anticompetitive behavior. Even more brazen was Twitter's decision to deny Gab—its direct competitor—access to its application programming interface, which simplifies the implementation and maintenance of software.

Facebook has also targeted its direct competitor, Minds, by labeling links to the website "unsecure."[2] It's amazing that tech companies, in the midst of intense scrutiny from antitrust investigators on both sides of the Atlantic, appear to believe such obvious targeting of their competitors will go unnoticed, or that their paid-off politicians and opinion formers will protect them.

The picture gets even bleaker when you consider the numerous services that alternative platforms like Minds and Gab must rely on in order to function. They need domain registrars to give them a web address (.com, .net, .org, and so forth). They need providers to host their websites and data. They need payment processors to deal with transactions from paying customers.

All of the main players in these services have displayed a willingness to engage in political censorship. Gab was effectively kicked off the internet in late 2018 after GoDaddy, its previous domain registrar, cut ties. PayPal and Stripe, the web's two main payment processors, have also cut ties with the free-speech platform.[3] Square, Inc.'s Cash App has also closed Gab's account, as has Coinbase, the web's leading cryptocurrency site.[4] Microsoft Azure, Gab's previous cloud-hosting provider, threatened to take the site offline for "weeks to months" if it did not remove specific instances of hate speech.[5] Asia Registry, the domain name provider Gab used to replace GoDaddy, once threatened to do the same.[6]

Through intense effort, Gab has found ways around this extraordinary corporate censorship. "Gab had to build every part of our infrastructure from scratch in order to exist," Torba told me. "From hosting to email to payment processing. It wasn't easy, but we did it. We hope to provide this infrastructure as a service to other alt-tech companies and build out an ecosystem of infrastructure beyond Silicon Valley's control."

But again, why is any of this necessary? Why are major tech platforms allowed to discriminate against their commercial and ideological competitors? Why are the basic services required to maintain a functioning website, like hosting providers and DNS registrars, able to cut off access for spurious reasons? Why are payment processors, of all things, acting as political censors? And how is this a "free market," when entry into it is nigh impossible if you've created an app intended to promote free speech?

If conservative lawmakers and influencers really care about competition, Torba has a few suggestions for how they can help.

"They can start by actually joining and promoting alternative-technology platforms," said Torba. "Secondly, if there's any opportunity for government to get involved, it's at the antitrust level. Specifically enforcing existing antitrust law against the Apple/Google App Store duopoly, which controls 98 percent market share of mobile app distribution channels.

"If Gab was on both app stores today, we would have tens of millions of users."

Even social media apps that aren't banned from app stores, like Minds and Parler, still face a significant hurdle. That is the natural monopoly problem. People do not want to use a social network that has few people on it. Take DLive, a live-video-streaming service that competes with the more mainstream Twitch (owned by Amazon). You would think that the presence of PewDiePie, YouTube's biggest star, would have catapulted DLive into the mainstream. It hasn't, which reveals an important truth—while PewDiePie is a special case in that he sometimes puts his values above profit seeking, internet celebrities wishing to build a social media following ultimately don't have an incentive to move to desolate platforms. Generally speaking, the audience doesn't follow them; they have to follow the audience. A mass exodus of internet personalities from a platform might achieve something, but it hasn't happened yet, and that isn't an accident. Especially for those involved in politics and the 2020 election, who need to reach a large audience *right now*, the incentives for remaining on the existing platforms are simply too strong.

Data-harvesting platforms like Google and Facebook enjoy the benefits of a similar network effect. As they grow larger and attract more users, they acquire more data about those users, which they use to offer those users a more personalized service. This is particularly important to Google, which bases its appeal on providing relevant and timely information to its users. Despite the virtues of privacy-respecting competitors like DuckDuckGo, Google is in a far better position to provide search results that are tailored to what you're interested in—because it knows everything about you. A search engine just entering the market simply can't compete with that depth of knowledge. And how could a competitor to Facebook or YouTube offer content to users that so accurately pinpoints what they're interested in? They would need the users and their data first, and they can't get those without offering a better service. On the data question, competitors to the Big Tech platforms are stuck in a catch-22.

Part of the problem is that the internet itself is built in a way that makes it vulnerable to centralization. I spoke to an entrepreneur who has been deeply involved in computer science since the 1990s. He is interested in models that are alternative not just to the Big Tech platforms, but to the internet itself. While he preferred to remain anonymous to escape blacklisting, he is well known in Silicon Valley for his radical ideas, both political and technological.

"The cause of the centralized internet is a technical problem," my source said. "Or perhaps an economic problem. The decision between shared and personal computing, which is what we're really talking about here, has gone back and forth for decades."

"Shared" computing, today, is what companies like Amazon, Facebook, Google, and Twitter use. You give them your data, which is then housed on their computer servers and owned by them. In exchange, you get a chance to use their services. My source says that the public's decision to accept this devil's bargain—convenience, in exchange for a loss of control over our data—is what led to the current predicament.

"I am old enough that I remember back in the '90s and even '80s, when people still believed in the real Internet. We certainly assumed everyone would have their own Unix box [a type of highly customizable personal computer] or something like it, though we thought it would be in their houses rather than in a data center. But the idea that the future was a return to shared computing was unthinkable.

"In the early 2000s, some smart people realized it was much easier to fake the future than actually build it—and created social 'networks' that were *logically* decentralized, but 'technically' just one big server, like AOL or Compuserve.

"Unfortunately, it turns out that while it's hard to pressure a network, it's easy to pressure a fake network. Simulated freedom turned out to be a dead end. Some of these simulated networks are rapidly reaching the point of tyranny where political nonsense starts to impose significant disutility on even apolitical actors."

My source said he believes that the only way back to internet freedom is to essentially replace the entire internet. Instead of the current model, where big companies own the data and the servers, my source imagines a future in which individuals own their own data and servers.

"Your digital self in 2030 will be a private virtual computer, running in a secure enclave (like Intel SGX [a set of codes allowing users to securely lock down enclaves of their computer memory]), owned by you on the blockchain, rented from your host with crypto[currency], standardized so that it can be transferred instantly or even routinely to any other host, and communicating over onion networks (like Tor).

"Because of the enclave, your host has no way of knowing what you are computing. No one who is talking to you has any way of finding you. This is a frightening level of freedom and I'm not sure society is ready for it, but I expect it to happen. There is nothing technically impossible or even especially difficult about it.

"How does a decentralized network succeed? Ultimately, a personal server should be superior because it has better usability. It should have better usability because its UI [user interface] has no conflict of interest: it is always working just for the user. For example, a personal server will never show its user ads. Another way to succeed is to have a better community. Still a third way is users who actually need privacy."

My source speaks at a very technical level—to break it down, what he envisages is a digital "you" that is your property, and thus transferable. Imagine if you could take all of your Facebook posts and move them to another server. You can't currently do that, because you don't own them—legally, they belong to Facebook, and as a technical reality, they exist on Facebook's servers. In the decentralized future imagined by my source, each of us has our own server, which hosts all our data. My source also imagines a future with true privacy—because the data exists on your own server, there is no way to permanently turn it over to advertisers or other third parties, and because my source predicts a growth in the use of onion networks (a highly decentralized form of computer networking that is undetectable, even to ISPs).

It's a rosy picture of the future, and there are already technologies that aspire to create it. Sandstorm (sandstorm.io), for example, is a software project that allows users to run internet apps on their own private servers, without the need for an Apple or a Google. It features a chat system for communicating with others on the network, a document- and file-storage system, and multiple other applications that normally rely on centralized, shared, Google-like servers.

There's also Urbit (urbit.org), a technology in its early stages. Urbit reimagines the internet as a network of digital "landowners"—everyone has a little piece of digital "land" on Urbit. Every user who joins, by default, will have a personal address (like a web URL), a personal cryptocurrency wallet, and a personal username, all on their own personal server. Everything that the centralized tech companies can take away from you—your account, your ability to process payments, your web URL—you own on Urbit by default. You don't need anyone's permission to run the software—you just need an internet connection.

I would certainly recommend that the more technically savvy among you take the time to explore Urbit and Sandstorm. They are in their early stages, but if successful, they promise to take the internet back to the way it was—decentralized and free. And, unlike the internet as it exists today, that decentralization is baked into the system from the start. There is no danger of takeover by a centralized entity like Facebook or Google.

But that's the future—what of the present? For those of you seeking alternatives to the current tech giants, I will briefly list some viable services.

1. Social Media

Gab (gab.com). Gab remains the gold standard of alternative social media platforms, having been built to offer the same kind of unfettered public square initially promised by the likes of Facebook and Twitter. Gab is committed to the First Amendment and is extremely unlikely to ban you unless you are advocating violence or posting illegal content. Pornography is banned on Gab, but there are plenty of other dark corners of the internet you can visit if that's what you're after.

Minds (minds.com). Minds is an open-source social network, meaning that its code is publicly viewable. This is a comfort to those who worry about being manipulated by hidden algorithms—Minds touts "radical transparency," endeavoring to hide as little as possible about its inner workings. With just over one hundred thousand active users, it won't give you the kind of audience you might expect on Facebook or Twitter, but you will get a social network that isn't built on harvesting personal data and is committed to free-speech principles that are similar to Gab's.

Parler (parler.com). Like other upstart social networks, Parler suffers from a dearth of users compared to the major platforms. However, its original and most active users come from "MAGA Twitter," a result of early promotion from conservative figures like Candace Owens. Grassroots conservatives who have been banned from Twitter or Facebook and still want to connect online to other Trump-supporting activists will find a decently sized network on Parler. Like Minds and Gab, Parler does not restrict "hate speech" and does not share the personal data of users with third parties.

2. Video

Bitchute (bitchute.com). A haven for those who have been banned from YouTube, Bitchute offers video hosting without censorship.

Its audience is small but growing. The biggest problem Bitchute faces is financial—video hosting is expensive, and it is forced to collect monthly donations from users in order to keep the site running. Bitchute might benefit from relaxing its privacy policies, not just to run targeted ads, but also to offer YouTube-style tailored content. I suspect users who just want a financially stable free-speech platform where people can easily find their videos will see it as a fair trade.

DLive (dlive.tv). An alternative to livestreaming services like Twitch and YouTube live, DLive has become popular among edgier, more politically incorrect online video personalities. While it did receive a huge boost in popularity after YouTube star PewDiePie joined the platform, don't expect a massive inbuilt audience—assuming you haven't been banned yet, DLive works best as a safe haven. Start on YouTube or Twitch, but also do occasional broadcasts on DLive so that your fans will have somewhere to go if you're banned from either of the established streaming services. DLive benefits from its system of cryptocurrency donations, allowing fans to contribute to their favorite content creators without having to go through chokepoints like PayPal and Stripe, which have censored right-wingers in the past. Be warned, though: DLive *does* ban "hate speech" on its platform. Thus far, its leadership has not demonstrated a willingness to launch the kind of partisan crackdowns seen on YouTube and other platforms, but keep in mind that DLive has given itself the option to do so.

3. Email

ProtonMail (protonmail.com). If you want an easy-to-use, encrypted email service that doesn't allow Google to read what's in your inbox and drafts folder, ProtonMail is a great option. The service was built with security and privacy in mind, offering encryption, password-protected emails, and self-destructing emails (emails that auto-delete once a set amount of time has elapsed). It may not have all the fancy fonts and search functions of Gmail, but I think that's a fair price to pay.

Tutanota (tutanota.com). *Tuta nota* is a Latin phrase meaning "secure message," which, as with ProtonMail, is the email service's selling point. For technically adept users, Tutanota offers a wide range of advanced features including a desktop email client (similar to Microsoft Outlook) and U2F two-factor verification for the most paranoid among you. (U2F verification uses a physical hardware device, often a USB drive, to unlock your email account—far more secure than a typed password.)

4. Search

DuckDuckGo (duckduckgo.com). With an Alexa rank of 166 (meaning it's the 166th-most-popular website in the world), DuckDuckGo is far ahead of other alternative-tech platforms in building a user base, even though it is still a long way off from Google, Yahoo!, and Bing. Unlike those search engines, however, DuckDuckGo has built its appeal on avoiding the kind of creepy profiling engaged in by Google, which finds out everything there is to know about you in order to show you personalized results. DuckDuckGo shows one set of results to everyone, on every search—something that also makes political bias in search results much easier to detect and correct for.

Yippy (yippy.com). Founded by Trump-supporting U.S. Navy veteran Rich Granville, Yippy also won't collect your data. It uses the power of supercomputers (IBM Watson, in particular) and "metasearch" (scraping search results from other search engines) to provide highly customized search results without collecting your personal data. It also has an interesting feature called "clusters," which displays a string of related topics to the left of a list of search results. Yippy doesn't have a huge user base (its Alexa rank is over 100,000), but it does have an influential user base—its ability to deliver tailored search results without the privacy risks of Google makes it ideal for security-conscious businesses and agencies.

The Internet Wasn't Built in a Day

Conservatives and other Trump supporters are in a difficult spot, to put it mildly. The alternative technologies described in this chapter will take years, maybe even decades, to fully mature. Whether the alt-tech platforms will ever overcome the overwhelming market dominance of Facebook, Google, and other established platforms is an open question.

That said, is there any guarantee that the state will provide a solution any faster? As we saw in the previous chapter, Washington is bought and paid for by the Big Tech companies. Alternative tech may not solve the censorship problem speedily, but government officials aren't exactly nimble either—even when they understand an issue. And many of the technical elements of Big Tech censorship are completely over the heads of the aging baby boomers who occupy America's elected offices.

Andrew Torba is convinced that only alternative tech can provide a real solution.

"Big Tech has Congress bought and controlled on both sides with lobbying dollars," he told me. "In fact, Big Tech is lobbying in favor of regulation because they know it will solidify their market dominance. The only solution is to build. We can't keep playing on a battlefield that the enemy controls and expecting them to enforce the rules equally. This is war. A war of information. A war of access technology. A war of control and power. He who controls the battlefield controls the outcome of the war. If conservatives want to win, we need to build our own battlefield. Which is exactly what we are doing and what we will continue to do."

I prefer a dual approach, one that encourages both political and technological solutions to the dominance of Big Tech. Indeed, the two can work in tandem—legislation from Congress to prevent political deplatforming from payment processors and hosting providers would be a great boost to alternative-tech platforms. So, too, would pro-competition policy to address unfair exclusions from the Apple- and Google-dominated app marketplaces.

That said, I see very little chance that either Washington or competing tech platforms will provide a viable alternative to the Silicon Valley giants in time for the 2020 election. Trump has some advantages that work in his favor, including profound stupidity on the part of the Democrats, who spent his first term going on a wild-goose chase called "impeachment." Trust in the media, his biggest opponent, continues to decline. And, unlike what happened in 2016, the president will go into this election with a Republican Party that is better funded, better organized, and almost 100 percent behind him. His opponents are lackluster, his supporters are energized, and for most of his term, the economy boomed. He's very fortunate to have all these factors working in his favor—because, while he has enjoyed some policy success in his first term, his administration has been unable to stop the systematic censorship of his supporters online, the deepening of search bias on Google and YouTube, and the rise of hidden censorship. It is too late for either alternative tech or changes in policy to fix the problem. The 2020 election, therefore, will be a key test of American democracy—can a presidential candidate win an election when the giants of Silicon Valley are arrayed against him? Can humans beat machines?

EPILOGUE:
The Typewriter That Did
as It Was Told

We're at a strange moment in human history, when we are unsure about whether we control technology or technology controls us. I closed the last chapter asking whether humans can beat machines, and that really is the challenge of 2020. Will enough voters be alert to the possibility of biased search results about political candidates? Will they break from the norm, do what 60 percent of Google users usually don't do, and go beyond the first three search results that appear?[1] Will enough of the digital grass roots go beyond Twitter and Facebook? Will they turn on browser-based notifications for their favorite conservative websites and sign up for email blasts to circumvent the tightening grip on information enjoyed by the top social media platforms? Will grassroots activists knock on ten extra doors per day to counter the turnout bias caused by Big Tech platforms? Remember, more Democrats than Republicans use social media. Even if tech platforms were to send out an equal number of voting reminders to all their users—something that they are not legally obliged to do—it would still favor the Democrats.

In 2020, Republican activists will have to consider not just how to beat the Democrats, but how to beat the most powerful technologies ever created for manipulating information and behavior. It is an enormous task, one that should not be underestimated. I'm on the right, so I hope Trump wins—but given what I know about the power of tech companies, I'm not optimistic. Of the 120 million votes cast in 2016, it was just over one hundred thousand votes in three key swing states that carried the election for Trump.[2] Having read this book, do you really think that Big Tech, with its vast deposits of information on all of us, can't identify exactly who those voters are, what they care about, and how to make them go blue in 2020? The Big Tech companies were caught napping in 2016, engaging only in minor acts of bias like censoring search suggestions about Hillary's health, and busing Latin American voters to the polls. They won't be caught napping again. Nothing less than a titanic, on-the-ground effort from Republican activists will stop them from stealing the election this time. And even that may not be enough.

If, by some miracle, Trump manages to overcome the forces of Big Tech bias that are arrayed against him, his next administration will need to get serious about the problem. Tinkering around the edges won't do—not just to safeguard American democracy and fair access to the digital public square, but also to safeguard consumer rights for everyone—Republican and Democrat alike. The relationship between tech platforms and their users needs to be completely recalibrated. As I've repeated throughout this book, it is unacceptable that Big Tech platforms can erase years of investment and work that you may have put into a social media account simply because they don't like your views. Without access to tech platforms, you are, in the modern world, effectively a second-class citizen. Due process must be imposed.

The right to free speech has always conflicted with the right to privacy, even though it's hard to have one without the other. There is a legitimate conversation to be had about harassment, incitement to violence, online mob behavior, doxing, and violations of privacy. The internet has undoubtedly made these problems more common and more severe. But, in order to have a serious conversation about them, we need to ignore the left-wing journalists who have hijacked these topics and turned them to political ends.

"Harassment" isn't a partisan topic—it affects everyone, Republican and Democrat. In extreme cases, it drives people to suicide—just read the Post Millennial's coverage of Alec Holowka's death for a recent example.[3] We can find an objective definition for the word, and create a fair, nonpartisan means to contain the problem. But that won't happen until politicians stop accusing their opponents' supporters of being "abusive" just because they created a Reddit meme to mock them. Opportunistic "national conversations" about the online behavior of Trump supporters, Bernie supporters, Corbyn supporters, or even Gamergate are instructive—they show us how *not* to debate the issue of online mobbing, harassment, and violations of privacy.

Privacy is something beloved by citizens and despised by journalists—especially the witch-finder general-style journalists who stalk the depths of social media, searching for old offensive jokes or edgy political positions that they can use to ruin people's lives. This makes anonymity all the more valuable—yet it is under threat from ad-tech companies, which want to tie anonymous content to real-world identities.

As we saw in chapter 12, "The World Wide Honeypot," technology exists right now that could tie your anonymous Reddit posts to your real identity on Facebook, by using computer programs to analyze your writing style, as well as seemingly unimportant minutiae like the speed of your keystrokes or mouse clicks.

In order to prevent a cancel-culture apocalypse, in which every anonymous post ever made is tied to a real identity, start deleting your old Reddit posts.

It's time for defenders of anonymity in the world of tech to step up their game—if anonymity is to be preserved, we need technology to both detect *and mask* our unique writing styles, the speed of our keystrokes, and every other factor used by the unmasking-bots. This may be the most important technology that freedom-loving techies can work on today—even more important, perhaps, than alternative social media platforms. In an increasingly censored, politically cor-rect world, anonymity is the last refuge of dissident thought.

However, you can't win political battles with anonymity alone. When the time has come for a new idea, it cannot remain in the shadows.

Yet, on the most powerful networks for organizing online politi-cal movements, Twitter and Facebook, censorship reigns. Twitter, Facebook, YouTube, and Instagram have, among them, engaged in an unprecedented assault on the free flow of information over the past four years. It seems sometimes as if every week has brought a new purge of social media wrongthinkers.

Even Google's own researchers can't deny it, describing Silicon Valley's new role as "The Good Censor."

YouTube casually admits to taking down more than three hun-dred of President Trump's videos in its disclosures, without any apparent consideration of how biased it makes them look.

Apple and Google bar politically inconvenient apps from their marketplaces, using the most threadbare of excuses, none of which are ever applied to Twitter, Facebook, or similar apps—despite the presence of even worse violations there.

If you're a conservative on Twitter, you can be banned for post-ing facts, but if you're a leftist you can threaten violence against a Trump-supporting high school kid and still get to keep your "veri-fied" checkmark.

Don't expect the top results of any Google search to tell the true story of internet censorship—you'll have to buy this book for your friends if you want to educate them on that topic. Indeed, don't look to the top results on Google to tell you the true story of *anything*. Most likely, what you'll find there is a link to an article on Wikipedia—the defamation engine itself.

If executives at tech companies are concerned about address-ing their employees' political biases, or at least stopping them from affecting their products, they might consider taking steps to increase viewpoint diversity in their workforces. They might encourage conservatives to be more vocal about their opinions and challenge leftists when they see attempts to take the company's products in a political direction.

Yet I'm not optimistic that will happen, given that the most prominent advocate of viewpoint diversity at Google, James Damore, was fired almost as soon as he made his position known.

At Facebook, meanwhile, my source tells me he has never seen a single workshop on the dangers of political bias—compared with dozens upon dozens about the dangers of racist, sexist, and homophobic biases.

At the very least, Big Tech companies might take a leaf out of Oracle's book and encourage their employees to leave their political values at the door. Business is business and politics is politics and never the twain should meet.

But I predict that Big Tech companies won't do that. They won't do anything to address conservative concerns, beyond paying them occasional lip service in public (and even in those cases, as my sources revealed in this book, they have to be careful about backlash from their own employees). The truth is, they don't need to care. Republicans held all three branches of government in 2016–18, and they used that time to pass tax cuts while doing nothing about the growing threat of Big Tech bias. They missed a golden opportunity to recalibrate the predatory relationship between Big Tech companies and their users.

Some of the braver Republican politicians, like Senators Cruz and Hawley, have correctly identified Section 230 as a target for reform. But will their efforts ever succeed? Might they be hijacked by special interests more concerned with taking down copyright violations than protecting free speech? It's the swamp, so my hopes aren't particularly high. Virtually every think tank in Washington is bought and paid for by Big Tech, and the ones that aren't are drowned out by the ones that are.

Really, dear reader, the person who can change things isn't a politician and it isn't the CEO of an alternative-tech platform. It is *you*. If you don't want Silicon Valley to steal the election in 2020, get your boots on and get campaigning. Censorship has already cost Republicans hundreds of millions of impressions on social media platforms, and who knows how many swayed opinions as a result of search bias. If you want to fight the powers of Big Tech, you'll have to do it the old-fashioned way—by getting out there and knocking on doors.

And if your favored congressional representative, senator, or president happens to win the election (perhaps you're lucky and all three will do so), don't stop there. Demand action. Tell your elected representatives that you don't want them to listen to the bought-and-paid-for think tanks, and that American democracy will never be safe until the people banned from the digital public square are given fair due process. Tell them that search giants (and there's really only one, Google) need to be overseen or broken apart. Tell them that if two companies want to control the smartphone app marketplace, they need to play fair. Tell them to make an account on alternative-tech platforms. Tell them to start talking about this issue—and to never let up until the battle is won. It can be won. And it should be won. As powerful as the machines are, they aren't as powerful as we the people. It's time to take back control of these uppity digital typewriters.

Acknowledgments

This book is the product of four years of investigation into the colossal power of Big Tech companies. It would not have been possible without the support of my friends, colleagues, and above all my sources, who have risked their careers to expose the inner workings of Silicon Valley.

I am grateful for the support of Alex Marlow, Colin Madine, Jon Kahn, Larry Solov, and all my colleagues at Breitbart News—the best news team in America.

A number of pioneers have been instrumental in making Big Tech's growing dominance an issue of national concern. James Damore, Kevin Cernekee, Mike Wacker, Zachary Vorhies, Greg Coppola, Brian Amerige, Harmeet Dhillon, Peter Schweizer, M. A. Taylor, and Dr. Robert Epstein deserve America's thanks.

I'd like to thank Marlene Jaeckel for introducing me to my first sources during the Damore controversy. I'd also like to thank whoever sent me that anonymous Dropbox link containing the Google tape—I still don't know your name, but that was quite the story!

Most of all, I'd like to thank the Silicon Valley underground— that ever-watchful network of anonymous Big Tech sources and whistle-blowers still stuck in the belly of the beast. Without them, many of my most important stories would not have been possible.

You'll find many interviews with them throughout this book. They are the Paul Reveres of Silicon Valley, the watchers on the wall, and the first line of defense against technological tyranny.

Notes

Foreword

1. Savvas Zannettou et al., "On the Origins of Memes by Means of Fringe Web Communities" (presentation, Zenodo, November 2018).
2. Investment Watch Blog, "The Suppression of r/The_Donald by Reddit," December 23, 2019.
3. Lucas Nolan, "Reddit CEO Admits Changing Comments to Direct Users' Insults at Pro-Trump Moderators," Breitbart News, November 24, 2016.
4. Allum Bokhari, "Reddit Censors 'The_Donald' Community of 750,000 Trump Supporters," Breitbart News, June 26, 2019.
5. Allum Bokhari, "Reddit's Pro-Trump Community 'The Donald' Claims Site Ignores Violent Left-Wing Threats," Breitbart News, August 2, 2019.
6. Allum Bokhari, "Exclusive: Rep. Jim Banks Demands Reddit End Censorship of Pro-Trump Community 'The_Donald,'" Breitbart News, October 22, 2019.
7. Allum Bokhari, "Reddit Purges Moderators of Largest Pro-Trump Community 'The Donald,'" Breitbart News, February 27, 2020.

Prologue: The Typewriter That Talked Back

1. Madison Malone Kircher, "Google Docs Is Terrifyingly Locking People Out of Their Documents," New York Magazine, October 31, 2017.
2. "Microsoft Services Agreement," Microsoft Corporation, July 1, 2019, https://www.microsoft.com/en-US/servicesagreement/. Note: the services agreement applies to Office 365, which includes Microsoft Word.
3. Van Gosse, "Why Are All the Conservative Loudmouths Irish-American?," Newsweek, August 24, 2017.
4. Mitchell Sunderland, "Facebook Blocked Me Because I Said 'Faggot,' Even Though I'm Gay," Motherboard, May 25, 2014; Allum Bokhari, "Gay Conservative Suspended from Facebook for Using the Word 'Fag,'" Breitbart News, August 10, 2016; Ben Bours, "Facebook's Hate Speech Policies Censor Marginalized Users," Wired, August 8, 2017.
5. Gary Lineker, "I was wrong when I called Farage a dick and I apologise. He's a lot worse than that," Twitter, June 28, 2016, https://twitter.com/GaryLineker/status/747729209586495488.

6. James Delingpole, "RIP Godfrey Elfwick, Murdered by Twitter for Being Too Woke," Breitbart News, June 21, 2017.

7. Allum Bokhari, "Twitter Takes 20 Minutes to Protect a Journalist's Feelings, but 48 Hours to Remove Death Threats Against Covington Kids," Breitbart News, February 5, 2019.

8. Charlie Warzel, "'A Honeypot for Assholes': Inside Twitter's 10-Year Failure to Stop Harassment," BuzzFeed, August 11, 2016.

9. Allum Bokhari, "New Whistleblower Allegation: YouTube Manipulated 'Federal Reserve' Search Results in Response to MSNBC Host's Complaint," Breitbart News, July 30, 2019.

10. Craig Timberg, "Could Google Rankings Skew an Election? New Group Aims to Find Out," *Washington Post*, March 14, 2017.

11. Arne Holst, "Subscriber Share Held by Smartphone Operating Systems in the United States from 2012 to 2019," Statista, June 14, 2019.

1. A Very Offensive Election

1. Allum Bokhari, "LEAKED VIDEO: Google Leadership's Dismayed Reaction to Trump Election," Breitbart News, September 12, 2018.

2. Sheera Frenkel, "Renegade Facebook Employees Form Task Force to Battle Fake News," BuzzFeed, November 14, 2016.

3. Allum Bokhari, "Google Lawsuit: Senior Engineer Alon Altman Wanted to Sabotage Trump's Android Phone, Ban His Gmail Account," Breitbart News, April 19, 2018.

4. Allum Bokhari, "Exclusive: Leftist Google Employees Conspire to Undermine Breitbart's Ad Revenue," Breitbart News, February 13, 2018.

5. David Dayen, "The Android Administration: Google's Remarkably Close Relationship with the Obama White House, in Two Charts," Intercept, April 22, 2016.

6. Jack Nicas, "Alphabet's Eric Schmidt Gave Advice to Clinton Campaign, Leaked Emails Show," *Wall Street Journal*, November 2, 2016.

7. Joe Schoffstall, "Google's Eric Schmidt Wore 'Staff' Badge at Hillary Clinton Election Night Party," Washington Free Beacon, November 16, 2016.

2. How the Web Was Lost

1. Dan Schawbel, "Alexis Ohanian: How the Internet Can Make Your Life Awesome," Forbes.com, October 1, 2013.

2. S. O'Dea, "Mobile operating systems' market share worldwide from January 2012 to December 2019," Statista.com, February 28, 2020; Shanhong Liu, "Global market share held by leading internet browsers from January 2012 to March 2020," Statista.com, April 17, 2020; J. Clement, "Worldwide desktop market share of leading search engines from January 2010 to January 2020," Statista.com, March 25, 2020.

3. "The Top 500 Sites on the Web," Alexa Web Rankings, accessed April 27, 2020, https://archive.fo/Jtt8f.

4. Lucas Nolan, "Google CEO Sundar Pichai Defends YouTube Censorship in Interview," Breitbart News, June 10, 2019.

5. "First Nation in Cyberspace," *Time*, December 3, 1993, international edition.

6. *Pruneyard Shopping Ctr. v. Robins*, 447 U.S. 74 (1980).

7. Max Roser, Hannah Ritchie, and Esteban Ortiz-Ospina, "The Internet's History Has Just Begun, *Our World in Data*, 2020, https://ourworldindata.org/internet#growth-of-the-internet.

8. David Emery, "Did Paul Krugman Say the Internet's Effect on the World Economy Would Be 'No Greater Than the Fax Machine's'?," Snopes.com, June 7, 2018.

9. "Newsweek Kills Story on White House Intern," Drudge Report, January 17, 1998, https://www.drudgereportarchives.com/data/2002/01/17/20020117_175502_ml.htm.

10. Kevin D. Williamson, "Our Tarnished Media," *National Review*, November 9, 2017.

11. Tom Parker, "YouTube Quietly Removes 'Broadcast Yourself' Motto from Its Official Blog," ReclaimTheNet.org, May 5, 2019.

12. Michael J. Coren, "Facebook's Global Expansion No Longer Has Its Mission Statement Standing in the Way," Quartz, June 22, 2017.

13. Hank Berrien, "Twitter CEO: That Quote About Twitter Being 'the Free Speech Wing of the Free Speech Party' Was a Joke," Daily Wire, October 18, 2018.

14. Kate Conger, "Google Removes 'Don't Be Evil' Clause from Its Code of Conduct," Gizmodo, May 18, 2018.

15. Allum Bokhari, "Aaron Swartz' Warning that Social Media Companies Could Censor the Net Rings Truer Than Ever," Breitbart News, January 11, 2016.

16. Julian Assange, Cambridge Union Society, March 5, 2011, https://www.youtube.com/watch?v=gkSPfBl5GV0&feature=youtu.be&t=297.

17. Julian Assange, Cambridge Union Society, March 5, 2011, https://www.youtube.com/watch?v=gkSPfBl5GV0&feature=youtu.be&t=396.

3. The Panic

1. Jason Pontin, "The Case for Less Speech," *Wired*, November 6, 2018.

2. Michael J. Robinson, "Public Affairs Television and the Growth of Political Malaise: The Case of 'The Selling of the Pentagon,'" *American Political Science Review* (June 1976).

3. David Mitch, "The Spread of Literacy in Nineteenth-Century England," *Journal of Economic History* (March 1983).

4. Josiah Woodward Leeds, *Concerning Printed Poison* (Philadelphia, 1885).

5. Kate Summerscale, "Penny Dreadfuls: The Victorian Equivalent of Video Games," *Guardian*, April 30, 2016.

6. Wendy Lee and Marissa Lang, "Fake News a Real Problem for Google, Facebook," *San Francisco Chronicle*, November 16, 2016.

7. Grace Duffy, "Who Are the Biggest Political Publishers on Social?," NewsWhip, June 15, 2016; Ben Kew, "Breitbart News 29th-Most Trafficked Site in America, Overtakes PornHub, ESPN," Breitbart News, February 19, 2017.

8. Time Staff, "President Barack Obama Says Fake News Is a Problem for 'Democratic Freedoms,'" *Time*, November 18, 2016.

9. Tess Townsend, "Mark Zuckerberg: Don't Blame Facebook for Trump's Election Victory," *Inc.*, November 10, 2016.

10. William Turton, "Facebook Employees Are in Revolt over Fake News," Gizmodo, November 15, 2016.

11. Alex Pfieffer and Peter Hasson, "Snopes, Which Will Be Fact Checking for Facebook, Employs Leftists Almost Exclusively," Daily Caller, December 16, 2016.

12. Joe Schoffstall, "Read the Controversial David Brock Memo Outlining Plans to Attack Trump," Washington Free Beacon, January 26, 2017.

13. Brendan Nyhan, "Trump Lost the Citizenship Debate, but He's Still Corroding Our Politics," Gen, July 15, 2019.

14. Brendan Nyhan, "Fake News and Bots May Be Worrisome, but Their Political Power Is Overblown," *New York Times*, February 13, 2018.

15. Brendan Nyhan and Jason Reifler, "When Corrections Fail: The Persistence of Political Misperceptions," *Political Behavior* (June 2010).

16. Josh Constine, "Facebook shrinks fake news after warnings backfire," Tech Crunch.com, April 27, 2018.

17. Dan Sperber et al., "Epistemic Vigilance," *Mind & Language* 25, no. 4 (August 20, 2010): 359–93, doi:10.1111/j.1468-0017.2010.01394.x.

18. Sperber et al., "Epistemic Vigilance."

4. Plausible Deniability

1. Vidya Narayanan et al., "Polarization, Partisanship and Junk News Consumption over Social Media in the US" (Computational Propaganda Research Project, Oxford University, February 6, 2018).

2. Allum Bokhari, "Ted Cruz Grills Mark Zuckerberg on Facebook Censorship: Who Moderates Your Moderators?," Breitbart News, April 10, 2018.

3. Allum Bokhari, "Exclusive: Trump's Facebook Engagement Declined by 45 Percent Following Algorithm Change," Breitbart News, February 28, 2018.

4. Paris Martineau, "Conservative Publishers Hit Hardest by Facebook Newsfeed Change," Outline, March 5, 2018.

5. Nick Clegg, "Facebook, Elections and Political Speech," Facebook Newsroom, September 24, 2019, about.fb.com/news/.

6. Allum Bokhari, "The Smoking Gun: Google Manipulated YouTube Search Results for Abortion, Maxine Waters, David Hogg," Breitbart News, January 16, 2019.

7. Susan Svrluga, "A Conservative Speaker Was Uninvited from Campus. And Then Re-invited," *Washington Post*, October 23, 2015.

8. Foundation for Individual Rights in Education, Disinvitation Database. www.thefire.org/research/disinvitation-database/.

9. Jennifer Kabbany, "Princeton Debate Club Disinvited Conservative Prof. Amy Wax from Event Dedicated to Free Speech," College Fix, January 7, 2019.

10. Samantha Harris, "'Disinvitation Season' Hits a New Low at Brandeis University," TheFire.org, April 9, 2014.
11. Greg Lukianoff and Jonathan Haidt, "The Coddling of the American Mind," *The Atlantic*, September 2015.
12. Nico Hines, "University College London's Nietszche Club Is Banned," Daily Beast, June 5, 2014.
13. Scott Jaschik, "George Will, Uninvited," InsideHigherEd, October 8, 2014.
14. Staff Report, "UNDERCOVER VIDEO: Twitter Engineers to 'Ban a Way of Talking' Through 'Shadow Banning,' Algorithms to Censor Opposing Political Opinions," Project Veritas, January 11, 2018.
15. Daniel Cox and Robert P. Jones, "'Merry Christmas' vs. 'Happy Holidays': Republicans and Democrats Are Polar Opposites," Public Religion Research Institute, December 19, 2016.
16. "Lord of the Rings, 2020 and Stuffed Oreos: Read the Andrew Bosworth Memo," *New York Times*, January 7, 2020.

5. Deleted

1. Natalie Jimenez Peel and Shachar Bar-on, "300+ Trump Ads Taken Down by Google, YouTube," CBS News 60 Minutes Overtime, December 1, 2019.
2. Robert Kraychik, "Facebook Caves to Left-Wing Journalists Demanding Removal of Trump Midterm Ad," Breitbart News, November 5, 2018.
3. Lucas Nolan, "4 Companies Move to Blacklist Project Veritas in Quick Succession after Big Tech Exposés," Breitbart News, June 27, 2019.
4. Allum Bokhari, "Twitter Blacklists Project Veritas from Running Ads," Breitbart News, November 25, 2019.
5. Andy Ngo, "Twitter Punishes You for Telling the Truth," Post Millennial, December 4, 2019.
6. Liam Deacon, "Tommy Robinson Suspended from Twitter for Stating Statistical Fact About Muslims in Grooming Gangs," Breitbart News, March 1, 2018.
7. Graeme Gordon, "We Talk to Patreon's CEO About Why Lauren Southern Got Banned," Canadaland, August 1, 2017.
8. Seamus Kearney, "Mediterranean Migrant Deaths Down in 2017," Euronews, January 7, 2018.
9. Doug Cuthand, "Importance of Indigenous Peoples March Got Overshadowed by 'the Face of White Privilege,'" CBC, January 26, 2019.
10. Allum Bokhari, "Twitter Still Hasn't Banned Accounts That Threatened High School Kids," Breitbart News, January 22, 2019.
11. Allum Bokhari, "Exclusive: Facebook's Process to Label You a 'Hate Agent' Revealed," Breitbart News, June 13, 2019.
12. Southern Poverty Law Center, New Black Panther Party, accessed June 2, 2020, https://archive.fo/w4mcX.
13. "Patreon Allows Armed Antifa Group to Raise Money for 'Revolution,'" Far-LeftWatch, December 17, 2018.

6. Robot Censors

1. Jim Waterson, "YouTube Blocks History Teachers Uploading Archive Videos of Hitler," *Guardian*, June 6, 2019.
2. Staff Report, "UNDERCOVER VIDEO: Twitter Engineers to 'Ban a Way of Talking' Through 'Shadow Banning,' Algorithms to Censor Opposing Political Opinions," Project Veritas, January 11, 2018.
3. Staff Report, "UNDERCOVER VIDEO: Twitter Engineers."
4. YouTube Community Guidelines Enforcement, Google Transparency Report, Alphabet Inc., https://transparencyreport.google.com/youtube-policy/removals?hl=en&total_removed_videos=period:Y2019Q3.
5. Allum Bokhari, "EXCLUSIVE: Leaked Messages Show Google Employees Freaking Out over Heritage Foundation Link," Breitbart News, April 4, 2019.
6. Nick Bastone, "Over a thousand Google employees have signed a petition calling for the removal of a member of Google's new AI ethics board over her comments on immigrants and trans people," Business Insider, April 1, 2019.
7. Lucas Nolan, "Member of Google's Canceled AI Board Furious at Company's Cave," Breitbart News, April 5, 2019.
8. Kelsey Piper, "Exclusive: Google cancels AI ethics board in response to outcry," Vox.com, April 4, 2019.
9. Kay Coles James, "I wanted to help Google make AI more responsible. Instead I was treated with hostility," *Washington Post*, April 19, 2019.
10. AI Now Institute, Research, https://ainowinstitute.org/research.html, https://archive.fo/v4fhC.
11. AI Now Institute.
12. "Machine Learning Fairness," Google Developers, Alphabet Inc., https://developers.google.com/machine-learning/fairness-overview/, https://archive.fo/6AvRS.

7. Human Censors

1. James Damore, "Google's Ideological Echo Chamber," July 2017, https://assets.documentcloud.org/documents/3914586/Googles-Ideological-Echo-Chamber.pdf.
2. Kate Conger, "Exclusive: Here's the Full 10-Page Anti-Diversity Screed Circulating Internally at Google," Gizmodo, August 8, 2017.
3. Lucas Nolan, "Google Engineer to James Damore: 'I Will Hound You Until One of Us Is Fired,'" Breitbart News, January 8, 2018.
4. Allum Bokhari, "SJW Backlash Against Google Staffer: 'I Would Beat the Sh*t out of Him,'" Breitbart News, August 7, 2017.
5. David Brooks, "Sundar Pichai Should Resign as Google's C.E.O.," *New York Times*, August 11, 2017.
6. Paul Lewis, "'I see things differently': James Damore on his autism and the Google memo," *Guardian*, November 17, 2017.
7. Lucas Nolan, "Rebels of Google: Employee Reprimanded for Describing Campus Streaker as 'Crazy Person,'" Breitbart News, September 4, 2017.

8. Allum Bokhari, "Rebels of Google: 'Senior Leaders Focus on Diversity First and Technology Second,'" Breitbart News, August 7, 2017.

9. Allum Bokhari, "Lawsuit: Google Instructed Managers That 'Individual Achievement' and 'Objectivity' Were Examples of 'White Dominant Culture,'" Breitbart News, April 18, 2018.

10. Robert Kraychik, "Exclusive—Harmeet Dhillon: Silicon Valley 'Actively Trying to Blacklist' Conservatives 'Through Some Hiring Engines,'" Breitbart News, April 20, 2018.

11. Adelle Nazarian, "Zuckerberg Scolds Facebook Employees for 'All Lives Matter,'" Breitbart News, February 26, 2016.

12. Allum Bokhari, "Exclusive: Facebook Employee Calls Out Leftists over Fox News Hire Outrage," Breitbart News, February 3, 2020.

13. Kirsten Grind and Keach Hagey, "Why Did Facebook Fire a Top Executive? Hint: It Had Something to Do with Trump," *Wall Street Journal*, November 11, 2018.

14. Jay Yarow, "How Larry Ellison Built an Empire—And Almost Lost It," Business Insider, December 10, 2010.

15. Theodore Schleifer, "Some Oracle employees plan to walk off the job to protest Larry Ellison's Trump fundraiser," Recode / Vox.com, February 19, 2020.

8. Financial Blacklisting

1. Kenneth P. Vogel, "Ron Paul Becomes $6 Million Man," Politico, December 16, 2007.

2. Charlie Nash, "Jordan Peterson and Dave Rubin Abandon Patreon in Protest of Censorship," Breitbart News, January 16, 2019.

3. Jamie Glazov, "GoFundMe Bans Glazov Gang from Accepting Donations," September 21, 2017, jamieglazov.com.

4. Elisha Fieldstadt, "Bakery That Refused to Make Cake for Lesbian Couple Raises Record-Breaking Donations," NBC News, July 17, 2015.

5. Liam Clancy, "Kickstarter Bans Swedish Academic from Crowdfunding Book Linking Immigration and Rape," Daily Caller, January 26, 2018.

6. IndieGoGo Community Guidelines, accessed March 9, 2020. https://archive.fo/eOC7L.

7. Anti-Defamation League. https://archive.fo/mGfrw; https://archive.vn/pncmA; https://archive.vn/fUAdN.

8. Bloodmoney.org, https://archive.md/kKjqr.

9. Mark DiStefano, "Activists Are Trying to Force Mastercard to Cut Off Payments to the Far Right," BuzzFeed, May 1, 2019.

10. Allum Bokhari, "The Terrifying Rise of Financial Blacklisting," Breitbart News, January 2, 2019.

11. A. W. R. Hawkins, "Wells Fargo Stems the Tide: Not a Bank's Job to Set U.S. Gun Policy," Breitbart News, April 15, 2018.

12. Michelle Malkin, "Is This Bank Chasing Away Conservatives?," *National Review*, April 15, 2019.

9. The World's Most Dangerous Company

1. Dr. Robert Epstein, "The New Mind Control," Aeon.co, February 18, 2016.
2. Robert Epstein and Ronald E. Robertson, "The search engine manipulation effect (SEME) and its possible impact on the outcomes of elections," *Proceedings of the National Academy of Sciences of the United States of America (PNAS)*, August 18, 2015.
3. Tom Ciccotta, "Epstein: 'Google Is the Most Powerful Mind-Control Engine Ever Created'," Breitbart News, October 11, 2018.
4. Dr. Robert Epstein, "Why Google Poses a Serious Threat to Democracy, and How to End That Threat," United States Senate Judiciary Subcommittee on the Constitution, June 16, 2019, https://www.judiciary.senate.gov/imo/media/doc/Epstein%20Testimony.pdf.
5. Ryan Shelley, "80 SEO & SEM Statistics That Prove the Power of Search [2019 Update]," SMA Marketing, October 16, 2019, https://archive.fo/TeBuz.
6. "Google Search Statistics," Internet Live Stats, February 7, 2020, https://archive.fo/u8WI0.
7. Craig Timberg, "Could Google rankings skew an election? New group aims to find out," *Washington Post*, March 14, 2017.
8. Mike Wacker, "Google's Manual Interventions in Search Results," Medium, July 2, 2019.
9. Staff Report, "Blacklisted: Leaked YouTube Doc Appears to Show Election Interference," Project Veritas, June 26, 2019.
10. Mark Goodman, "Are you Taking Advantage of the 2nd Largest Search Engine in the World?," Walker Sands. https://archive.fo/Lnhoy.
11. J. Arthur Bloom, "EXCLUSIVE: Documents Detailing Google's 'News Blacklist' Show Manual Manipulation pf Special Search Results," Daily Caller, April 9, 2019.
12. Project Veritas, Google Document Dump, https://www.projectveritas.com/google-document-dump/.
13. President Donald J. Trump, "Google search results for 'Trump News' shows only the viewing/reporting of Fake News Media. In other words, they have it RIGGED, for me & others, so that almost all stories & news is BAD. Fake CNN is prominent. Republican/Conservative & Fair Media is shut out. Illegal? 96% of…results on 'Trump News' are from National Left-Wing Media, very dangerous. Google & others are suppressing voices of Conservatives and hiding information and news that is good. They are controlling what we can & cannot see. This is a very serious situation-will be addressed!," Twitter, August 28, 2018, https://twitter.com/realDonaldTrump/status/1034456273306243076.
14. Paula Bolyard, "96 Percent of My Google Search Results for 'Trump' News Were from Liberal Media Outlets," PJ Media, August 25, 2018.

10. Censorship Killed the YouTube Star

1. Robert Moran, "Who Is PewDiePie, YouTube's Record-Setting Personality?," *Sydney Morning Herald*, August 27, 2019.

2. Suzanne Ault, "Survey: YouTube Stars More Popular Than Mainstream Celebs Among U.S. Teens," *Variety*, August 5, 2014.

3. PewDiePie, "This Man Has −1000 Respect for Women and the Reason Why Might SHOCK You," YouTube, July 13, 2017, https://www.youtube.com/watch?v=rrDD5NTnoU4.

4. Leonardo DiCaprio, "Great news for our oceans! Today, #Starbucks announced plans to eliminate plastic straws from its 28,000 stores worldwide! Starbucks distributes more than 1 billion straws a year, so this news is a great step in breaking free from plastic," Instagram, July 6, 2018, https://www.instagram.com/p/BlCJnVmHDOr/.

5. Philip DeFranco, "LOL @WIRED changed their headline calling @pewdiepie racist. Garbage coverage. Garbage two dimensional flawed arguments. So pathetic," Twitter, February 16, 2017, https://twitter.com/PhillyD/status/832308782252253184, https://archive.fo/YyI6W.

6. Rolfe Winkler, Jack Nicas, and Ben Fritz, "Disney Severs Ties with YouTube Star PewDiePie after Anti-Semitic Posts," *Wall Street Journal*, February 14, 2017.

7. Alexi Mostrous, "Big Brands Fund Terror Through Online Adverts," *Times*, February 9, 2017.

8. Alexi Mostrous, "Google Faces Questions over Videos on YouTube," *Times*, February 9, 2017.

9. Julien Rath, "Analysts Predict the YouTube Advertiser Boycott Will Cost Google $750 Million," Business Insider, March 27, 2017.

10. Ben Kew, "YouTubers in Uproar After Company Notifies Them of Advertising Policy Violations," Breitbart News, September 1, 2016.

11. Peter Hasson, "EXCLUSIVE: YouTube Secretly Using SPLC to Police Videos," Daily Caller, February 27, 2018.

12. Kent Walker, "Four Steps We're Taking Today to Fight Terrorism Online," Keyword, blog.google, June 18, 2017.

13. Charlie Nash, "Report: YouTube Goes After Ron Paul, Demonetizes Videos Criticizing Afghanistan Policy," Breitbart News, August 27, 2017.

14. Charlie Nash, "YouTube Continues Demonetization Censorship, Affecting Liberal Dave Rubin and Fast Food Guru 'Reviewbrah,'" Breitbart News, September 7, 2017.

15. YouTube search, "Maxine Waters," YouTube.com, accessed January 27, 2020, https://archive.fo/WazvE.

16. Lucas Nolan, "Watch the Pro-Life Videos YouTube Doesn't Want You to See," Breitbart News, January 16, 2019.

17. Allum Bokhari, "'The Smoking Gun': Google Manipulated YouTube Search Results for Abortion, Maxine Waters, David Hogg," Breitbart News, January 16, 2019.

18. Staff Report, "Blacklisted: Leaked YouTube Doc Appears to Show Election Interference," Project Veritas, June 26, 2019.

II. The Defamation Engine

1. "Sean Hannity," Wikipedia.org, December 24, 2019, https://web.archive.org/web/20191224020808/https://en.wikipedia.org/wiki/Sean_Hannity.

2. John Nolte, "Rachel Maddow's 17 Most Audacious and Paranoid Russia Hoax Lies," Breitbart News, May 2, 2019.
3. Henry J. Gomez, "Rachel Maddow Says That Ohio Budget Includes Requirement for Transvaginal Ultrasound," Politifact, July 9, 2013.
4. "Breitbart News," Wikipedia.org, November 30, 2019, https://web.archive.org/web/20191130162533/https://en.wikipedia.org/wiki/Breitbart_News.
5. T. D. Adler, "Breitbart Blacklisted from Use on Wikipedia as 'Reliable Source,'" Breitbart News, October 3, 2018.
6. "Have White People Lost Their Minds?," Daily Beast (aggregated from Village Voice), September 29, 2010; Ruben Navarette Jr., "Dear White People: After El Paso, You Should Pipe Down and Listen to Us," Daily Beast, August 21, 2019; Dean Obeidallah, "The Unbearable Whiteness of Congress," Daily Beast, January 8, 2015.
7. Leyland Cecco, "Trudeau Says He Can't Recall How Many Times He Wore Blackface Makeup," *Guardian*, September 20, 2019.
8. Allison Lampert, Kelsey Johnson, "UPDATE 3-Canada's SNC-Lavalin settles Libya bribery case that shook Trudeau government," Reuters, December 18, 2019.
9. Danny Goodwin, "Wikipedia Appears on Page 1 of Google for 99% of Searches [Study]," Search Engine Watch, February 13, 2012.
10. Justin Deyell, "Why Does Wikipedia Rank So Well?," Techwyse, March 2, 2016.
11. Charlie Nash, "Big Brother: YouTube to Fact-Check 'Conspiracy Theory' Videos with Wikipedia," Breitbart News, March 14, 2018.
12. Lisa Seitz-Grewell, "Google and Wikimedia Foundation Partner to Increase Knowledge Equity Online," Wikimediafoundation.org, January 22, 2019.
13. "Wikipedia: Deprecated Sources," Wikipedia.org, accessed February 19, 2020, https://en.wikipedia.org/wiki/Wikipedia:Deprecated_sources.
14. "Wikipedia: Reliable Sources," Wikipedia.org, accessed December 8, 2019, https://archive.md/KE8ie.
15. T. D. Adler, "CNN Blackmail Controversy Buried on Wikipedia with Help of Partisan Editors," Extranewsfeed, November 20, 2017.

12. The World Wide Honeypot

1. Sir Roger Scruton, *How to Be a Conservative* (London: Bloomsbury Continuum, 2014).
2. Kate Eichorn, "Why an Internet That Never Forgets Is Especially Bad for Young People," *MIT Technology Review* (December 27, 2019).
3. Hilary Andersson, "Social Media Apps Are 'Deliberately' Addictive to Users," BBC, July 4, 2018.
4. Matthew Boyle, "Exclusive—'Crappy Jew Year': New York Times Editor's Anti-semitism, Racism Exposed," Breitbart News, August 22, 2019.
5. David Ng, "New York Times Fact Checker Used Racist, Homophobic Slurs on Twitter," Breitbart News, September 17, 2019.
6. Haris Alic, "Exclusive—Another New York Times Editor Made Racist, Anti-semitic Comments," Breitbart News, September 22, 2019.

7. Regini Rina, "Deepfakes Are Coming. We Can No Longer Believe What We See," *New York Times*, June 10, 2019.
8. Mike Ciandella, "Study Suggests the Media Have Begun Adopting the Language of Social Justice Warriors," Blaze, June 7, 2019.

13. The "Free Speech Wing of the Free Speech Party"

1. Taylor Lorenz, "It's Impossible to Follow a Conversation on Twitter," *The Atlantic*, February 15, 2019.
2. Yoree Koh and Jack Marshall, "The Problem with Twitter Ads," *Wall Street Journal*, April 30, 2015.
3. Chris Baynes, "Donald Trump Says He Would Not be President Without Twitter," *Independent*, October 22, 2017.
4. Sasha Lekach, "Over 12,000 Tweets Are Calling for Trump's Assassination. Here's How the Secret Service Handles It," Mashable, February 2, 2017.
5. Mario Trujillo, "Death Threats Against Senators Remained on Twitter for 2 Weeks," Hill, June 28, 2016.
6. Ezra Dulis, "Talib Kweli Explains Why He's Not Violating Twitter's Rules: 'Calling a Coon a Coon Ain't an Attack,'" Breitbart News, July 20, 2016.
7. Amanda Hess, "Why Did Twitter Ban Chuck C. Johnson?," *Slate*, May 28, 2015.
8. Allum Bokhari, "Project Veritas Video Shows Former Twitter Employees Discussing 'Shadow Banning' Users," Breitbart News, January 11, 2018.
9. Alex Thompson, "Twitter appears to have fixed "shadow ban" of prominent Republicans like the RNC chair and Trump Jr.'s spokesman," Vice News, July 25, 2018.
10. Del Harvey and David Gasca, "Serving Healthy Conversation," Twitter, May 15, 2018, https://blog.twitter.com/en_us/topics/product/2018/Serving _Healthy_Conversation.html.
11. Tom Parker, "Leaked Facebook documents suggest the company throttles live videos on conservative pages," Reclaim The Net, February 28, 2019.
12. Steven Musil, "Man who deleted Trump's Twitter account reveals himself," CNET, November 29, 2017.
13. Catherine O'Donnell, "New study quantifies use of social media in Arab Spring," UW News, University of Washington, September 12, 2011.
14. Josh Halliday, "Twitter's Tony Wang: 'We are the free speech wing of the free speech party,'" *Guardian*, March 22, 2012.
15. Laura Sydell, "On Its 7th Birthday, Is Twitter Still the 'Free Speech Party'?," NPR, March 21, 2013.
16. Charlie Nash, "Twitter CEO Jack Dorsey: Our Free Speech Motto Was a 'Joke,'" Breitbart News, October 18, 2018.

14. When Facebook Kills Your Business

1. Lucas Nolan, "Facebook Deletes Disabled Veteran's Page Without Warning— After Taking $300,000 for Ads," Breitbart News, October 16, 2018.
2. Allum Bokhari, "Facebook Blacklists Conservative News Organization with 3.4 Million Followers," Breitbart News, November 13, 2019.

3. Will Oremus, "Republicans Couldn't Stop Thanking Mark Zuckerberg for His Contribution to Capitalism," *Slate*, April 11, 2018.

4. Elisa Shearer and Katerina Matsa, "News Use Across Social Media Platforms 2018," Pew Research Center, September 10, 2018.

5. Hannah Kuchler, "Facebook Faces Questions over Role in Donald Trump's Rise," *Financial Times*, November 14, 2016.

6. Olivia Solon, "2016: The Year Facebook Became the Bad Guy," *Guardian*, December 12, 2016.

7. Shanika Gunaratna, "With Trump's Election, Facebook Wrestles with the Power of Fake News," CBS News, November 11, 2016.

8. Caitlin Dewey, "Facebook Fake-News Writer: 'I Think Donald Trump Is in the White House Because of Me,'" *Washington Post*, November 17, 2016.

9. Mike Allen, "Sean Parker Unloads on Facebook: 'God Only Knows What It's Doing to Our Children's Brains,'" Axios, November 9, 2017.

10. Julia Carrie Wong, "Former Facebook Executive: Social Media Is Ripping Society Apart," *Guardian*, December 12, 2017.

11. Ed Pilkington and Amanda Michel, "Obama, Facebook and the Power of Friendship: The 2012 Data Election," *Guardian*, February 17, 2012.

12. Kashmir Hill, "Facebook Manipulated 689,003 Users' Emotions for Science," *Forbes*, June 28, 2014; Kramer et al., "Experimental Evidence of Massive-Scale Emotional Contagion Through Social Networks," *Proceedings of the National Academy of Sciences* (June 17, 2014).

13. Josh Constine, "Facebook Changes Mission Statement to 'Bring the World Closer Together,'" TechCrunch, June 22, 2017.

14. Mark Zuckerberg, Facebook, January 11, 2018, https://www.facebook.com/zuck/posts/10104413015393571.

15. Arjun Kharpul, "Facebook Shares Fall 4% After It Announces Big Changes to the News Feed," CNBC, January 12, 2018.

16. Summer Meza, "Zuckerberg Loses $3.3 Billion After Facebook Changes News Feed," *Newsweek*, January 13, 2018.

17. Allum Bokhari, "EXCLUSIVE: Trump's Facebook Engagement Declined by 45 Percent Following Algorithm Change," Breitbart News, February 28, 2018.

18. "Report: Facebook Algorithm Change Hits Fox, Breitbart, Conservative Sites—CNN, New York Times Unaffected," Breitbart News, March 6, 2018; Allum Bokhari, "Report: Establishment Media Soaring on Facebook, Conservative Media in Decline Following Algorithm Change," Breitbart News, April 9, 2018.

19. Charlie Nash, "Facebook to Fund News Programming, Including CNN's Anderson Cooper," Breitbart News, June 6, 2018.

15. When Silicon Valley Met Washington

1. Costs of War Project, "U.S. Spending on Post-9/11 Wars to Reach $5.6 Trillion by 2018," Watson Institute, Brown University, November 7, 2017, brown.edu.

2. Communications Decency Act of 1996, "Protection for Private Blocking and Screening of Offensive Material," 47 U.S.C. § 230.

3. Communications Decency Act of 1996, "Protection for Private Blocking and Screening of Offensive Material," 47 U.S.C. § 230, subsection c(2).

4. Communications Decency Act of 1996, "Protection for Private Blocking and Screening of Offensive Material," 47 U.S.C. § 230, subsection c(1).

5. Mark Epstein, "Could America's Big Tech Industry Create Free Speech Problems?," National Interest, April 5, 2018.

6. *Laura Loomer v. Facebook Inc.*, U.S. District Court for the Southern District of Florida.

7. Sam Levin, "Is Facebook a Publisher? In Public It Says No, but in Court It Says Yes," *Guardian*, July 3, 2018.

8. Jared Taylor, *New Century Foundation v. Twitter Inc.*, June 14, 2018, Superior Court of the State of California, in and for the City and County of San Francisco, Reporter's Transcript of Proceedings.

9. Aditi Roy, "Google Is Tech's Top Spender on Lobbying—Facebook and Amazon Are Also at Record Levels," CNBC, June 9, 2019.

10. Google, Alphabet Inc., Accessed June 3, 2019, https://web.archive.org/web/201 90603185909/https://services.google.com/fh/files/misc/trade_association _and_third_party_groups.pdf.

11. Turning Point USA, "Big Gov SUCKS! #iHeartCapitalism," Twitter, June 21, 2019, https://archive.md/4oY6T.

12. Nitasha Tiku, "Leaked Audio Reveals Google's Efforts to Woo Conservatives," *Wired*, December 10, 2018.

13. Allum Bokhari, "Leaked Audio: Google Discusses 'Steering' the Conservative Movement," Breitbart News, March 7, 2019.

14. Ending Support for Internet Censorship Act, S. 1914, 116th Cong. (2019), https://www.hawley.senate.gov/sites/default/files/2019-06/Ending-Support-In ternet-Censorship-Act-Bill-Text.pdf.

15. David French, "Josh Hawley's Internet Censorship Bill Is an Unwise, Unconstitutional Mess," *National Review*, June 20, 2019.

16. Allum Bokhari, "EXCLUSIVE: Leaked Messages Show Google Employees Freaking Out over Heritage Foundation Link," Breitbart News, April 4, 2019.

17. Paul Matzko, "The Real Reason Facebook and Netflix Support Net Neutrality," Foundation for Economic Education, June 15, 2018.

18. Bernie Sanders, Twitter, December 14, 2017, https://archive.md/uA46O.

19. Joe Concha, "CNN Headline Declares 'End of the Internet as We Know It' After Net Neutrality Vote," Hill, December 14, 2017.

20. M. J. Okma, "The Repeal of Net Neutrality Is an Attack on the LGBTQ Community," GLAAD, December 17, 2017.

21. "Tell the FCC and Congress That Net Neutrality Matters to Reproductive Freedom," NARAL, https://archive.md/3ek8L.

22. Mark Zuckerberg, Facebook, https://archive.md/3oIMv, July 12, 2017.

23. Google Take Action, "The Net Neutrality Rules That Protect the Open Internet Are in Danger of Being Dismantled," https://archive.md/AfTXR.

24. Charlie Kirk, "It's Time to Treat Tech Platforms Like Publishers," *Washington Post*, July 11, 2019.

25. "Joe Rogan Experience #1258 - Jack Dorsey, Vijaya Gadde & Tim Pool," March 5, 2019, https://www.youtube.com/watch?v=DZCBRHOg3PQ.

26. Glenn Greenwald, Twitter, September 7, 2018, https://archive.md/Qq5Rk.

27. Glenn Greenwald, Twitter, June 1, 2019, https://archive.md/WokQ8.

28. Allum Bokhari, "Infowars Ban: CNN, Democrats Successfully Lobby Big Tech to Censor Their Critics," Breitbart News, August 6, 2018.

29. Sean Moran, "Sen. Ron Wyden Demands 'Consequences' for Social Media Platforms That Don't Censor People Like Alex Jones," Breitbart News, August 22, 2018.

30. Allum Bokhari, "DNC Demands More Censorship by Facebook of 'Misinformation,'" Breitbart News, December 5, 2019.

31. Lucas Nolan, "Tulsi Gabbard on Joe Rogan: Silicon Valley Is 'Throwing Free Speech Out the Window,'" Breitbart News, May 15, 2019.

32. Allum Bokhari, "Fake 'Big Tech Critic' Elizabeth Warren Calls for More Tech Censorship," Breitbart News, July 1, 2019.

33. Kathleen Hunter and Ben Brody, "Trump Warns Google, Facebook and Twitter to 'Be Careful,'" Bloomberg, August 28, 2018.

34. Allum Bokhari, "Trump: 'A Free Society Cannot Allow Social Media Giants to Silence' Free Speech," Breitbart News, September 24, 2019.

16. "Just Build Your Own"

1. "Mobile Operating System Market Share Worldwide, Mar 2019 – Mar 2020," Statcounter GlobalStats, accessed March 19, 2020, https://gs.statcounter.com /os-market-share/mobile/worldwide.

2. Stephanie Dube Dwilson, "Yes, Facebook Is Blocking Minds Links as 'Unsecure,'" Heavy.com, October 13, 2018.

3. Adi Robertson, "Gab is back online after being banned by GoDaddy, PayPal, and more," Verge, November 5, 2018.

4. Corin Faife, "Square's Cash App Didn't Reauthorize Gab, Will Continue to Block Accounts, Says Source," BreakerMag, January 7, 2019.

5. Russell Brandom, "Microsoft threatened to drop hosting for Gab over hate speech posts," Verge, August 9, 2018.

6. Michael Edison Hayden, "Nazis on Gab Social Network Show There Is No Such Thing as a Free Speech Internet," Newsweek, September 22, 2017.

Epilogue: The Typewriter That Did as It Was Told

1. "90% of people don't go past page 1 of the Google Search results when searching for you," Conversion Guru, May 29, 2017, https://www.conver sionguru.co.za/2017/05/29/90-people-dont-go-past-page-1-google-search -results-searching/.

2. Tim Meko, Denise Lu, and Lazaro Gamio, "How Trump Won the Presidency with Razor-Thin Margins in Swing States," Washington Post, November 11, 2016.

3. Diana Davison, "Allegations that led to Alec Holowka's suicide need proper scrutiny," Post Millennial, September 3, 2019.

Index

"Abusive," 7, 78, 79, 80, 82–83, 243
ACORN (Association of Community
    Organizers for Reform Now),
    32–33
Advanced Technology External
    Advisory Council (ATEAC), 84–88
Aeon (magazine), 114
Alcoff, Joseph, 203
Algorithms, 25, 75–90
    categorizing "hate speech," 75–77,
        83, 137
    corrupt content-moderation of, 77–83
    Facebook, 76–77, 78, 90, 186–87
    Google, 33–34, 64, 76, 84–88
    political machines, 77–83
    robot overlords, 83–90
    Twitter, 76, 78, 80, 81–83
    YouTube, 10, 76, 77, 83, 136–37, 140
Ali, Ayaan Hirsi, 58, 137–38, 156
"All Lives Matter," 97–98
Alphabet Inc., 22–23. *See also* Google
Altman, Alon, 20–21
American Border Patrol, 108
American Civil Liberties Union
    (ACLU), 85, 86, 87
American Conservative Union, 213–14
American Enterprise Institute, 214, 215
American Ingenuity Award, 100
American Institute for Behavioral
    Research and Technology, 116
Americans for Immigration Control, 108
Americans for Legal Immigration
    (ALIPAC), 108
American Spectator, 124

America Online (AOL), 29
Anning, Fraser, 200, 201
Anonymity, 129, 170–74, 243–44
Anti-Defamation League, 80, 101, 107,
    157
Apple, 101, 244
Apple App Store, 11–12, 227–28, 244
Apple Pay, 108
App marketplaces, censorship of,
    11–12, 227–28, 244
Arab Spring, 182–83
"Argumentative theory of reasoning,"
    51–52
Artificial intelligence (AI), 9, 84–90, 91
Asia Registry, 230
Asimov, Isaac, 170
Assange, Julian, 36
Atlantic Council, 214
AT&T, 213, 219, 221
"Automated flagging," 83

Bachmann, Lutz, 201
"Backfire effect," 50
Banks, Jim, 222
Bannon, Steve, 145, 150
Baron-Cohen, Simon, 92, 93
Beck, Glenn, 124
Bell Telephones Co., 2, 4
Benjamin, Carl "Sargon of Akkad," 65,
    107, 109, 142, 201
Benkler, Yochai, 151
Berners-Lee, Tim, 28–29, 30
Beykpour, Kayvon, 60
Biddle, Sam, 167–68

Biden, Joe, 55, 190
Big Conservatism, 213–15, 218, 221
Big Tech, 7–8, 9. *See also specific Big Tech companies*
AI systems, 9
Big Conservatism ties to, 213–15, 218, 221
community guidelines, 59–61
gatekeeping, 26–27
political links of, 22–25
political lobbying of, 213–315, 238–39
Section 230 and, 206–19
vested interests of, 21–25
Bitchute, 235–36
Black-box algorithms, 76
Blackburn, Marsha, 222
Blacklists (blacklisting). *See also* Financial blacklisting
Google, 94–95, 119–26, 181
YouTube, 56–57, 138–40
Black Lives Matter, 59, 95, 97–98, 101, 178, 182
Blind, 129, 130
Bolsonaro, Jair, 183
Bosworth, Andrew "Boz," 61, 62
"Bots," 49, 81–82
Brandeis University, 58
Brave, 129
Brave New World (Huxley), 13
Breitbart, Andrew, 32–33
Breitbart News, 8–9, 94, 96, 217
Facebook News Feed change, 197, 198
"fake-news" panic, 44, 54
Google's censorship, 20–21, 126
Wikipedia entries, 144–45, 150, 151, 154
YouTube's "blacklist" file, 56
Brin, Sergey
election of 2016 and Trump, 15–16, 21, 23, 62, 131
political links, 23–24
British Broadcasting Corporation (BBC), 17, 163
Brooks, David, 92, 93
Brooks, Shawn, 145–46
Buckley, Colm, 93
Bugler, 3–4

"Build your own" conservatives, 225–39
email, 236–37
search, 237–38
social media, 235
video, 235–36
Bush, George W., 32
BuzzFeed, 10, 18, 125, 157, 192
"fake-news" story, 44–45

California Republican Party, 158
Cambridge Analytica, 194
Cambridge Union Society, 36
Cambridge University, 92
Campus wars, 57–58
Camus, Renaud, 201
"Cancel culture," 162, 166–69, 168, 243
Carlson, Tucker, 218, 222
Carome, Patrick J., 211–12
Cato Institute, 213–14
Censorship, 7–8, 37–38. *See also* Algorithms; Human censors; "Shadowbans"; *and specific Big Tech companies*
of app marketplaces, 11–12, 227–28, 244
Chinese, 11
digital-era fearmongering, 44–50
financial blacklisting, 105–11
Google's "The Good Censor," 26–28, 30, 34, 35, 126–28
overt, 63–64, 74, 178–79
rise of "good censors," 33–36
YouTube, 132–42
Center for American Liberty, 96
Central Intelligence Agency (CIA), 3
Cernekee, Kevin, 19–20, 21
Chase Bank, 110–11
Cherelus, Gina, 166
Chicks on the Right, 124
Chinese censorship, 11
Christchurch mosque shootings, 228–29
Christi, 66–67
Christie, Agatha, 170
Ciaramella, Eric, 188
Clegg, Nick, 23, 55

Clickbait, 41, 186, 187–88, 191
Clinton, Bill, 30–31
Clinton, Chelsea, 69
Clinton, Hillary, 27, 107, 183
   election of 2016, 10, 22–24, 116, 155, 242
CNN, 9, 51, 125, 132, 154–55, 220
Coinbase, 229–30
Color of Change, 108–9
Comcast, 221
Competitive Enterprise Institute, 214, 215, 218
Compulsory education, 39
CompuServe, 29
Concerning Printed Poison (Leeds), 39–40
Confirmation bias, 51–52
Connor (alias), 77–80
Conservatism (conservative instinct), 161–62
Conservative Political Action Conference (CPAC), 185, 213–14
Conservative Tribune, 9, 44, 124
Cook, Tim, 101
Corbyn, Jeremy, 183
Costolo, Dick, 184
Coulter, Ann, 58, 222
Covington Gate, 71–72, 74, 145, 166, 176–77
Crowder, Steven, 124, 137
Crowdfunding, 106–7
Cruz, Ted, 97, 101, 115–16, 126, 222, 245

Daily Beast, 145–46, 157, 166
Daily Caller, 44, 46, 54, 123–24, 124, 150, 156
Damore, James, 20, 91–96, 214, 245
Darcy, Oliver, 177
Dartmouth College, 49
Davidsen, Carol, 194
Decentralized networks, 232–34
Defense Advanced Research Projects Agency (DARPA), 1
DeFranco, Philip, 135
Democratic National Committee, 55, 155, 223
De Niro, Robert, 177

Depp, Johnny, 177
Dhillon, Harmeet, 96
DiCaprio, Leonardo, 133
Digital currency, 12
Digital-era fearmongering, 44–50
Digital pillory, 164–70
Digital revolution, 26–27, 28
Dissenter, 228
Dixon, Dwayne, 203
DLive, 231, 236
Dobbs, Lou, 156
Dole, Bob, 31
Dorsey, Jack, 33, 184, 226
Dowson, Jim, 201
"Doxing," 71, 145–46, 242
Drudge, Matt, 31
Drudge Report, 31–32, 54
DuckDuckGo, 129, 231, 237
Dungeons & Dragons, 38
Dystopia, 7, 13

Economist, The, 8
Eichhorn, Kate, 162
Election of 1968, 3
Election of 2000, 32
Election of 2012, 23, 193–94
Election of 2016, 15–25, 242
   alleged Russian interference, 155–56, 183–84
   Facebook and, 17–19, 45–46, 61, 62, 64, 191–93
   Google and, 15–17, 19–24, 62, 116
Election of 2018, 116–17, 182
Election of 2020, 239, 241–42
Electronic Frontier Foundation (EFF), 109–10
Ellison, Larry, 102–3
Encyclopedia Britannica, 112
End of Forgetting, The (Eichhorn), 162
Enlightenment, 208
"Epistemic vigilance," 51
Epoch Times, 65
Epstein, Jeffrey, 27
Epstein, Robert, 10, 113–18, 119
European migrant crisis, 69–70
European Organization for Nuclear Research (CERN), 28–29

Facebook, 7–8, 12, 13, 186–205
  addictive power of, 163–64
  algorithms, 76–77, 78, 90, 186–87
  alternatives to, 227, 229
  "an extremely left-leaning place,"
      97–101
  censorship, 35, 37, 38, 44, 45–46, 64,
      66, 72–73
  community guidelines, 59–61
  content moderation, 76
  "deboosting," 181, 217
  digital currency, 12
  election of 2012 and, 23, 193–94
  election of 2016 and, 17–19, 45–46,
      61, 62, 64, 191–93
  "fake news" and, 45–46, 50
  "hate agents" review list, 72, 73, 181,
      199–205
  human censors, 101
  ideological echo chamber, 101–2,
      103–4
  Luckey scandal, 99–101
  making the world more closed, 195–99
  net neutrality and, 220
  News Feeds, 46, 55, 186–87, 195–99
  plausible deniability, 55–56
  political ads, 55–56
  political links, 23–25
  Section 230 and, 209–10
  shaming campaign against Trump
      and, 191–95
  terminating whole businesses, 186–91
Facebook Messenger, 77
"Fact checkers" ("fact-checks"), 4–5,
    46, 55
Fairness Doctrine, 217, 221
"Fake news," 3–4, 7, 8–9, 18, 32
"Fake-news" panic, 41–42, 54, 58–59,
    128, 191
  digital-era fearmongering, 44–50
  virtue of partisanship, 50–53
Family Research Institute, 108
Farrakhan, Louis, 72–73, 74, 203
Fearmongering, digital-era, 44–50
Federal Communications Commission
    (FCC), 21, 219–20, 221
Federalist Society, 214

Federal Reserve, 10, 22, 140
Federal Trade Commission (FTC), 216
FedEx, 6, 11
Feministing, 125
Fields, J.T., 40
Financial blacklisting, 105–11
  Chase Bank, 110–11
  Mastercard and Visa, 108–10
  Patreon, 69–70, 73, 106–7, 109
  PayPal and Stripe, 107–8, 109, 229
Financial Times, 191–92, 193
First Amendment, 30, 211–12
Fischer, Ford, 74
Fiverr, 134
Ford, Henry, 149
Forgetfulness, 161–62, 169–70
Forgiveness, 161–62
Fox News, 132, 143, 157, 188, 198, 218
Free market, 11, 12, 221
Free speech, 35–36, 126–27, 242
Free Thought Project, 74
French, David, 216–17
FrontPage Magazine, 124

Gab, 11–12, 227–30, 235
Gabbard, Tulsi, 116, 118, 223
Gabriel, Brigitte, 108, 201
Gadde, Vijaya, 60
Gaddhafi, Muammar, 147
Gaetz, Matt, 222
Gaffney, Frank, Jr., 108
Gamergate, 59, 155, 182, 243
Gates, Bill, 26, 28
Gateway Pundit, 124, 150, 198
Gawker, 167–68
Geller, Pamela, 108
Gender disparities in tech employment,
    92
Gennai, Jen, 64, 74
Gilmore, John, 30
Gizmodo, 46, 92
Glackens, Louis M., 41–42, 43
Glazov, Jamie, 107
Glick, Caroline, 124
Gmail, 20, 112
GoDaddy, 229, 230
GoFundMe, 106, 107

Gohmert, Louie, 222
Goldberg, Zach, 166–67
Goldman Sachs, 24
"Good Censors," 26–28, 33–36, 126–28
Google, 7–8, 12, 112–31. *See also* YouTube
   algorithms, 33–34, 64, 76, 84–88
   alternatives to, 129–30, 231
   anti-Trump plotting, 19–21
   "blacklists," 56–57, 94–95, 119–26, 181
   community guidelines, 59–61
   corporate lobbying, 213–15
   Damore scandal, 20, 89, 91–96, 245
   dumb f**ks, 129–31
   election of 2016 and, 15–17, 19–24,
     62, 116
   election of 2018 and, 116–17, 182
   "The Good Censor," 26–28, 30,
     33–34, 35, 126–28, 244
   "knowledge panels," 123, 124,
     148–49, 158
   license to lie, 157–58
   manual interventions, 118–23
   net neutrality and, 24, 221
   news blacklists, 123–26
   plausible deniability, 56–57, 59–62
   political bias of, 113–23
   search engine manipulation effect
     (SEME), 113–23
   Section 230 and, 209–10
   terms of service, 7, 8–9
   vested interests, 21–25
   Wikipedia favoritism, 148–49
Google Android, 112
Google Chrome, 112, 129
Google Docs, 7, 8
Google Home, 112
Google Now, 124, 125
Google Play, 11–12, 227–28, 244
"Google's Ideological Echo Chamber"
   (Damore), 91–92
Gore, Al, 32
Gosar, Paul, 116, 222
GotNews, 178
Government regulation, 14, 115–16,
   206–24. *See also* Section 230
   net neutrality, 24, 219–21
Granville, Rich, 237

Greenblatt, Jonathan, 107
Greene, Talib Kweli, 177
Greenwald, Glenn, 222
Grewal, Paul, 100
Griffin, Kathy, 71, 155
Guardian, 40–41, 93, 192, 193
Gulf of Tonkin, 3
Gullibility, 51

H-1B visa, 55
Hannity, Sean, 143–44, 153, 156
Harris, Sam, 107
Harvard University, 92, 151, 190
Harvey, Del, 184
Hassan, Olinda, 60, 74, 79
"Hate agents" review list, 72, 73, 181,
   199–205
Hate facts, 68–74
"Hateful conduct," 57, 58, 59, 69–72, 85
"Hate groups," 108
"Hate journalism," 69–70
"Hate speech," 7, 8, 11, 37, 58, 59, 90,
   200, 228–29
   algorithms and, 75–77, 83, 137
Hawley, Josh, 115–16, 215–18, 221–22, 245
Hayes, Chris, 10, 140–41
Hearst, William Randolph, Sr., 41–42,
   43, 43–44
Hearst Communications, 42
Heritage Action, 214
Heritage Foundation, 84–87, 185,
   213–14, 217–18
Hess, Amanda, 178
Hidalgo, Alex, 92–93
Hitler, Adolf, 77
Hogg, David, 56, 138
Holowka, Alec, 243
Hopkins, Katie, 156
Horowitz, David, 108
Houston Chronicle, 42
Http (hypertext transfer protocol), 29
Hudson, Jerome, 177
Huffington Post, 125
Human censors, 91–104
   Damore scandal, 20, 89, 91–96
   Facebook, 97–101
   ideological echo chamber, 101–4

Human Rights Campaign, 69
"Hyperpartisanship," 38, 52, 59

Ideological echo chamber, 101–4
Illegal immigration, 69–70, 108
InBlondWeTrust, 66–67
Indiegogo, 106, 107
Industrial revolution, 26, 39
Infowars, 65, 223
Insight Labs, 26, 126
Instagram, 36, 66, 209–10
Interactive Advertising Bureau,
    46–47
Intercept, the, 8, 22, 222
"Intersectionality," 167
Irish jokes, 2, 5–6, 9

James, Kay Coles, 84–87, 90, 217
Jeong, Sarah, 72, 88, 165–66, 177
Jigsaw, 16
Jihad Watch, 108, 109
John Birch Society, 140
Johnson, Boris, 156
Johnson, Chuck, 178
Johnson, Gary, 100
Jones, Alex, 10, 11, 51, 68–69
    bans on, 56, 65, 68–69, 74, 201, 223
    Twitter ban on, 177, 178, 218
Jones, Leslie, 127
Jordan, Jim, 222
"Junk news," 54
Juola, Patrick, 170–71

Kahn, Gabriel, 42
Kasich, John, 144
Katz, Diane, 217–18
Kerry, John, 106
Kickstarter, 106, 107
King, Stephen, 170
Kipling, Rudyard, 46
Kirk, Charlie, 222
Klein, Ethan, 135
Kolfage, Brian, 187–88
Kompromat, 164–65
Kotleba, Marian, 201
Kovacevich, Adam, 215
Krugman, Paul, 30

LaCorte News, 65, 188–89
Lanier, Jaron, 84
Latin American voters, 242
Leaks, 13
Leeds, Josiah Woodward, 39–40
Levatino, Anthony, 139
Lewinsky, Monica, 31
Lewis, C. S., 170
Liberty, 161–62
Libra coin, 12
Limbaugh, Rush, 124
Lineker, Gary, 9–10
LittleThings, 186–87, 188, 191
Locke, John, 208
Long, Billy, 222
Loomer, Laura, 56, 65, 68, 156, 178, 201,
    202
Luckey, Palmer, 99–101

McCarthy, Kevin, 158
McInnes, Gavin, 56, 65, 110, 156, 201
McKesson, DeRay, 178
"Machine Learning Fairness," 87–88
Maddow, Rachel, 143–44
Madonna, 177–78
"Make America Great Again," 75–76
Malkin, Michelle, 58, 110, 222
Mallory, Tamika, 203
Manafort, Paul, 155
Massie, Thomas, 140
Mastercard, 108–10
Maxwell, R. C., 65
Mazurek, Milan, 201
Media Matters, 47–48, 54, 125, 157
Mediterranean Sea refugee smuggling,
    69–70
Meechan, Mark "Count Dankula," 142
Mercier, Hugo, 51–52
Microsoft Azure, 230
Microsoft Word, 8
Military Grade Coffee, 187–88
Minds, 229, 230, 235
MKUltra, 3
Monroe, Nick, 65
Moody, John, 188
Moral panic, 38–42
Mostrous, Alexi, 136

Motivated reasoning, 50–51
Mozilla, 228
MSNBC, 10, 132
Mubarak, Hosni, 183
Mullin, Markwayne, 222
Mulvaney, Mick, 140
Murphy, Meghan, 210–11
Mussolini, Alessandra, 201

NASA, 1
National Enquirer, 3
National Review, 215, 216–17
National Review Institute, 214
National Taxpayers Union, 214
Nation of Islam, 203
Natural language processing, 171–73
Natural monopoly, 230–31
Naughton, Eileen, 16, 20
Nawaz, Maajid, 69
Nehlen, Paul, 201
Netflix, 24, 219
Net neutrality, 24, 219–21
News Corp, 136
NewsGuard, 49
Newsstand bans, 8, 304
Newsweek, 31
New York Journal American, 43
New York Times, 3, 9, 24, 30, 56, 61, 88, 92, 93, 125, 140, 151, 165–66, 177, 198, 209
New York World, 43
Ngo, Andy, 69, 72, 88, 178
Nietzsche, Friedrich, 58
"Nigger," 76–77
Nimble America, 100
1984 (Orwell), 13
Nixon, Richard, 3, 4
Norai, Mo, 81, 82–83
Northwestern University, 9
Nyhan, Brendan, 49–50

Obama, Barack, 22, 44–45, 59, 84, 183, 193–94
Occupy Democrats, 125
Oculus Rift, 99–100
Odeh, Rasmea, 203
Ohanian, Alexis, 26

"OK boomer," 67
O'Keefe, James, 32–33, 64, 222
Omar, Ilhan, 178
Oracle, 102–3, 245
Oremus, Will, 189–90
Overt censorship, 63–64, 74, 178–79
Owens, Candace, 201, 235

Page, Larry, 23
Paglia, Camille, 93
Pai, Ajit, 219–20
"Pajamas media," 32
Palihapitiya, Chamath, 193
Panic, 37–53. *See also* "Fake-news" panic
  moral panic, 38–42
Parler, 230, 235
Partisanship, virtue of, 50–53
Patreon, 69–70, 73, 106–7, 109
Paul, Logan, 127
Paul, Ron, 106, 137
PayPal, 107–8, 109, 229
Peace Now, 2–3
Pearlman, Leah, 163–64
Pelosi, Nancy, 146, 166
Penny dreadfuls, 39, 40–41
Pentagon Papers, 35
Peterson, Jordan, 107
PewDiePie (Felix Kjellberg), 132–36, 231, 236
Phillips, Nathan, 71–72
Pichai, Sundar, 16, 28, 93–94, 118–19, 123–24, 130, 131
Pinker, Steven, 92, 93
PJ Media, 125
Plausible deniability, 54–62
Podesta, John, 23
Political censorship. *See* Censorship
Political correctness, 59, 90, 94, 155
Political neutrality, 54–55, 62
PolitiFact, 144
Pontin, Jason, 37–38
Pool, Tim, 222
Porat, Ruth, 16, 131
Postal service, 4–6, 8, 9
"Post-truth era," 51, 153
PragerU, 198, 209–10

Prince Harry and Meghan Markle, 168–69
Princeton University, 58
Privacy, 161–63, 166–69, 170–74, 243
Privacy arms race, 174
Problematic social media use, 163–64
Project Dragonfly, 218
Project Veritas
    Chase Bank investigation, 111
    Google investigations, 64, 124
    Twitter investigations, 81–82, 179
    YouTube investigations, 119–20, 141
"Property rights," 208, 218–19
PROTECT IP Act, 224
ProtonMail, 236–37
Proud Boys, 110–11, 201
Pseudonymity, 170–74
"Public servants" standard, 206, 207
Pulitzer, Joseph, 43
Putin, Vladimir, 144
PyCon, 168

"Quality ranking," 78–79

Rebel Media, 124, 156
Reddit, 26, 159, 209, 228, 243
Red Guards Austin, 73
RedState, 124
Regulation, 14, 115–16, 206–24. See also Section 230
    net neutrality, 24, 219–21
Republican Attorneys General Association, 214
Republican Governors Association, 214
Republican Legislative Campaign Committee, 214
Richards, Adria, 168
Right Side Broadcasting, 54
Right Side News, 124
"Right wing," 89
Right Wing News, 65, 187–88
Right Wing Watch, 125, 157
Ripon Society, 214
Robertson, Ronald E., 113–14
Robinson, Tommy, 10, 56, 65, 69, 72, 200, 201, 202

Robot censors. See Algorithms
Rogan, Joe, 222
Romney, Mitt, 23
Roof, Dylann, 108
Rothenberg, Randall, 46–48
Rowling, J. K., 170–71, 173
R Street Institute, 214
Rubin, Dave, 107, 137
Rubio, Marco, 102
RuneScape, 7

Sacco, Justine, 167–68, 169
Salvini, Matteo, 183
Sanders, Bernie, 10, 35, 183, 220, 222
Sandmann, Nicholas, 71–72
Sandstorm, 234
San Francisco Chronicle, 42
San Francisco Examiner, 41–42
Sarsour, Linda, 202–3, 204
Schmidt, Eric, 22–24, 125
"Scraping," 172
Scruton, Roger, 161
Search engine manipulation effect (SEME), 113–23
Search engine optimization (SEO), 116–17
Search engines, 34. See also Google
    alternatives, 237–38
    political effects of bias, 113–18
Second Treatise on Government (Locke), 208
Section 230, 14, 158, 159–60, 206–19, 221–24, 245
    Hawley's reform proposal, 215–18, 221–22
Shabazz, Malik Zulu, 72–73, 203
"Shadowbanning," 178–84
"Shadowbans," 63–74, 175
Shapiro, Ben, 139
"Shared" computing, 232
Silicon Valley. See also Big Tech
    Big Conservatism ties to, 213–15, 218, 221
    community guidelines, 59–61
    election of 2016 and, 15–17, 19–24
    gatekeeping, 26–27

plausible deniability, 54–62
vested interests of, 21–25
"Similarity score," 79
Singh, Pranay, 81–83
60 Minutes, 63–64
Slate (magazine), 10, 56, 139, 178, 189
Sleeping Giants, 20–21
Smosh, 133
SNC-Lavalin affair, 147
Snowden, Edward, 36
"Snowflakes," 60
Social media, alternatives, 235
Social media addiction, 163–64
Solomon, John, 155
Sommers, Christina Hoff, 137
Soros, George, 48
South Africa Project, 108
Southern, Lauren, 69–70, 107, 156, 201
Southern Poverty Law Center, 49, 73,
    80, 135, 157
Spambots, 79
Speiser, Joe, 186–87
Spencer, Robert, 108, 109
Sperber, Dan, 51–52
Stone, Roger, 65
Stop Online Piracy Act, 224
Stripe, 107–8, 229
Strong, Anthea, 23
Suhler, Linda, 66, 67, 82
Super PACs, 105–6
Swan, Jonathan, 179
Swartz, Aaron, 35, 36
Sweet Cakes, 107

Tapper, Jake, 155
Tarrio, Enrique, 65, 110–11
Taylor, Jared, 211
Telephone, 4–5, 12
Terms of service, 2, 5–6, 78–79
    Google, 7, 8–9
    Twitter, 180–81
Thune, John, 189–90
Time (magazine), 8, 30
Torba, Andrew, 227–28, 230, 238
Totalitarianism, 12, 202
Trudeau, Justin, 146, 147
Trump, Donald, 13–14, 54–55

"bricked" phone, 20, 21
election of 2016, 15–20, 45–46, 59,
    191–93, 242
election of 2020, 102, 103, 239,
    241–42
Facebook page, 55, 197–98
Google search results, 125
Section 230 executive order, 223–24
shaming campaign of Facebook
    against, 191–95
Twitter use, 176, 181
Wikipedia entry, 146–47
YouTube censorship of, 63–68, 141
TrumpGirlOnFire, 66–67
Turning Point USA, 156, 214, 222
Tutanota, 237
Twitch, 231
Twitchy, 124
Twitter, 7–8, 175–85
    algorithms, 76, 78, 80, 81–83
    alternatives to, 225–26, 227, 229
    celebrity bias of, 9–10
    censorship, 13, 35, 65–67, 69, 71–72,
        101, 175–78
    community guidelines, 59–61
    content moderation, 76
    "conversational health," 179–80, 185
    "free speech wing" comment, 35,
        184–85
    "hate speech," 11, 37, 72
    "off-site behavior" rule, 176–78
    Section 230 and, 209–12
    "shadowbanning," 178–84
    terms of service, 180–81
    Trump ban, 181
    verified checkmarks, 10, 39, 72, 74,
        177, 244
Typewriters, 1–2, 6–7

United States–Mexico–Canada
    Agreement, 223–24
University of California, Berkeley, 95
Urbit, 234

Vadrevu, Abhinav, 179
Venker, Suzanne, 57, 58
VentureBeat, 72

Verizon, 24, 219, 221
Vice News, 140, 179, 200
"Video malaise," 38–39
Virtual Private Networks (VPNs), 170
Visa, 109–10
Vox, 125, 156, 157, 198

Wacker, Mike, 118–19, 120
Walden, Greg, 190
Walker, Kent, 16–17, 21, 62, 74, 131, 137
Wall Street Journal, 100, 135, 176
Walsh, Matt, 124
Wang, Tony, 184
Warren, Elizabeth, 223
Washington Free Beacon, 54
Washington Post, 3, 8, 9, 87, 101, 117,
    150, 159, 192, 193
Watergate, 35
Waters, Anne-Marie, 201
Waters, Maxine, 56, 138–39
Watson, Paul Joseph, 56, 65, 68, 72, 74,
    156, 200, 201, 202
Wax, Amy, 57–58
Western Journal, 198
"Whiteness," 166–67
"White privilege," 71, 166–67
Whittaker, Meredith, 85–87
WikiLeaks, 32–33, 35–36, 109
Wikimedia Foundation, 149, 158, 160
Wikipedia, 143–60
    as alleged "reliable sources," 149–51,
        154
    "Anyone Can Edit" slogan, 151–56
    character assassination of, 155–57
    defamation engine, 149–50
    license to lie, 156–60
    political bias of, 143–48, 158–59
    renegade editors, 151–56
Will, George, 58
Williams College, 57

Winklevoss twins, 190
Women's March, 202–3
World Wide Web, 28–33
    rise of "good censors," 33–36
Wright-Piersanti, Tom, 165–66
Wyden, Ron, 223

Yaniv, Jessica, 210–11
"Yellow journalism," 42–43, *43*
Yellow Kid, The, 42–43, *43*
Yiannopoulos, Milo, 65, 201, 202
Yippy, 237–38
York, Dwight D., 203
Young, Toby, 156
YouTube, 112, 132–42
    algorithms, 10, 76, 77, 83, 136–37, 140
    "blacklists," 56–57, 138–40
    censorship, 10, 13, 28, 34, 63–65,
        141–42, 244
    content moderation, 76
    demographics, 132–33
    "hate speech" clampdown, 37
    PewDiePie hatchet job, 132–35, 136,
        231, 236
    Section 230 and, 209–10
    shift in platform's policies, 135–38
    the smoking gun, 138–42
    Trump censorship, 63–68, 141
    "trusted flagger" program, 137

Zuckerberg, Mark, 186, 189–90,
    196–97, 199
    "an extremely left-leaning place" of
        Facebook, 97–101
    censorship and Facebook, 33
    Congressional hearings, 189–90, 194
    "fake news" and Facebook, 18, 45,
        184, 192
    net neutrality and Facebook, 220
    political ads and Facebook, 55–56

About the Author

Allum Bokhari currently serves as the senior technology correspondent at Breitbart News, one of America's leading news websites, and the leading source of conservative tech coverage.

Bokhari has published explosive material from Silicon Valley whistleblowers exposing Big Tech's lurch toward censorship, including Google's "The Good Censor" document, Facebook's "Hate Agents" review list, and YouTube's search blacklist.